A
POLITICAL HISTORY OF JAPAN
DURING THE MEIJI ERA 1867-1912

A POLITICAL HISTORY OF JAPAN DURING THE MEIJI ERA
1867-1912

Walter Wallace McLaren

NEW YORK
RUSSELL & RUSSELL · INC
1965

FIRST PUBLISHED IN 1916
REISSUED, 1965, BY RUSSELL & RUSSELL, INC.
BY ARRANGEMENT WITH FRANK CASS & CO. LTD., LONDON
L. C. CATALOG CARD NO: 65-17910

8/70   BCh

Printed in Great Britain

PREFACE

AT no time since the Russo-Japanese War has the interest in Japan's foreign policy been so widespread as at present, and seldom, if ever, has it been more difficult to comprehend Far Eastern affairs. In 1904 and 1905 the sympathy of the whole Anglo-Saxon world was given unreservedly to the Japanese in their struggle with Russia, mainly because it was popularly, though erroneously, believed that they were engaged in a quixotic enterprise, the aim of which was to defend the integrity of China and preserve the independence of Korea against the aggressive designs of the Colossus of Northern Europe. But during the past decade that judgment has been reversed, and the combat is now regarded as having been a war of expansion upon the part of Japan no less than that of Russia. Korea and the three Eastern provinces had been the prey of Russia, but as a result of the war they became the quarry of Japan. In what other light are subsequent events—the annexation of Korea and the consolidation of Japan's interests in Manchuria—to be interpreted?

Ever since September 1914 Japan's action as a member of the Entente Allies group has been shrouded in mystery. The military expedition against Kiao-chau obviously was undertaken by the Japanese in order to rid themselves and their allies of the menace of a German naval base in the Pacific. But why was the successful issue of that exploit followed almost immediately by an attempt to settle their differences with China? And why were the Japanese terms presented at Peking so ambiguously worded that for the time

5

being it was impossible to tell exactly what they were? Why was an ultimatum forwarded, and backed up by a display of force? And why did the Japanese Government at the very last moment withdraw the most objectionable group of its demands? These questions and many others of similar import were asked in almost every capital of the Western world, but no satisfactory answers were forthcoming from responsible authorities. In the House of Commons Sir Edward Grey said no more than that to the best of his knowledge no accurate version of the Japanese demands had been published. Was it that he did not know what they were at the time he spoke and had not been consulted or informed by the Japanese Foreign Office before the drive against China had been initiated? The State Department at Washington issued a brief statement to the effect that Japan's action involved no breach of the existing treaties, a note which if not particularly informing was at least reassuring. Why was the British Foreign Secretary even less explicit? Had the Japanese Government violated the spirit of the Anglo-Japanese Alliance? If not, then the British Government must have approved all of Japan's demands, Group V₁ as well as the others.

In Japan itself there was almost as great uncertainty as to the significance of the Cabinet's action at Peking. Were the demands and the ultimatum merely a device to win the support of a chauvinistic nation for the Government, a pre-election policy to be discarded as soon as it had served its purpose, or was it an outcome of the stampeding of the Cabinet by its "strong-policy" members? Some countenance is lent the former hypothesis by the fact that as soon as the election campaign had terminated successfully for the Government the drive upon China slackened ; but if this interpretation be accepted, then why did the Cabinet, even though it enjoyed the support of a majority of the members of the Lower House, resign a few months later? Was Count Okuma's resigna-

Preface

tion the consequence of his foreign policy, or of the bribery scandal which involved one of the members of his Cabinet, Baron Oura, the Minister of Agriculture and Commerce? If the former, who exerted the pressure? Certainly not the people, for there were no popular demonstrations of hostility against the Government's Chinese policy in Tokyo or elsewhere. Was it a case of the interference of the Elder Statesmen to curb the exuberance of the ultra-stalwarts, Oishi, Kono, and the others, in the Doshikai? If so, why did the Elder Statesmen, who are notoriously militarist in their sympathies, object to taking advantage of China's weakness and Europe's preoccupation? Did they object to Okuma's foreign policy because it was too strong or not strong enough? Or was it a warning from London or Washington that caused them to refrain from seizing the advantages almost within their grasp? Publicly, the downfall of the Okuma Cabinet was explained as the result solely of the discovery of Oura's guilt in disbursing 50,000 yen among the members of the Diet in the interests of the military party's programme for the creation of two new army divisions in Korea. But if such was the case, why was Baron Kato, the Minister of Foreign Affairs, as well as Oura left out of the reconstructed Okuma Cabinet? These are questions which the Japanese asked themselves and could not answer ; for undoubtedly the failure of the Government to settle definitively with China was a real disappointment to the masses, to whom expansion on the continent of Asia is the first, last, and only object of foreign policy.

In this book I have endeavoured to supply the information which is essential to the formation of accurate judgments as to the meaning of Japanese policy by reviewing her modern political history, describing her system of government, and explaining her national ambitions. In Part I, entitled " The Reconstruction Period," I have presented a careful survey of the evolution of the existing political institutions of Japan and

Preface

an enumeration of the powers exercised by the various authorities, the Emperor, the Elder Statesmen, the Privy Council, the Cabinet, the Diet, and the bureaucracy. For that study I have used a collection of the laws and ordinances illustrative of the organization of government, central and local, which I edited for the Asiatic Society of Japan and published as Volume XLII, Part I, of the *Transactions* of that Society. I have been compelled to refer the reader to this source book for the texts of the essential documents because no other collection exists except in the Japanese language.

In Part II, entitled " The Parliamentary Régime," I have followed the history of the Japanese Diet from its establishment in 1890 until the beginning of 1913. The political parties, their internal dissensions as well as their struggles with the various oligarchic Cabinets, have occupied a large part of my space, as have also the rise and growth of the military faction in the oligarchy. Why the brilliant exploits of arms have synchronized with the decline in the popular interest in domestic politics and the demoralization of the party politicians I have likewise attempted to explain.

Much of what is said may seem an unnecessarily severe indictment of the Japanese " Constitutional Monarchy," but my severity is not unparalleled by Japanese opinion as expressed by their most influential writers. I have stated, for example, that bribery is " a national institution," not in order to convey the impression that the Japanese differ in that respect, except perhaps in degree, from other peoples, but merely because the same conclusion has been drawn from the facts by the Japanese themselves. My main criticism of their system is directed against the appalling lack of principle displayed, not only in connection with their domestic but also their foreign policy. That there is a tendency toward an increase rather than a diminution of unprincipled action, and that a remedy will not be found except in an abatement of the intense chauvinism of

Preface

the race, *especially of the ruling military caste,* is my
settled conviction. All true friends of the Japanese
—and as such those of us who have lived some years
among a people so admirable in many respects will
wish to be classed—can only hope that they will heed
the voices of their own prophets, if not the plain
teachings of history, so that they may rise superior to
those national faults which create alarm and distrust
in their neighbours, and move forward steadily along
the path of honourable progress, deservedly respected
by the nations of the world.

W. W. McLAREN.

WILLIAMSTOWN,
　　MASSACHUSETTS,
　　　　January 1916.

CONTENTS

PART I

THE RECONSTRUCTION PERIOD

PART II

THE PARLIAMENTARY RÉGIME

Contents

PART I

THE RECONSTRUCTION PERIOD

A Political History of Japan During the Meiji Era

CHAPTER I

THE RESTORATION MOVEMENT

THE Japanese *coup d'état* of 1867, commonly called the Restoration, was as swiftly executed as it had been elaborately prepared for by the supporters of the Imperial cause. The forces which finally thrust the Emperor forward into the position of an active ruler were of varying degrees of power and of diverse origin, intellectual, sentimental, political, and military, some at work for several centuries, and others the result of the two decades immediately preceding the event. Of the methods adopted to ensure the success of this movement, some were the devices of men of high qualities who were loyally and unselfishly devoted to the national ideal, while others were obviously those of jealous and reckless samurai, bent on revenge or improvement of their own fortunes.

Among the actual promoters of the movement for the Emperor's restoration there were two very different views of its meaning. To the Conservatives it was a return to antiquity (*Fukko*), to the Radicals a renovation (*Isshin*). As time went on and the exigencies of change began to exert their inherent force, it became apparent that the more conservative directors of the movement could no longer fashion it upon the pattern of antiquity. To set up in the

15

middle of the nineteenth century for the government of a nation of thirty millions a polity which had been unsuited to even the needs of a small tribe in the year 645 was an impossible task, and eventually the views of the more radical reformers prevailed. When once it came to be seen clearly that nothing short of a complete " renovation " of the Government of Japan would meet the changed circumstances of the times, the way was opened for the introduction of those remarkable reforms at which the world, often ignorant of their true significance, has never ceased to wonder.

The immediate object of the League of the Western Clans in 1867 was to destroy the Shogunate, whose origin dates back as far as 1192, when the Emperor Go Toba appointed Minamoto Yoritomo *Sei-i-tai-Shogun* (Foreign - Barbarian - Repressing Great General). The nature of that institution and its effects upon the monarchy require some explanation.

The Shogunate, which exercised the executive powers of the national Government, was founded upon the feudal order. Without feudalism it could never have existed, for the Shogun would necessarily have become a supplanter of the Emperor, and could not have permitted his deposed rival to continue even as spiritual head of the nation, with a Court of his own at Kyoto. The campaign which set Yoritomo upon his pedestal of power at Kamakura was fought out between two great rival military clans, the Minamoto and the Taira, and the Emperor, who was without military resources, was not brought into the conflict directly. He was merely the spectator of a struggle between two groups of his nominal subjects, and stood ready to confer any powers or titles which might be demanded of him by the victorious clan. Thus it was that after the Taira had been crushed on land and sea at Minatogawa and Dan-no-Ura, Yoritomo made a triumphal entry into Kyoto, and proceeded to set the Imperial house in order and receive from the Emperor

The Restoration Movement

Go Toba Tenno, a boy of his own nomination, and from the retired emperor, Go Shirakawa, such honours as he chose to ask. It is true that the Taira for a brief space in the twelfth century, under the leadership of Kiyomori and his son Munemori, held possession of the person of the Emperor and were, therefore, *Kwangun*—the loyal defenders of his cause. But the Minamoto had not been blind to the fiction by which a rival clan could claim the status of supporters of the throne, nor did they hesitate to acquire by force that same status for themselves. In the holocaust which destroyed the Taira the young Emperor Antoku Tenno, who had succeeded to the title at the age of three, and was but eight years old in 1185, lost his life. Yoritomo had immediately placed on the throne as Antoku's successor Go Toba Tenno, a boy of eight years of age. In this way the Imperial house was affected by the strife of its subjects ; but however much royal individuals might suffer accidentally, or however much interference there might be in the succession, the feudal warriors were careful to refrain not only from usurping the throne for themselves or scions of their houses, but from going outside of the Imperial line for candidates for royal honours.

If Minamoto Yoritomo was capable of branding as a sham the Taira claim that in taking up arms against them he became a rebel in the eyes of the Court, why was he, like his predecessors and his successors through the whole history of feudal Japan, so careful to nominally preserve intact in the succeeding generations of one family the succession to the throne? Modern Japanese writers point to this fact with an immoderate pride. " The Imperial throne of Japan," they say with a show of truth, " has been occupied by a single line through generations unbroken from the beginning." The reason commonly ascribed —that the Imperial ancestors from the heavenly sphere have directed the progress of their race, and, however much purely human forces have been permitted to

17

prevail, have at least shielded the Imperial line from dishonour and destruction—is not accepted by intelligent Japanese themselves, much less by foreign students of their history. To cast doubt upon the claim of an unbroken succession would not be difficult unless we are prepared to believe that adoption into the Imperial family did not constitute a break in the actual line ; unless what we call and what the Japanese themselves now call illegitimacy is as serviceable as legitimacy for the perpetuation of an Imperial line. Concubinage was the universal habit of royalty and the nobility in Japan until the Restoration. The reigning Emperor to-day is not the child of the Empress, the legal consort of the Meiji Tenno, but of the Lady Nakayama. So little did the Japanese, even of the early years of Meiji, condemn the practice of polygamy that documents published by the Imperial Household Department and translated officially into English gave the names of the Imperial concubines and their offspring. Whatever may be said in palliation of these facts, the claim of unbroken descent can only be substantiated by acknowledging the prevalence of customs which the Japanese of to-day would willingly forget.

Moreover, even though we might be willing to accept adoption as conferring royal lineage upon a member of the Imperial family outside of the direct line, or illegitimacy as a substitute for legitimacy, there remain the plain facts of history, which show that throughout the whole of the long period from the twelfth to the nineteenth centuries the Shoguns, the military usurpers, displayed for the Court an astonishing contempt. Emperors were placed upon the throne or compelled to make room for successors as the Shogun and his Council saw fit. At all times, whether the Shoguns resided in Kamakura or Yedo, or the Taiko in Osaka, the Imperial palace in Kyoto was guarded like a prison. Funds for its maintenance were provided by the Shogunate, and sometimes so meagre

The Restoration Movement

was that provision that the Emperor was in actual want. Of so little importance was the Imperial person in the days of early foreign intercourse that the Jesuits hardly knew of the Emperor's existence. They seem to have thought of him as a Japanese counterpart of the Pope of Rome, except that he had no aspirations for temporal power. The Dutch writers likewise were in the habit of referring to the Shogun as "his Majesty," and on their annual pilgrimage from Deshima to Yedo, Kyoto was the only city which they were permitted to examine freely. The privilege was probably accorded by the Tokugawa to show the foreigners how lightly the Court was regarded. Commodore Perry delivered to the Shogun in Yedo the autograph letter to the Emperor of Japan from the President of the United States, and none of the ambassadors of the Western Powers seemed to have entertained any suspicion that in dealing with the authorities in Yedo they were not approaching the throne.

In the light of these facts, some other explanation of the relations between the Shogunate and the Imperial Court must be sought than that which depends upon the claim now made by Japanese historians of the official type, that the throne throughout this whole period was divinely preserved by the Heavenly Gods. We naturally turn to look for the truth in feudal institutions and in the monarchy itself.

The origins of feudalism [1] on its institutional side are to be found not only in the Constitution of *Taikwa* (645 A.D.) but in the political society of Japan previous to the seventh century, a society composed largely of patriarchal units, each of which had its chief who exercised authority over the members of the group and the land on which they lived. The Emperor was in theory the head of the entire tribe, but his power rested upon the military strength of the members of his own immediate unit. In case of a weak or non-

[1] See Asakawa, K., *Origin of Feudal Land Tenure in Japan. American Historical Review*, October 1914.

19

military Emperor the theoretical sovereignty which he exercised over the people might not only fall into abeyance but be transferred to the head of some other unit. The tendency was thus wholly toward decentralization, the breaking up of the tribe into units or groups, which were feudal to all intents and purposes, though the headship of the units was not necessarily bestowed for military genius. It was to offset this alarming process of decentralization, which threatened the position of the Emperor and the strength of the tribe, that the reforms of *Taikwa* were introduced. The State socialism of China, the country which threatened the national existence of Japan in that day, was copied. The adopted form of government provided for the division of the free people of the tribe into the *governing* and *supporting* classes. The governing class consisted of the holders of high civil offices, and attached to those offices were grants of rice-land to be held during tenure, the holders enjoying exemption from the payment of tribute to the Emperor. The supporting class was provided with grants of rice-land which were subject to periodic redistribution, and in return for their land the people of this class owed the Government taxes and the performance of military services. In this way the free element in the population was destined to become not only the administrative class but the basis of the military power of the State in all national contests with foreign Powers.

The first effect of these reforms was to turn the former heads of units into civil officials of the reorganized State, to change the name but not the reality of the former régime except in one respect—that certain of the officials were supposed to exercise control over all the units of the tribe or nation. In the second place, the fact that only the rice-lands were allotted and provision was made for their periodic redistribution left out of account by far the larger part of the national domain, and thus opened the way

The Restoration Movement

for the growth of estates (*Sho*) which subsequently became the nuclei of the fiefs of the powerful territorial lords. By the end of the eighth century the equality which was supposed to be maintained by periodic redistribution of rice-lands had given place to inequality, partly because that redistribution had not been rigidly carried out in all parts of the national domain, and partly because of the freedom with which individuals alienated their lands. The immunity of the higher officials from taxation and the greed of the Buddhist sects were also factors operating to destroy the Constitution of Taikwa shortly after its adoption. Out of the failure of this early Japanese experiment in State socialism feudalism grew, for it is only necessary to point to the methods by which men were able to add acre to acre in building up their fiefs, and to the natural process by which those fiefs came under the control of a military class, to see the civil power, represented by the Imperial house, dominated by first one and then another of the military clans, the Taira, Minamoto, Hojo, Ashikaga, and finally Tokugawa.

When the landed estates had begun to multiply, as they did rapidly even in the eighth century, by taking new lands into cultivation and by acquiring by purchase or otherwise the original allotments, the process was accelerated by a variety of devices with which every student of European feudalism is familiar. The practice of commendation—the granting of real rights in his property by a peasant to a more powerful neighbour in return for protection—was considered illegal during the ninth century, but nevertheless a rapid movement in that direction took place, especially during the tenth and eleventh centuries. The opposite tendency, the granting of benefices by a superior to an inferior, in return for services of a military or fiscal nature, completed the development of the institution of feudalism. The motives, in so far as they were acquisitive, are easily understood. To obtain land as the basis of wealth was the ambition of every enterprising magnate, and to found upon that land a race of military servitors was merely to insure the perpetuation of his tenure. But there were other motives, too, which hastened the development of feudalism. As we have already pointed out, the rice-lands allotted at the beginning of the eighth century to the high civil officials were immune from taxation, and that immunity not only stimulated imitation but caused the burden of taxation for the support of the State to lie all the heavier upon those whose lands were taxable. The new estates carved out of unoccupied and unregistered lands enjoyed fiscal immunity, and the result was that as population grew, and with it the expenses of the Government, the sources of revenue remained almost stationary and the rate in consequence tended to increase. To escape this burden of taxation was one of the peasant's objects when he transferred the title of his land to a powerful neighbour. As the practice of commendation grew, not only did the revenues of the State diminish, but the officials in their efforts to refill the empty treasury were compelled to lay fresh levies upon those who had not secured immunity. It is easy to see, therefore, how the land-greed of the rising feudal chiefs was seconded by the desire of small holders to escape taxation. And it is also obvious that the central government, for lack of revenue, was not in a position to extend its control over the whole nation as the population increased. The revenues from the royal lands hardly sufficed to defray the expenses incurred in their administration. Less and less pressure was exerted by the central government over outlying districts, and as that pressure diminished the feudal lords became more independent, until in the end a condition of complete decentralization was arrived at.

While this process was going on, another no less essential to feudalism was at work. Not only was the accumulation of land necessary to the growth of the feudal chiefs' power, but the development of a body of armed retainers was imperative. Beneficing did not necessarily imply military service ; oftentimes taxes in the form of rice were the compensation given in exchange for the protection of the magnate. The creation of a military class in the fiefs was at least partly due to other causes than these, the most important of which was undoubtedly the appearance of a class of landless and lawless men, recruited in part from the original land-owning free citizens, who deserted their lands to obtain relief from the growing burden of taxation. These men not only became the material for a military class supported by the fief, but made such a class necessary as the surest means of defending the estate against marauding expeditions from outside. But a band of warriors upon an estate was not only useful for defensive but for offensive purposes, and by the eleventh century the practice of violence against nearby fiefs in order to acquire their lands was as common as evasion of the law had been in the eighth and ninth for the same purpose.

With this development of military forces in connection with the estates of the great landed proprietors, several changes occurred which it is important to notice. The civil nobility of the eighth century gave place to a military nobility. Enterprising men of the lower orders sought to commend themselves only to the military leaders of the time. The great offices of State which had been hereditary in the Fujiwara family no longer carried with them the prestige necessary to attract the support of the people. Moreover, the domain over which the civil officials exercised control was relatively diminishing. Even the capital itself was not free from disturbances caused by the feuds of supporters of rival military houses, and along with the decline of the civil authority went that of the Imperial Court. The only part which it could play—and a dangerous rôle it proved to be—was to intrigue first with one military commander and then another, in an attempt to keep always on the winning side. As a result, the history of the Imperial house from the twelfth century onwards presents an almost unbroken record of misfortune. Emperors were assassinated, deposed, retired, and their power was always overshadowed by that of some military upstart. How it came about that the succession to the throne remained hereditary in one family, in the limited sense that it did, can only be explained by the force of the cult of its descent from the gods. That the various Shoguns should not have usurped the name as well as the substance [1] of royalty was certainly not due to any lack of power, nor to the possibility of resistance on the part of the Court.

Another development which followed close upon the rise of a military feudalism was the changed status of the people. By the *Taikwa* reforms the *free* citizens of the kingdom were divided into the ruling and the supporting classes. The proportion between the ruling caste and the unprivileged orders, as distinguished from the slaves, was something like 1 to 200, the former constituting about one-half per cent. of the free people. The *unfree* or slaves amounted to about 4 or 5 per cent. of the total population, which numbered in 700 A.D. about 3,000,000 or 3,500,000 people. From these figures it would appear that the main body of the nation was composed of a peasantry employed in the cultivation of the soil, of which they owned and occupied small but equal holdings, for which they paid taxes to the sovereign in rice, silk, and textile products, who were in addition liable to forced labour or *corvée* when not conscripted to serve in the Imperial Guard of the capital. But with the growth of military feudalism a startling change

---

[1] *Vide* Article 2 of the Constitution of September 1615, defining the authority of the Shogun: "The Shogun . . . having been entrusted with the government of the country, has complete authority over the three Imperial Princes, the five *Sekke* families, the Court nobles, and the feudal nobility." (See Gubbins, J. H., *The Progress of Japan, 1853-71*, p. 269. Oxford, 1911.)

took place in their status. The ownership of land passed out of their hands by the processes of alienation or commendation to the feudal lords, nor was this divorcing of the peasantry from the ownership of soil counteracted by the practice of conferring benefices or by subinfeudation, which became common in the tenth century and continued thereafter, for the benefice or sub-fief was conferred not upon the peasant but upon the warrior. Except for the small number of peasants who became members of the warrior class in the beginning, the free citizens of *Taikwa* were reduced to a condition of serfdom. We may be sure, too, that as soon as the warrior class became a recognized factor in the feudal system, a caste arose the iron rules of which afforded but few opportunities for the peasants to break into it. Some notable exceptions there were, of course, such as that of Hideyoshi, the son of a wood-cutter, who by virtue of his great military genius worked his way up under Oda Nobunaga, finally succeeding to that great chieftain's position under the title of Taikosama. As a general rule the peasants became serfs attached to the soil of the fief, supporting by their labour on the land the military and ruling class. That such was the outcome of the process was proved by the census reports issued shortly after the Restoration. Out of a population of some 31,000,000 in 1870, the ruling class was composed of about 280 Daimyo families and 400,000 samurai households, in addition to the 150 families of Court nobles, in all not more than 2,000,000 people, and the changes which took place, by which the original 5 per cent. of slaves and 95 per cent. of free people were turned into 93 per cent. of serfs and 7 per cent. of free citizens, could only have been the result of feudalism.

But the transformation of the political society of Japan through the rise of a feudal order, however much light it throws upon the problems we are considering, does not serve completely to explain the growing hatred

A Political History of Japan

of the Western clans for the Shogunate in the period preceding the Restoration. In feudalism anarchy is the ordinary rule. Every chieftain's hand is raised against his neighbour, and might to hold what is possessed is seconded by a covetous desire to seize what is another's. In the rough-and-tumble of such a régime individual prowess is the factor of prime importance. Possession of a mighty arm or military skill is the surest guarantee of success. There is a certain rough justice in the rule that might makes right, provided that it is individual might that counts, for old age saps the strength of the strongest, and heredity plays strange pranks by giving great soldiers weakling sons. Thus honours are won and lost, families rise and fall, and talent and enterprise have their reward. There was in the never-ending strife of feudalism in Japan something of the zest of a game, which seemed to satisfy the participants. The rules of that game do not appeal to the minds of the present generation of men, who are revolted by its cruelty as manifested in the indiscriminate slaughter of the women and children of a beaten foe or the assassination of his own kin by a jealous chieftain, or the worship of mere physical force ; but if the moral and social ideas inevitably pertaining to those early times cannot be offered as an excuse, they at least explain such practices. The Minamoto after the defeat of the Taira sought out and exterminated as far as they could every scion of that house. Yoritomo was not only not content with completely destroying his Taira rivals, but turned almost immediately upon his own brother Yoshitsune, his greatest general, and caused his death to secure for his own sons the succession to his great office. Yet it was less than a score of years after his death that the Minamoto made room for another and more powerful family, the Hojo.

During all the earlier centuries of the feudal period there never was a time when any one military clan

The Restoration Movement

had reduced the whole country to submission. There
were always outlying remote districts where it was
possible to successfully defy the authority of the
Shogunate. The south-western extremity of the
Empire, the Island of Kyushu, the home of the
Satsuma clan, was until the end of the sixteenth century an independent principality, and so haughty had
Shimadzu, the Prince of the house, become, that when in
1586 the Taiko Hideyoshi sent a demand for his submission, the ruling Daimyo tore to pieces his letter
and packed his messenger back to Osaka. That insult
was in due time avenged by Hideyoshi, who swept
with a conquering host from Kokura on the Straits of
Shimonoseki to the very walls of Kagoshima, Satsuma's
capital, and there dictated terms of peace. There was
thus until the beginning of the seventeenth century a
fighting chance for predominance, at least for the more
powerful of the clans. The histories of Nobunaga,
Hideyoshi, and Tokugawa Iyeyasu alike prove that
genius and ambition might still raise an individual to
the very top of the feudal hierarchy. But at the beginning of the seventeenth century, with the rise of the
Tokugawa, conditions changed. A system or organization took the place of the individual. The Shogunate,
founded by military power, strengthened itself by
means of codes of law, canons of religion and art,
rules of etiquette, policies of administration, and the
creation of an all-pervading civil bureaucracy, and held
all the Daimyo, great and small, in its grip. Against
this system no individual could make headway. The
game and zest of feudal anarchy disappeared, and
the highest honours thereafter fell by the rule of
inheritance to the members of the Tokugawa clan,
and the system persisted in spite of the lack of great
leaders. Only Iyemitsu, the third of the line, approached at all the capacity of Iyeyasu, and of the
other thirteen Tokugawa Shoguns only two have left
their names in history—Yoshimune, the eighth, and
Yoshinobu, the fifteenth and last. So conspicuous was

A Political History of Japan

the weakness of the descendants of Iyeyasu that just as Yoritomo's two sons were ruled by Hojo Tokimasa, and the last two members of the Ashikaga dynasty by Oda Nobunaga, so the Tokugawa Shoguns, as befitted their system, ruled in name and name only through the Go-roju or Council of State. Nominally too exalted to take any active part in the government of the country, the later Tokugawa Shoguns were actually unfitted for such an exercise by reason of their incapacity. It was natural that the clansmen, if not the Daimyo of the feudal principalities, should chafe against the perpetuation of an organized tyranny which not only overshadowed the Imperial house, but shut them out from any adequate participation in the conduct of the nation's affairs.

It has been often implied by Japanese historians that there is a miraculous element in the method by which the throne was preserved throughout the earlier and ruder feudal period as well as during the two centuries and a half of the highly refined Tokugawa régime. The story of the monarchy gives little ground for such a claim. But there was an element of reality in the appeal of the throne which has to be reckoned with in trying to understand the Restoration movement. If the successful elevation of the monarch to the position of a ruling sovereign in 1867 stood alone as the sole incident of its kind in Japanese history, the event might be explained on the basis of the myths of divine descent and the miraculous interference of the Heavenly Gods. But there had been various earlier and unsuccessful attempts to accomplish a similar purpose. As far back as 1219 the Emperor Go Toba Tenno considered the time opportune for the restoration of the sovereign's prerogatives. In that year the last of Yoritomo's sons had been assassinated and the direct line had come to an end. Go Toba Tenno, therefore, summoned the nobles of the West to support his cause, and with a considerable army moved upon Kamakura, the capital and stronghold of the Minamoto.

The Restoration Movement

Though Yoritomo's line had failed, his wife Masago, still the guiding spirit at Kamakura, gathered together her supporters and defeated the Imperial forces. Go Toba Tenno was banished to the island of Oki, and his sons Tsuchi Mikado and Juntoku to Awa and Sado respectively, and the nobles who had rallied to his standard were stripped of their lands. About a century later an attempt was made by Go Daigo Tenno to accomplish the Restoration, and his forces overthrew the Hojo and destroyed Kamakura, and for three years he ruled in Kyoto. But at the end of that period Ashikaga Takauji, who had been one of Go Daigo's generals, rebelled against his Imperial master because Go Daigo refused to revive the office and dignity of the Shogunate. Takauji was successful in defeating the royalists. Go Daigo Tenno fled from Kyoto, carrying with him the Imperial regalia, and established himself in the mountain fastnesses of Yoshino, where he continued to hold his Court, though not to rule the Empire, until his death, in 1339. In Kyoto a new line of sovereigns was started by the dictator Takauji, and from his first nominee he secured the coveted title of *Sei-i-tai Shogun*. With Takauji began the domination of the Ashikaga, which lasted for 238 years.

It seems fairly obvious from these early attempts to restore the power of the State to the throne that the real stumbling-block was the strength of the various dynasties of usurping Shoguns or regents. Why the title of Shogun should have been more desirable than that of Emperor is not difficult to understand, for, as we have seen, there never was a time after the ninth century when the Emperor and the Court enjoyed real power : it was power that the various usurpers sought, and the last place they would be inclined to look for it was in the Imperial palace. The monarchy, therefore, persisted in one family since no one outside of that stock thought it worth while to usurp an office which, however high and sacred, had no attraction for a successful military leader.

A Political History of Japan

If, in seeking the causes of the Restoration movement, great importance is to be attached to the jealousy
of the Western clansmen, there were other and hardly
less significant forces at work bringing on the event,
chief among them being the intellectual movements
of the eighteenth and nineteenth centuries in the fields
of religion, history, and science, as well as the disintegration of the Tokugawa power and the foreign
policy of the Shogunate.

One of the features of the Tokugawa policy which
is most frequently commented upon was the encouragement of learning among the samurai. The object of
that particular measure was doubtless not only to
advance knowledge by a diligent search after truth
in certain directions, but to occupy the minds of a
restless class of men whose natural occupations had
disappeared in an era of universal peace. By direction of the authorities the samurai became interested
in Chinese learning. They not only revived the ancient
classics of Confucius and Mencius, but busied themselves with the writings of Chu-hi and other school-
men of the Sung dynasty (960-1278). The seventeenth
century witnessed such zeal for Chinese literature,
philosophy, and religion among the upper classes in
Japan, that the native classics were forgotten and
Japanese Buddhism was neglected. The climax of
this Chinese movement was reached in the eighteenth
century, and was followed by a revival of interest in
the ancient literature of Japan. This Japanese renais-
sance was led by Kada, Mabuchi, and Motoöri, and
carried on in the nineteenth century by Hirata. A
patriotic desire to see the ancient national literature
revived and appreciated inspired their work. Com-
mentaries on the *Kojiki*, the *Nihongi*, and the
Manyoshu, and exegetical treatises upon the difficult
texts of the Japanese classics make up the bulk of
their work. Motoöri's principal contribution to this
movement was the *Kojiki Den*, " in which he lost no
opportunity of attacking everything Chinese and of

exalting the old Japanese customs, language, and religion in a spirit of ardent and undiscriminating patriotism." [1]   Hirata, Motoöri's greatest pupil, was similarly engaged in the exaltation of Shinto and the ancient literature of Japan, until the Shogunate realized that its power was being undermined by his zeal in advocating the claims of the Emperors, whose mythical history and divine origin form so large a part of the *Kojiki* and *Nihongi*.   Hirata thereupon was proscribed and exiled to his distant home in Dewa.   This reactionary movement, led by the men whom we have just mentioned, interested and instructed thousands of the educated classes in Japan, and played a large part in preparing the minds of the people for the restoration of the Emperor in 1867.   As a religious movement, the attempt to revive " Pure Shinto " was a failure, however, because of its reactionary nature: the theology which it sought to found upon the Japanese classics was impossible of belief among a people steeped in the philosophy of the Sung dynasty.

The second of the intellectual movements arose in the very midst of the Tokugawa family toward the close of the seventeenth century.   Mitsukuni, second in the line of the Mito Daimyo, and a grandson of Iyeyasu, gathered around him in his capital a great body of historical scholars, and under his direction and encouragement they explored the annals and traditions of the Imperial house from the time of the mythical founder of the line, Jimmu Tenno (660 B.C.), to Go Komatsu Tenno at the close of the fourteenth century. The product of all this research was a great work, completed in 1715, called the *Dai-Nihonshi* (*History of Japan*).   The Shogunate opposed the progress of these studies to the extent of prohibiting their publication, but the history circulated freely in manuscript form, as did many another proscribed work, and wherever it was studied it revived interest in the ancient polity of the country, in the cult of the divine ancestry

[1] Aston, W. G., *Shinto, the Way of the Gods*, p. 373.   London, 1905.

of the Imperial house, and in the true relation between the Emperor and the Shogun.

Encouraged by the example of the Mito scholars, a history of the Shogunate from its foundation by Yoritomo in the twelfth century to the accession of Iyeyasu was completed in 1827. This work was called the *Nihon Guaishi* (*The External History of Japan*). Like its predecessor, its teaching was highly derogatory to the exalted pretensions of the Shogun. The Emperor was represented as the only legitimate sovereign, allegiance to whom was the duty of every Japanese, while the Shogun was declared a usurper whose position depended upon the power of the sword.

The influence of these historical works upon the literati connected with the various feudal Courts, even though they were written in difficult classical Chinese which prevented the common people from understanding them, must have been as great in its way or even greater than that of the theological teachings of Mabuchi, Motoöri, and Hirata, and the ferment of new and disquieting thought undoubtedly began to work in the minds of the educated classes. Along with these studies of the native classical theology and history must be grouped a variety of scientific books which emanated from the busy students [1] of Dutch learning. The work of the Japanese scholars of Western sciences, particularly military and medical, began in the second half of the eighteenth century. To what extent this large and rapidly growing body of students of Western knowledge prepared the people for the new régime is still an unsettled question, for the materials necessary to the formation of an exact judgment are still withheld from publication. Some years ago a more or less complete collection of reminiscences was published by one of the prominent leaders of the Restoration, but the whole edition was bought by the Imperial House-

---

[1] For the Life of one of the group of Dutch scholars see Greene, D. C., *Takano Nagahide*. *Transactions of the Asiatic Society of Japan*, vol. xli. Part III. Yokohama, 1913.

The Restoration Movement

hold and suppressed. It is obvious, however, that such influence as the students of the Dutch language exerted was of a very different nature from that of the Mito historians or the leaders of the theologico-philosophical movement known as the "Revival of Pure Shinto." Their work tended to break down the barriers of seclusion which had been one of the main defences of the Shogunate against radical changes in thought and life in Japan. As in the case of the two intellectual movements mentioned, the Shogun's Government sought to hamper the spread of Western learning by persecuting its protagonists, and a long list of martyrs to the cause of Dutch learning could be cited, Watanabe, Takano, and Sakuma being among the best known of those who were done to death.

As we shall see later, the movement to restore the Emperor was coupled with a form of chauvinism or intense nationalism which may be summed up in the expression "Exalt the Emperor! Away with the barbarians!" (*Kinno! Joi!*) From this it would appear that the Dutch scholars' work in enlightening the nation upon the subject of foreign scientific attainments was anathema, but a conclusion of that kind must not be hastily arrived at. The cry, "Away with the barbarians!" was directed against Perry and the envoys of other foreign Powers, but there was nothing in that slogan which indicates a general unwillingness to emulate the foreigners' achievements in armaments or military tactics. In fact, for a number of years previous to 1853, Satsuma and Choshu and other Western clans had been very busily engaged in manufacturing guns and practising gunnery : to that extent at any rate the discoveries of the students of European sciences had been deliberately used by those men who were to be foremost in the Restoration.

In one respect at least the Dutch scholars contributed directly to the intellectual results achieved by the native historians. In all their reading of the histories of foreign countries they found no counterpart for the

33

A Political History of Japan

Shogunate. Western countries were governed directly, so they discovered, by their various Kings and Emperors, and it was natural to suppose that that fact had some connection with the progress in arms and knowledge which they had made. Reflections of such an order were, however, only ancillary at most in the Japanese minds to the more powerful convictions as to the righteousness of the Emperor's cause supplied by the students of the ancient classics of Japan. It is not easy, therefore, to determine the importance, on its intellectual side, of the study of Dutch in bringing about the Restoration. Some Japanese of the present day tend to emphasize the value of the movement, but it is probable that the thought is fathered more by desire than a critical knowledge of the facts. For example, Professor Ukita,[1] of Waseda University, states that new Japan was born on the 4th day of March, 1771, the day on which the superiority of Western anatomical science was incontestably proved. It is a long way, however, from the dissection of a criminal's body by a group of Japanese physicians, who found that a Dutch book on anatomy was accurate in its descriptions and the Chinese books were not, to the Restoration, and it requires a considerable effort of the imagination to see the connection. Present-day Japanese students of the Restoration period are prone to over-emphasize the part played by science, and to minimize the power of the superstitions and myths so deliberately and effectually propagated in the name of history by the native Japanese historians and theologians, as well as that of the opportunist policies of the promoters of the Restoration. It is interesting, however, to point out the fact that the Western clansmen, by their adoption of Western military methods and arms, were more than a match for the Shogun's forces, not only in the wars of the Restoration, but in the contests between the Tokugawa and Choshu which raged during the middle sixties.

How inextricably intermingled were fanaticism and

[1] Okuma, *Fifty Years of New Japan*, vol. ii. p. 140. London, 1910.

The Restoration Movement

enlightenment during the working up of the movement may perhaps be best seen in the so-called " Patriotic Schools " which sprang up in every town and village throughout Western Japan during the second quarter of the century. The staples of education in those schools were theologico-military—the exaltation of the Emperor as the descendant of the Sun-goddess, and therefore the rightful ruler of Japan, the destruction of the power of the usurping Tokugawa Shoguns, and the expansion in Asia of the Japanese Empire, to be accomplished by force of arms. To ensure success for the contemplated changes, instruction was given in military science, and actual training went on both in the old and in the new and Western style. The influence of these schools depended naturally upon the character and capacity of the masters. Doubtless many were mediocre in ability and disingenuous in their rampant loyalty, but here and there a prodigy was developed, such as that striking figure Yoshida Shoin, a member of the Choshu clan. Yoshida died at the hands of the Shogunate in 1859, at the age of twenty-nine, having been taken in an attempt to assassinate the Shogun's representative (Sho-Shi-Dai) in Kyoto, yet in his brief span of life he had profoundly influenced many of the Choshu leaders, and among his friends and pupils were numbered Kido, Ito, Inouye and Shinagawa. It is said of him by his biographer, Mr. Tokutomi, that his development was extraordinarily early, and it is claimed that he gave lectures on tactics before his Daimyo when less than ten years of age. His courage was that of a fanatic, and his whole life a protest against the disorder of the times in the sense of the usurpation by the Shogun of the powers which rightfully belonged to the Emperor.

In attempting to sum up the causes of the Restoration movement, enough has been said with regard to its intellectual and sentimental causes, but there remain to be dealt with the political and military forces immediately at work.

A Political History of Japan

On its political side the Restoration movement was the product of a reaction, based on superstition and fable in the guise of history, as well as on genuine scientific truth, against the duarchy implied by the existence of the Shogunate. It is doubtful whether the whole feudal system was involved, for, strange as it may seem, some at least of the clans held that the authority of the monarch ruling the whole country in the place of the Shogun was not incompatible with the continued existence of the feudal magnates and their exercise of sovereign powers over their fiefs and people. It is even probable that Satsuma, the most powerful of the Western clans, was prepared to enter the field against the Shogun in the hope of itself usurping the power exercised by the Tokugawa. The confusion of political ideas which existed at the time can hardly be overstated.

It would perhaps be fair to say that without the decline of the virility of the Shogunate by a process of internal disintegration, and a synchronous increase of the military power of such clans as Satsuma, Choshu, Tosa, and Hizen, as well as others of lesser note, a successful issue to the anti-Shogunate revolution would have been impossible. Certainly, without unity of action among the leading anti-Shogun clans the plan to destroy the dual system was hopeless. How and by whom the League of the Western Clans was formed is perhaps the question of greatest interest yet to be cleared up. The difficulties in the way of united action were very great, and that they were overcome is a tribute to the ingenuity of the men who formed this coalition. That it fell to pieces as soon as the immediate object was accomplished is a proof that agreement was reached only on a few matters of policy. To Kido Takayoshi is usually attributed the honour of persuading the Western Daimyo to unite their strength in behalf of the Imperial cause, but to any one conversant with the government of a clan, the task which he successfully accomplished was very different from what the

36

The Restoration Movement

description suggests. The Daimyo were only nominal rulers in their clans ; the real authority did not even lie with the karo, the members of the clan council, but with the yonin, the business men of the fief. Kido belonged to this class himself, and, like all the members of his class in the various daimiates, he was directly affected by the propaganda of the patriotic schools. Undoubtedly in Kido's case loyalty to the Imperial cause was genuine, and it is probable that he saw the inevitable result of the Restoration upon the feudal order. To the yonin the destruction of the daimiates was not the end of all things, but the beginning of a real career, bounded not by the narrow limits of their fiefs, but by the wide extent of the Empire alone. But how many of these matters were discussed at the meetings between Kido and Saigo Takamori, the representative of Satsuma, is not known, for Saigo was not the man to reveal what was in his mind. However, from subsequent events it would seem possible to infer that Saigo, too, saw the future opening up in a wonderful vista in which he appeared as the first military leader of the nation.

Having persuaded the yonin to concerted action against the Shogunate, it was not a difficult matter to get the consent, *pro forma*, of the Daimyo, for they could be easily persuaded that their future was assured. It is hardly possible to explain the League of the Clans on any other ground, for it is not likely that proud men, wholly conservative in their instincts, such as Shimadzu Hisamitsu (Saburo), the uncle of the reigning Prince of Satsuma, would have voluntarily supported a cause sure to involve in its successful issue the destruction of their feudal powers, without believing in the prospect of still greater honours in the reconstructed State of the future.

Be this as it may, to presuppose some such designs for personal aggrandizement seems a more correct reading of human nature than the usual explanation of the events, which asks us to believe that the Daimyo

A Political History of Japan

plunged blindly into the cause of the Emperor without a thought for their own future.

If it were not for the projection into the political arena of the problem of foreign intercourse raised by the advent of Commodore Perry, no further analysis of the political forces behind the Restoration would be necessary, and the movement could be set down as a revolution for the purpose of overthrowing the Tokugawa Shogunate. But Perry's mission, whatever its real purpose as conceived in the United States, was not an accidental phenomenon, but part of the general Western movement of trade towards the Orient. China and its resources had been known to and partially exploited by Europeans for some centuries, and by Americans since 1784. To obtain humane treatment for American sailors who reached the shores of Japan, whether voluntarily or through storms and shipwreck, and to secure the privilege of exchanging commodities, were the main objects of the Perry embassy. Other similar missions shortly afterwards arrived, bringing representatives of England and Russia. It happened in all cases, so great was the ignorance of the Japanese polity among foreigners, that the Shogun was approached as the supreme authority. Their mistake, natural enough in itself, proved a calamity to the Shogunate, since it afforded an opportunity for the partisans of royalty to make capital for their cause and bring fresh difficulties upon the already embarrassed Yedo Government. It is easy enough to see that so long as Japan was closed to foreign intercourse, and the Shogunate restricted to dealings with its own people, the difference between a government in the name of the Emperor or of the Shogun remained only a matter of domestic import, but when the Shogun's Government was compelled to treat with the representatives of other Powers, its true position became a far wider question. In the eyes of those Japanese who wished to regard it as such, the signature of the Shogun, or Taikun—a title invented for the occasion—upon en-

The Restoration Movement

gagements binding the country in its dealings with foreign Powers was a forgery as well as a deliberate reversal of the national policy of seclusion. However we may be disposed to appraise the culpability involved in the deception practised by the Yedo authorities in signing the early treaties with the American and English representatives, we are disposed to leniency by a fuller knowledge of the circumstances. The foreign representatives insisted upon concluding treaties, the Shogun could not secure their ratification by the Emperor, and there was nothing left to do but to affix his own signature. Moreover, if the Shogunate had been obdurate, and Perry had carried out his threat of securing his demands by force, the attack must necessarily have been made against Yedo, and the loss in property and lives would have been borne by the Shogun's people, the citizens of Yedo, and, what was more important, the loss in prestige in the eyes of his countrymen would have caused the fall of the Shogunate then and there. To have confessed to Perry the truth about the native polity, and to have directed him to the Imperial Court, would have been equally fatal for the Shogunate. It is difficult to see what else could have been done in the name of the Shogun by Ii Naosuke, the President of his Council of State, than to sign the treaties, and perpetuate the fiction that the Taikun was in reality the Emperor of Japan.

After the signing of the treaties, and the arrival of the Ministers of foreign Powers, still knottier problems arose to embarrass the Yedo Government. The most conspicuous of the complications, easily enough created by the *Kinno* party, were those known as the Kagoshima and Shimonoseki affairs.[1] In both cases the diplomatic agents of the Treaty Powers demanded the punishment of the offenders and money compensation for the damage done, and in both the Shogunate had to confess its weakness and commission the offended parties themselves to execute vengeance

[1] See Longford, J. H., *Story of Old Japan*, pp. 323-4.

39

A Political History of Japan

by force of arms. Neither of these punitive expeditions, the one against Satsuma, the other against Choshu, was wholly successful, and in the latter case, at any rate, the Shogun's Government was mulcted for a considerable amount. The effect of these and numerous other unfortunate incidents which involved the death of various innocent persons connected with the foreign embassies was to wear down the respect in which the Yedo Administration was held both in Japan itself and among the Treaty Powers.

Furthermore, the ranks of the Tokugawa party were split in two by dissensions over the question of a successor to Iyesada, who died in August 1858. The two factions were headed respectively by Ii Naosuke, Prince of Hikone, and Nariaki, Prince of Mito, the former supporting the claims of Iyemochi, the Prince of Kii, the latter those of his own son Yoshinobu (Keiki, Hitotsubashi). By vigorous action Ii carried the day for his candidate, and Nariaki and his supporters were confined to their palaces and ordered to refrain from further interference in the affairs of State. A lack of unity again appeared a decade later, when Owari and Echizen, two of the great Tokugawa clans, attached themselves to the royalist cause in the wars of the Restoration.

The complications attendant upon the opening of the country to foreign trade may be said to have precipitated the downfall of the Shogun's Government. Not only was the military weakness of the Tokugawa régime evidenced by its powerlessness to enforce its will upon the Western clans, but suspicion was cast upon its loyalty to the interests of the nation. Japanese began to be fearful for the independence of their country. Rightly or wrongly, they suspected that the nation's existence was menaced by the weak truckling of Yedo to the foreigners. Doubtless the *Kinno* party did not fail to propagate such suspicions among the clans, and advocate a union of the whole nation under the banner of the Emperor as the only means

40

The Restoration Movement

of defence against the encroachments of the "barbarians."

But it was specifically on its military side that the greatest weakness of the Shogunate lay. The Yedo Government established by Iyeyasu in the early part of the seventeenth century was primarily a government of force, and its security lay in the domination of each and every clan by the Tokugawa. How and why this power of might was honeycombed and destroyed during the seventeenth and eighteenth centuries by substituting a régime of peace for one of war, by exchanging the sword for the pen, by the creation of an all-embracing civil bureaucracy for the administration of the nation's affairs, has been related and discussed by every historian of Japan, and it can be assumed that such was the fact, without any further examination of the processes. As time went on the military power and prestige of the great clans, especially those remote from Yedo, had increased, and particularly in the second quarter of the nineteenth century, by the very practice which we have seen had so great an influence in the formation of military feudalism. The members of the warrior class had begun to desert their lords and reach the status of ronin or masterless men, from whence it was easy for them to pass into the ranks of the armies of any Daimyo. In this way considerable bodies of men were added to the fighting strength of the Western clans. So strong had Choshu become in 1864 that the clan openly defied the Shogun. For some years a fruitless war dragged on, and finally the Shogunate was glad to secure peace without effecting any other result than the temporary disgrace of the two Choshu Princes and the exclusion of their retainers from Kyoto. It was this disastrous civil strife that broke the last remnants of the Yedo power.

Among the remoter causes of the Restoration, the place of first importance must be given to the existence of a sectional and feudal jealousy, the West against the East. The main object of the movement was to destroy the domination of the Tokugawa over Choshu and Satsuma, and incidentally to place the Emperor once more in the position of an active sovereign. In the same category, but as of secondary importance, may be mentioned the intellectual and sentimental causes, no doubt essential and of no small importance in preparing the educated classes for the changes contemplated, but nevertheless distinctly ancillary. Among the immediate causes the arrival of the Western nations and the breaking down of the policy of national seclusion probably take first place, because of the influence they exerted toward the overthrow of the Shogunate and the unification of the Empire under the monarch as the surest means of preserving the nation's independence.

CHAPTER II

THE POLICY OF THE RESTORATION PARTY

THE incidents of the closing years of the old régime afford an insight into Japanese political characteristics, and merit closer study, especially for the light they throw on subsequent events. The *Kinno* party being out of power by reason of the Tokugawa predominance and desirous of getting the reins of office into their hands, displayed an almost criminal willingness to adopt any and every means to overthrow the Yedo authorities. In 1864 Choshu laid plans to carry off the Emperor, Komei Tenno, who was privy to the plot, to the Western provinces, and by appealing to the people's loyalty to the throne contest by force of arms the Shogun's right to rule. When owing to the vigilance of the Shogun's representative that *coup de main* failed, and in consequence Choshu was exiled from Kyoto and the Mori deprived of their rank and office, the Emperor, in feigned indignation at the affront to his person, but really to discomfit the Shogun, ordered that Choshu should be punished. Thus there was forced upon the Tokugawa the necessity of undertaking a punitive expedition against Choshu, the expense of which exhausted the Yedo treasury, while its virtual failure destroyed the last fragments of the Shogun's military prestige. Nor did the Imperialists stop with fomenting internal disturbances, for by working on the sentiments of the fanatical ronin with the cry " Expel the barbarians ! " they brought about the murder of several foreigners, thus jeopardizing peaceful relations between the Yedo authorities and the Treaty Powers. As it turned out,

43

the wisdom, or perhaps the timidity, of the Shogunate deprived the situation of its most dangerous elements, and no clash with the Powers occurred.

In 1867, near the close of the year, the Western clans forwarded a joint letter to the Shogun demanding his resignation from office. Backed by the power of the Royalist clans, and supported by two of the most powerful of the branches of the Tokugawa house, Owari and Echizen, refusal of such a demand was impossible, and it is probable that the Shogun and his Council of State, harassed as they were by fears and foes on every side, welcomed the opportunity of making their exit. The terms of the letter were therefore readily complied with, in a note [1] dated November 3, 1867, and the resignation was formally accepted in the name of the Emperor on the 12th of the same month.

The position of the Tokugawa party in this crisis was plainly indicated in official statements issued at the time. The letter of resignation itself pointed to the coming of the foreigners as creating a situation which demanded the restoration of the administrative authority to the Emperor and unification of the whole people in support of the throne. It plainly implied also that foreign intercourse was inevitable, but that the danger of aggression by foreign Powers against the independence of the State had been overestimated. As far as his clan was concerned, the Shogun pledged it to the support of the monarch, and evidently expected that, in stepping down from the high office which he had inherited from his ancestors, he and his people would take their places again in the feudal hierarchy under the sovereign. In a letter [2] addressed to the members of the diplomatic corps the Shogun explained the circumstances which had elevated his ancestor to

---

[1] McLaren, W. W., *Japanese Government Documents, 1867–89*, pp. 1, 2 ; *Trans. A. S. J.*, vol. xlii. Part I. Yokohama, 1914. (This collection of documents is referred to hereafter by the abbreviation *J. G. D.*)

[2] Gubbins, *op. cit.*, pp. 306–11.

the position of administrative authority in the nation, and after formally accepting, as the result of his own misconduct, the troubles and perplexities of the period, announced his intention of giving up entirely his rule over the land and restoring to the Emperor the powers of his high office. The only open protest against the Shogun's course in resigning his power came from the citizens of Yedo, in a long document in which they described the unfortunate plight into which they would fall if the seat of government were removed from their midst. This protest was mainly the complaint of the merchants, who anticipated their own ruin and the decline of their city.

When the Tokugawa thus gave up their peculiar position in the State, it was with the understanding, on their part at least, that the Emperor would assume control of the administration, and, relying upon the advice and support of *all* the clans, their own included, would strive to effect a solution of the problems which had arisen through the renewal of intercourse with foreign countries. But the designs of the Western clansmen were not compatible with the survival of any shreds of the Tokugawa power, and it soon became apparent that the Court, reflecting the sentiments of the dominant party, was determined to ignore the former Shogun's claims. The Tokugawa were willing to surrender their hereditary position of priority in the feudal order, but they were not disposed to degrade themselves still further. Rather than tamely submit to their own complete humiliation, the Tokugawa samurai determined to fight out the issue with their enemies, the Western clans. Hence, in the opening days of 1868, Keiki sent a written protest [1] to the Court, pointing out that though he had taken such measures as were possible to ensure the safety of the Imperial person, Kyoto was rapidly filling up with " lawless men "—the Choshu samurai—and that in order to avoid a clash between his own retainers and these " low fellows " he had

D
[1] *J. G. D.*, pp. 3, 4.

determined to remove himself and his party to Osaka. The meaning of this protest, though couched in terms of highest respect and solicitude for the Imperial person, was plainly a declaration of war between his followers and the Western clans.

As no notice of his letter was taken by the Court, and no attempt was made by the Government to mollify the injured feelings of the Tokugawa, hostilities commenced. The Satsuma yashiki in Osaka was destroyed, and thereafter the forces of the Shogun marched on Kyoto, only to meet with defeat at Fushimi. Although Keiki himself took no part in the hostilities, the struggle thus commenced dragged on during the year, and did not end till the spring of 1869. At no time was there any doubt as to the result of this civil war, for the Tokugawa, who, four years before, with immensely greater resources and the support of public sentiment, were unable to make headway against the Choshu clan, could not hope to triumph over a coalition of all the Western clans, commanding as they did the whole power of the State.

Much might be said in extenuation of the folly of precipitating the war of the Restoration. Doubtless the long endured usurpation of the Shogunate had generated in the Western clans a hostility all the fiercer for being so long pent up. Doubtless, too, the Tokugawa party, in unconditionally resigning, displayed a simplicity that was not warranted in the circumstances if they expected anything at the hands of the new régime but the immediate and complete destruction of their influence in the State. Yet, if the Western leaders had in 1867 and 1868 shown even a tithe of the moderation which they displayed a few years later, when Admiral Enomoto, the last of the rebels to surrender, was appointed to office in the Government, the costly military operations need never have been undertaken.

When the civil war was over, the Government, with commendable clemency, allowed the ex-Shogun to live

The Policy of the Restoration Party

quietly in Shizuoka, from which city the founder of his line, Iyeyasu, after his retirement from office in favour of his son, had watched over and directed the destiny of the nation in the early years of the seventeenth century. A few of the ringleaders of the rebellion were executed, and the Aidzu clan was cruelly dispersed, but for the remainder of the rebels a general amnesty was declared.

If the events of those years leaves upon the student an impression of wanton opportunism, coupled as such a policy must always be with complete repudiation of principles and policies assumed for the occasion when their immediate purpose has been served, or if the actions of the Restoration leaders during this period reveal the short-sightedness of a group of samurai obsessed with a passion for the destruction of their enemies and a selfish ambition to elevate themselves to places of influence and power, much must be said on the other side of the case. The Shogunate was a complete usurpation of the Emperor's administrative powers, and, more than that, the administration over which the Shogun nominally presided was no longer efficient. There was neither peace nor order in the country, and the very existence of the Empire seemed to be threatened by the fleets of foreign Powers off the shores of Japan. Apart from the element of loyalty to the throne, which, so far as it existed as a genuine sentiment, was entirely praiseworthy, there was a profound anxiety for the safety of the State. The Restoration leaders saw clearly that to preserve its independence it was necessary to unify the forces of the country. Under the feeble control of the Shogunate, whose weakness had been amply demonstrated, there could be nothing but a continuation of the civil strife of previous years, entailing a further weakening of the Empire, and if Japan was to continue to exist as a sovereign State, its whole strength must be gathered under the direction of a single authority, the Emperor.

In choosing the Imperial throne as the centre around

47

which to rally the nation, the Imperialists could not have acted more wisely, though it is unnecessary to presuppose any particular loyalty to the person of the reigning sovereign, for the position of any individual Emperor had been, in fact, among the most uncertain in the State. However, if the monarch was the plaything of the Shogunate and the Court, the throne was a real institution and its appeal was universal. That it had been established by the gods and occupied for generations in an unbroken line was the belief of the people, and the Western clansmen had by no mere accident chosen a policy which ensured the success of their project. Yet it is impossible to decide how far that watchword of the Royalists, " Exalt the Emperor," was dictated by genuine loyalty or by shrewd political opportunism. Readers familiar with the versions of the events of this period as narrated by foreigners [1] will be well aware of the policy of the Imperialist party and its results, as far as the foreign relations of Japan were concerned. The tradition in Japan for practically the whole of the Tokugawa period had been opposed to all friendly and open intercourse with any foreign Power. National seclusion, intended to prevent all immigration of foreigners or emigration of Japanese, was one of the items of policy adopted by the third Tokugawa Shogun Iyemitsu in his attempt to secure a lasting era of peace for the Japanese people. The explanation of the adoption of such a measure [2] as well as the reasons for permitting a very limited infraction of the strict rule of isolation by means of the Dutch factory at Deshima do not concern us here. What is important to remember is the fact that

[1] The best of the recent books dealing with this period is J. H. Gubbins's *The Progress of Japan, 1853-71* ; Oxford, 1911. Among the contemporary accounts, those most worth reading are : Oliphant, L., *Narrative of the Earl of Elgin's Mission to China and Japan*, two vols., London, 1859 ; Alcock, Sir R., *The Capital of the Tycoon*, two vols., London, 1863 ; Adams, F. O., *The History of Japan*, two vols., London, 1875 ; Griffis, W. E., *Townsend Harris: First American Envoy to Japan*, Boston, 1895.

[2] For a discussion of this question see Longford, J. H., *op. cit.*, chap. xv.

The Policy of the Restoration Party

the effect of isolation, when combined with the historical studies and the theologico-political propaganda of the revivalists of Pure Shinto, was to make the Japanese of the Restoration period not only extraordinarily insular, but provincial to a degree seldom seen among civilized peoples. To them non-Japanese of whatever race or origin, whether Chinese, Europeans, or Americans, were barbarians—" ugly, red-haired barbarians." The thought of intercourse with foreigners was therefore peculiarly obnoxious and distasteful to those members of the race who were of political importance. As has been pointed out, the tradition of national seclusion, so strongly intrenched in the minds of the people, was responsible for one of the greatest obstacles with which the Shogun's Government had to reckon in signing the treaties with the American and European Envoys. Moreover, the hatred of foreigners was encouraged by the Court and its adherents, both because the Emperor Komei Tenno and his immediate circle, ignorant of the history of or actual conditions in foreign countries, were pleased to entertain such prejudices, and because the Shogun's administration could be greatly embarrassed by such a course. Samurai were encouraged to believe that to murder a foreigner was an act of patriotism, whereas such acts only led to demands for punishment and compensation, the former of these at any rate not always being in the power of the Yedo authorities to satisfy. The *Kinsé Shiriaku* and the *Genji Yume Monogatari*, both of which narratives cover more or less completely the decade previous to 1867, present from the Japanese viewpoint the character and results of the contemporary propaganda in favour of " expelling the barbarians."

Furthermore, the long period of isolation had furnished no precedents to guide the authorities in their dealings with foreigners, and lacking these, the Japanese of that day, except when direct pressure by display of armed force was exerted, fell back upon the resource of all Oriental minds in such an emergency—delay, subterfuge, and mental reservation. It is amusing to find the first American Envoy to Japan stationed at Shimoda, a little fishing town on the extreme end of the Idzu peninsula, as remote from Yedo as he could well be. Likewise that Hakodate, four hundred miles or more north of Yedo on the island of Hokkaido, should have been solemnly agreed upon as one of the Treaty Ports must have greatly amused the authorities, for at that time it was probably only a rare Japanese who could have told where that village was situated. We can sympathize, too, with the lament of Sir Rutherford Alcock that it was one thing for Lord Elgin to come to Japan accompanied by an escort of warships and force a treaty upon the Shogun, but a very different undertaking for the resident British Minister in Japan to see that the treaty stipulations were carried out. Townsend Harris, the first American Envoy to Japan, as patient and courteous a man as ever represented one country in another, said [1] of the Japanese officials : " I know enough of them to be aware that to lie is the rule, to tell the truth is the exception."

With the death of Komei Tenno early in 1867 and the succession of Mutsuhito (the Meiji Tenno), the Imperialist party reversed its former policy in its dealings with the Western Powers. The antagonists of intercourse became its protagonists. The passing of the old Emperor, who it would seem entertained a bitter hatred of foreigners, may partly account for the change. But in the main it may be said that the anti-foreign propaganda had served its purpose, and to continue it any longer would have been only a source of embarrassment to the new Government about to take over the administrative power of the Shogun. This *volte-face* from anti- to pro-foreign sentiment was swiftly executed by the Court, but not without some incidents which to those who participated in them were serious enough. The whole body of foreign repre-

[1] Griffis, W. E., *op. cit.*, p. 300.

The Policy of the Restoration Party

sentatives had come down from Yedo to Osaka by sea to attend the function of the opening of Osaka to foreign trade, to take place on January 1, 1868. They were still in Osaka when the battle of Fushimi was fought, and as the flying Tokugawa forces entered Osaka with the royalists in pursuit it was necessary for the envoys to make a hurried departure for Kobe, then a mere fishing village. But upon arrival at Kobe they found that the local officials had fled, and it was feared that a general massacre of the foreigners might ensue, for the long-standing hostility of the royalists was far better known than their recent conversion to friendliness. A clash did occur between a body of Bizen samurai and a detachment of French marines, and as a consequence guards were landed from the foreign ships in the harbour, and a joint demand from the Powers for the punishment of the offending samurai was forwarded to Kyoto. The result was that the commanding officer of the Bizen detachment was given over and condemned to death by *hara-kiri*. While the representatives of the Powers were still in Kobe, guarded by an international force, a messenger arrived from Kyoto to announce that the young Emperor had taken over the control of all the affairs of state and had sanctioned the treaties with the Powers. Under such dramatic circumstances was made the public announcement of the radical change of the policy of the Court toward the Powers, an announcement which legitimized the status of the foreign envoys *vis-à-vis* the new régime. The marine guards were immediately withdrawn from Kobe, and the whole party returned to Osaka. Shortly afterwards, as an earnest of its intentions, an invitation to the Court was extended to the Ministers of all the Powers.

The six weeks which elapsed before this audience were filled with events, some of which were not calculated to inspire confidence in the minds of the foreign representatives. An unprovoked assault upon a French man-of-war's boat was made near Osaka by a party

51

of Tosa samurai, and resulted in the death of eleven of the crew. This incident was closed by the execution of eleven of the samurai who participated in the attack, an ample apology from the Emperor, and the disbursement from the Imperial treasury of a large sum of money as compensation to the widows and children of the murdered men. But the most startling of all the events was an attack upon the British Minister, Sir Harry Parkes, and his escort as he was on his way to the audience at the palace in Kyoto on March 22. Fortunately, no one was killed except one of the two Japanese assailants, but a number of Sir Harry's guards were seriously wounded, and the Minister himself escaped death largely through the adroitness of Goto Shojiro, an Imperial representative who walked at his side. The audience was postponed, the Emperor made a humble apology and offered compensation to the wounded men, and the surviving, though wounded, assailant was executed, not by the honourable method of *hara-kiri*, but by decapitation and gibbeting, as a warning to others of his class that the anti-foreign policy of the past had been given up. The exciting story of this adventure was told by Sir Harry in a report to his Government, and was published in a contemporary Blue Book on Japan.

Nothing thus far has been said as to the nature of the treaties between the Shogunate and the foreign nations which were ratified by the Restoration Government in 1868. The earliest of the treaties was that signed by Commodore Perry on behalf of the United States on March 31, 1854, at Kanagawa. It provided for the immediate opening of the port of Shimoda in Idzu, and after one year the port of Hakodate in the Hokkaido, and for permission not only to purchase at these places supplies necessary for ships, but to exchange commodities ; for assistance to be tendered to American sailors shipwrecked on any coast of Japan ; for the appointment, after eighteen months, of an American consul or agent to reside at Shimoda, and for most-favoured-nation treatment. In a series of additional regulations agreed upon in September of the same year, it was provided that Americans violating the laws of Japan should not be dealt with according to Japanese law, but be taken on board their own ships by Japanese police. The earliest British convention, dated Nagasaki, October 14, 1854, and signed by Rear-Admiral Stirling, followed very closely the lines of the Perry treaty, and secured the immediate opening of the port of Nagasaki. It likewise stipulated that most-favoured-nation treatment should be accorded to Great Britain, and for the punishment of British offenders against Japanese laws by the commanders of their ships. In the following year Russia and the Netherlands entered into negotiations and secured treaties with Japan. The Russo-Japanese convention differed from the two above-mentioned in that it delimited the boundaries of the two countries by dividing the Kurile Islands and Saghalien almost equally between them. In respect to the punishment of Russian offenders against Japanese laws, and the most-favoured-nation treatment, its provisions were similar to the American and British conventions of 1854. The Netherlands " Preliminary Convention of Commerce," signed at Nagasaki on November 9, 1855, secured for the Dutch all the concessions accorded to Americans, British, and Russians, but the treaty differs from the others in many respects, which may be accounted for by the fact that the Dutch had always enjoyed trading privileges in Japan, though under stringent and in many ways humiliating regulations.

It was not, however, until 1858 that the treaties, with one important exception, assumed the form they bore at the beginning of the Meiji Era. A carefully worded " Treaty of Amity and Commerce between the United States and Japan " was signed in Yedo on July 29 of that year on behalf of the United States by Townsend Harris,[1] who has left a minute and often

---

[1] Griffis, W. E., *op. cit.*, chaps. xiii–xv inclusive.

amusing account of the progress of the negotiations.
Among other matters, the fourteen articles and seven
appended regulations which comprise the convention
provided for consular courts, religious liberty, a
tariff of import and export duties, and the revision of
the treaty, after July 4, 1872, " upon the desire of
either the American or the Japanese Government, and
on one year's notice given by either party." According
to the tariff of customs duties on imports, the free list
contained gold and silver, coined or uncoined, wearing
apparel in actual use, household furniture and printed
books not intended for sale, but the property of
persons coming to reside in Japan. Dutiable articles
were divided into three classes, (1) those paying
5 per cent. *ad valorem*, mainly articles necessary for
building or repairing ships or houses, steam machinery,
food-stuffs, coal, tin, lead, zinc, and raw silk ; (2) those
paying 35 per cent. *ad valorem*, spirituous and malt
liquors ; (3) all commodities not otherwise provided
for paying 20 per cent. *ad valorem*. A 5 per cent.
ad valorem duty was to be levied on all Japanese commodities exported as cargo, except gold and silver coin
and copper in bars.

Of similar import were the four other treaties with
Great Britain, Russia, the Netherlands, and France
which were negotiated about the same time, and such
differences of arrangement and other minor divergencies
as exist in the main reflect either the circumstances
under which the negotiations took place or the
idiosyncrasies of the envoys. For example, Harris,
who was peculiarly impressed with the capacity of the
Japanese for interposing delays, stipulated that the
American treaty should come into force at the
appointed time even if ratifications had not then been
exchanged.

In 1866 a Tariff Convention was signed at Yedo by
the representatives of Great Britain, France, and the
Netherlands, providing for a revision of the Harris
tariff of customs duties on imports and exports which

The Policy of the Restoration Party

reduced the import duties to a 5 per cent. basis. This measure may be explained partly by the desire of European Powers to hold the Shogun to the terms of the Shimonoseki Convention of 1864, and partly by the general Free Trade movement in Europe. While the reduction of the duties was greatly in the interests of both the foreign merchants in Japan and the Japanese themselves, yet it meant for the time being a diminution of the revenues of the already financially embarrassed Shogunate treasury. After the Restoration these tariff regulations grew more and more objectionable to the Japanese, not only because they were considered an invasion of the nation's sovereign rights, but on account of the pressure which it was believed the Powers had brought to bear upon the Shogunate at the time the convention was signed. How this question of tariff autonomy was finally settled will appear later.[1]

A knowledge of the nature of the functions which were taken over from the defunct Shogunate in the name of the Emperor by the leaders of the Restoration movement is essential to any understanding of the domestic problems which confronted the new administration. Probably no better analogy to the relations between the Shogunate and the Daimyo could be found than in the Chinese system under the Manchus, but even then the similarity is not by any means complete. The power of the Shogun, as well as that of the Daimyo, was founded upon possession of land, and over the people resident in their fiefs they exercised sovereign control. In practically all matters of local interest the will of the Daimyo, with the modification already stated, was law within the fief, and his power, represented by the military class, was the only sanction known. Thus the various branches of the Tokugawa family were scattered over the country upon great domains, the three most illustrious houses being those of Kii, Owari, and Mito. In addition to the domains presided over by cadets of the Tokugawa family, there were

[1] See below, Chapter X, pp. 237.

certain territories which were ruled directly by the Shogunate through officers appointed for the purpose, such as the cities of Yedo, Osaka, and Nagasaki. In this way the territory of the State was divided up into areas which for the purposes of local government were under the control of the feudal magnates, whether Tokugawa or otherwise. The Shogun was always a scion of a feudal house, and by direction of the founder of the Tokugawa line the choice was limited to the Daimyo families of Kii, Owari, and Mito. When a cadet of one of these houses succeeded to the office of Shogun, he was removed from his province to Yedo, and at the head of his Government exercised a limited administrative authority over the whole nation. To a certain extent the jurisdiction of the Daimyo in his own fief and that of the Shogunate were mutually exclusive, and it depended largely upon the power of the Daimyo whether the Shogunate interfered much or little in the government of the various fiefs. Iyeyasu in the zenith of his power was able to make and unmake Daimyo, and his commands were obeyed perforce, but the case was very different with most of his successors. The question thus arises : By what distribution of power among the various so-called sovereign authorities was a *modus vivendi* achieved? No answer which would be equally accurate for all cases can be given, for in feudalism armed force is the only sanction of law. It is probable, however, that throughout the whole Tokugawa régime the less powerful Daimyo were never in a position to resist interference in their affairs by the Shogunate, whereas the exact opposite was the case with the great feudatories, whether Tokugawa or not. As we have seen, a Prince of Mito in the seventeenth century was in a position to defy the Shogun in the matter of his historical studies, and in the nineteenth the Lords of Satsuma and Choshu openly challenged the Yedo authorities by refusing to surrender members of their clans who had been guilty of violence against foreigners.

The Policy of the Restoration Party

On the other hand, there were certain functions performed by the Shogunate in regulating the inter-clan relations. They were not permitted to enter into alliances with one another, nor with foreign Powers. Moreover, codes [1] of laws had been promulgated in the seventeenth and eighteenth centuries for the purpose of preserving the *status quo* of the various clans and for the administration of justice in civil and criminal cases.

Not only was the administration of justice peculiarly a matter of interest to the Shogunate, but so also were relations with foreign countries and the defence of the Empire against its enemies. It was the purpose of the Shogun Iyemitsu to cut off all intercourse with strangers, and hence an " Edict of Seclusion " (1636) had been promulgated, but no Shogun could arbitrarily determine that attacks upon the country by its enemies should not take place. Hence the fortification and defence of the sea coasts of Japan had constituted one of the conspicuous activities of the Shogunate. Those Daimyo whose territories were situated on the sea were compelled by the Yedo authorities to make provision against attack, and whenever foreign ships approached the coast, as they often did after the middle of the eighteenth century, it was the Shogunate which ordered them to be driven away. When this policy of strict non-intercourse began to be modified after 1825 the right to deal with foreigners was jealously guarded by the Shogun, and it was mainly for this reason that foreigners thought that Yedo was the seat of the Imperial authority. Likewise, it was natural that in its declining years the Shogunate should have been connected by foreigners with the direction of the foreign policy of the nation to the exclusion of practically everything else. Hence it is that Western students of Japan have but few sources [2] of information at hand for the study of that most in-

[1] Hall, J. C., *Tokugawa Legislation. Trans. A.S.J.*, vols. xxxviii., Part IV ; xli., Part V.
[2] See Wigmore, J. H., *Materials for the Study of Private Law in Old Japan. Trans. A.S.J.*, vol. xx., Supplement, Part I, *passim.*

teresting question, the administrative power of the Yedo authorities.

It is to be inferred, however, from the early regula-tions [1] issued by the Emperor's Government that the internal organization of the various clans was left entirely to their own discretion ; that the assessment and collection of rice taxes as well as other feudal dues of every kind were matters of local control ; that the bestowing of honours, coining of money, fixing of weights and measures, and regulation of inter-fief trade, were likewise within the discretion of the rulers of the clans. And finally, that during the period in which the Shogun's power was crumbling, the feudal lords had contracted alliances with each other and had exercised their discretion in securing the services of foreign teachers and advisers.

It is obvious, therefore, that during the course of the Tokugawa régime, and with particular rapidity toward its close, there was in process a decentralizing tendency, and it would not be far from the truth to say that that tendency had culminated by the middle of the nineteenth century in complete local autonomy, except in the territories directly controlled by the Shogunate and some of the branches of the Tokugawa family. For some months after the fall of the Shogun the customs of the past, so far as they concerned the local affairs of the clans, remained unmolested. The administration of the territories, however, belonging to the Shogunate or the numerous rebel members of the Tokugawa family presented a problem which the new Government had to face, though even that task did not become a pressing one for some time. In such matters as were not purely local, in which the action and the support of a central authority were necessary, it was relatively easy to transfer jurisdiction from Yedo to Kyoto by the creation, in connection with the Court, of a tentative administrative body, called the Sanshoku [2] (Three Offices of the Central Government).

[1] *J. G. D.*, p. 10.   [2] *Idem*, p. 4.

The Policy of the Restoration Party

It will, therefore, be obvious that during the months which immediately followed the transfer of the supreme authority from the Shogun to the Emperor, no small amount of confusion and uncertainty must have prevailed, especially in the ex-Shogun's domains, from which all the officials had fled at the news of the battle at Fushimi. For this reason many of the most important cities of the country, including all the ports, were left for the moment without any administrative machinery. But in the domains belonging to the royalist Daimyo, and in the theatre of the war of the Restoration, it is quite conceivable that conditions remained practically without change. The affairs of the great majority of the loyal Daimyo proceeded as usual. Only gradually was the control of the central Government extended to the remoter districts, and that such was the case is clearly evident from the official documents of the period.

The personnel of the Government set up in Kyoto in January 1868 is far more significant than its organization, which was intended to be temporary only. The " Three Offices of the Central Government " already referred to were those of the Sosai (Supreme Head), the Gijo and the Sanyo (Councillors of the First and Second Classes). Prince Arisugawa was made the Sosai, and associated with him as deputies were Sanjo Saneyoshi and Iwakura Tomomi. Under these three men, the first of whom was a Prince of the Blood, the other two Kuge, there served a number of men whose names fill the pages of subsequent history, especially Kido, Okubo, Komatsu, and Goto, in whose hands from the very beginning the real power of the Government rested. Subordinate to the office of the Sosai were those of the Gijo and Sanyo ; of the Gijo (First Class Councillors), half were nominated from the ranks of the Kuge, and half drawn from the Daimyo of the leading clans in Owari, Aki, Echizen, Tosa, and Satsuma. This list was as remarkable for the provinces it included as for those which it excluded, since it contained the names of only two, Tosa and Satsuma, of the four Western clans, which we have so often referred to as the chief promoters of the Emperor's cause. Owari and Echizen were Tokugawa clans which had gone over to the Imperial side upon the accession of the ex-Shogun Yoshinobu (Keiki or Hitotsubashi), and remained loyal to the throne during the war. Also, Choshu was excluded because the clan was still in disgrace, its two Princes deprived of rank, and its clansmen forbidden to enter Kyoto in consequence of the affair of 1864. The Gijo were intended to perform the functions of a deliberative and administrative body. Of the Sanyo (the Second Class Councillors), five were Kuge, and fifteen were samurai from the provinces mentioned above.

Another striking feature of the earliest organization of the central Government after the Restoration was the inclusion of such a large Kuge element. By this means the liability to friction between the Court and the Daimyo was diminished, for it is not inconceivable that the Court nobles looked forward to the Restoration as an event that would place all power in their hands. It is true that the Kuge regarded themselves in both rank and station as far above even the greatest of the Daimyo, and would therefore be liable to manifest considerable sensitiveness in the matter of the distribution of offices. The loyal Daimyo, on the other hand, were conscious of their prestige as feudal magnates, for it was undoubtedly by their assistance, or at any rate owing to the strength of their clans, that the Restoration was successfully accomplished. Difficulties of this sort were skilfully met by appointing to the highest post a royal Prince, against whose primacy no objection could be taken, and bestowing all the other great offices upon the Kuge and the Daimyo. The real master minds of the movement contented themselves, as had been their wont in the past, with offices inconspicuous, yet so close to the centre of authority that they could easily direct the progress

The Policy of the Restoration Party

of events. Hence we find Kido, Okubo, and many others of the real promoters of the Restoration attached to the Sosai's office. It is noteworthy, too, that of all the loyal Daimyo only those of the five provinces mentioned found places in the ranks of the Gijo and Sanyo. Whatever may have been the principle upon which this selection was made, the fact that a few were chosen and the rest overlooked has a significance that it would be difficult to exaggerate, for here at the very outset appeared a characteristic of the Meiji Government which has been the cause of almost constant friction between the official class and the politicians. "Clan government" does not refer so much to the continuance of the feudal spirit as to the monopolizing of power by the representatives of a few of the clans to the exclusion of the others. It is an over-statement of the truth, of course, to say that all the offices of state have been kept in the hands of the henchmen of a few Western clans, for as time went on the area from which public servants were drawn speedily widened, and yet the student of the Meiji Era, especially of its closing years, is constantly coming upon the politicians' efforts, both in the Diet and outside of it, to get rid of the domination of the "Sat-Cho" combination.

No sooner had the Sanshoku been established than important changes in its organization began to be made. In February 1868, after hostilities between the Tokugawa forces and the new Government had broken out, two separate attempts were made at organizing the Gijo for the better performance of administrative business. The first set up seven [1] Departments of State and the second added a Presidential Board,[2] making in all eight. At the head of each of these Departments was placed a Prince of the Blood or a Kuge who was a Gijo, and attached to each office were several

[1] *J. G. D.*, pp. 4, 5.
[2] *Idem*, pp. 5, 6. These arrangements were a faithful copy of the Chinese system which had been adopted by Japan in 701 A.D.

E

Sanyo. The eight departments were the Presidential Board, the offices of Shinto Religion, Home Affairs, Foreign Affairs, Army and Navy, Finance, Justice, and Laws. A somewhat elaborate attempt was made at the same time to define and delimit the functions to be exercised by each department. The relations which existed between the Gijo and Sanyo, or between either of these and the Sosai, cannot be accurately described. In a general way it is obvious that the Sosai was the executive authority, the Gijo the administrative body, and the Sanyo either administrative or advisory. Probably the Sosai determined what measures should be undertaken, and consulted the Gijo and Sanyo on the methods to be adopted in each case.

Such questions of detail are, however, not of any serious importance, for in June 1868, when the Tokugawa rebels had been driven into the remote regions of the north, and peace had been restored throughout that part of Japan which the Japanese of the day thought of as Japan proper, a complete revision of the organization of the Government was announced. The Sanshoku were abolished, and the Daijokwan was established as the repository of " all power and authority in the Empire." The proclamation [1] by which this change was announced is the most interesting of its kind appearing previous to the year 1889, and for that reason a somewhat detailed analysis of it follows.

In the preamble to this Constitution, for that was the word used as the title of the main part of the document, an explanation of the circumstances which had caused such frequent changes in the organization of the central Government was offered. " These arrangements (the Sanshoku, etc.), made during a time of civil commotion, were necessarily hurried and imperfect." The principles upon which the proposed Constitution had been based were embodied in the Imperial oath, and the purposes to be effected thereby were first, to establish laws and regulations which had

[1] *J. G. D.*, pp. 7–15.

The Policy of the Restoration Party

hitherto remained undetermined, and second, to ensure the permanent security and comfort of the people.

Then followed as the first article a recital of the Imperial oath : [1]

" The practice of discussion and debate shall be universally adopted, and all measures shall be decided by public argument.

" High and low shall be of one mind, and social order shall thereby be perfectly maintained. It is necessary that the civil and military powers be concentrated in a single whole, the rights of all classes be assured, and the national mind be completely satisfied.

" The uncivilized customs of former times shall be broken through, and the impartiality and justice displayed in the working of nature shall be adopted as a basis of action. Intellect and learning shall be sought for throughout the world, in order to establish the foundations of the Empire."

The second and third articles provided for the establishment of the Daijokwan (Council of State) for the purpose of concentrating all authority, whether executive, legislative, or judicial, in a single body, by which means " the difficulty of divided government " was to be obviated. Provision was made at the same time for division of the powers of the Daijokwan into three categories, and for the exercise of those three groups of functions by three separate bodies, which while distinct from one another were nevertheless integral parts of the Daijokwan. The fourth article announced the nature of the system by which appointments to office were to be made. The highest offices were to be given to the Court and territorial nobles, so that " due affection " might be shown to the relatives of the Emperor and respect to the feudal magnates, and offices of the second and lower rank were to be given to the samurai, that " honour may be given to wisdom." The fifth article announced the intention of establishing an assembly into which were to be

[1] For the modern form of this Imperial oath see *J. G. D.*, p. 8, footnote.

gathered representatives of the clans, cities, and Imperial domains. Article six provided for a system of ranks among the officials of the Government, so that each officer should realize the relative importance of the position to which he was appointed, " and not bring it into contempt." In article seven the display of pomp and grandeur universally connected with the movements of great personages was forbidden ; the retinues of Princes of the Blood, nobles of the Court and territorial nobles were not to exceed six samurai and three lackeys, while those of persons of lesser note were reduced to two samurai and one lackey. Article eight provided that all persons who had advice to offer on any matters of public interest should be afforded an opportunity of communicating their ideas to the authorities, and such persons were to be accorded interviews by the officials of the appropriate department, in their departmental offices, full discussions of the matters in question being allowed to take place ; otherwise than as thus provided Government officials were not permitted to discuss public questions with the unofficial public. Article nine stated that the term of office of all officials should be four years, one-half retiring every two years, except in the cases of those men who " cannot conveniently be dismissed because they have won general approval." Provision for a revenue for the State was made in the tenth article : the Daimyo, samurai, farmers, artisans, and merchants were to be taxed for the upkeep of the Army and the support of the Government. Government officials and persons possessing rank were to contribute one-thirtieth of their incomes. The eleventh and concluding article provided for the conduct of the local government, not according to a uniform system, but in accordance with the principles of the Imperial oath. It likewise limited the sovereign powers of the feudal authorities by denying them, without permission from the Daijokwan, the right to confer honours, coin money, or employ foreigners, and under no circumstances were they to contract alliances with a foreign Power or with

The Policy of the Restoration Party

other feudal magnates. These limitations were imposed so that there might " be no conflict of greater and lesser authority, no confusion in the Constitution."

The appendices contained a list of the offices and departments of the central Government, and the names and ranks of the men who were appointed thereto. A Council of State (Daijokwan) was set up and divided into seven departments: the Deliberative Assembly, consisting of Upper and Lower Houses ; the Lords President of the Council ; the Departments of Shinto Religion, Finance, War, Foreign Affairs, and Justice. During the following year the Department of Civil Affairs was created, only to be abolished in 1871, and those of Public Works and Education were added, and the Department of Justice was reorganized so as to perform the functions of the Board of Censors (Danjo-dai) in addition to those originally assigned to it. The main changes effected by this reorganization concerned the two bodies mentioned first in the list of component parts of the Council of State, viz. the Deliberative Assembly and the office of the Lords President of the Council. The Upper House of the Deliberative Assembly was composed of the former Gijo and Sanyo, and its powers included the establishment and amendment of the Constitution, the enactment of laws, the exercise of supreme judicial authority, appointment to high offices, the conclusion of treaties, and generally the decision of all matters of policy. From this enumeration it is evident that practically all powers except those of administration were concentrated in this body. The Lower House was composed mainly of the representatives of the feudal clans, and it was provided that these should deliberate upon matters of policy under the direction of the Upper House. As a matter of fact, when this Lower House met, as it did in both Kyoto and Tokyo in 1868 and 1869 under the names Kogisho and Shugi-in, its discussions were confined strictly to items of domestic policy, and were of no particular significance. The second department

65

of the Daijokwan, which was evidently designed as a substitute for the first of the offices of the Sanshoku, the Sosai, was composed of the two chief Ministers of State (Hosho) and various subordinates, and their functions seem to have been in the first place to act as a connecting link between the Daijokwan and the Court, and in the second to supervise the work of the entire administration. Outwardly this office has the appearance of being a second supreme authority, but all danger of friction between it and the Upper House of the Deliberative Assembly was precluded by making the members of the former members of the latter body also. There is no reason to suppose that this apparently anomalous office of the two chief Ministers was anything else than an institution intended to provide a convenient means of communication between the Government and the Imperial Court, in order that the measures of the former might obtain the sanction of the latter. In reviewing the details of the next general reorganization of the Government, which occurred in 1871, we shall have occasion to revert to the subject of this office in connection with its abolition. The five departments require no comment, unless it be to draw attention to the prominent position accorded in the list to Shinto Religion. In all five the details of the organization were identical—a Minister, a Vice-Minister, and a staff of subordinate officials and clerks. The functions to be performed by each were outlined, and were evidently intended to be strictly administrative in character.

The personnel of the Government is interesting as showing the consideration paid to the nobility, both Kuge and Daimyo, as well as the predominance of the Western clans. The highest offices were distributed among the Princes of the Blood, the Kuge and the Daimyo, the principal addition to the list of Gijo being that of Nabeshima, the Lord of Hizen. But, as hitherto, the real power rested with the samurai of the Western clans, Kido, Okubo, Goto, Soyejima, and Itagaki, whose names were found in the list of the

The Policy of the Restoration Party

Sanyo. During the course of the years 1868 and 1869 a number of changes in the offices were made, and further additions to the members of the Government. Sanjo Saneyoshi was created *Daijodaijin* ; Iwakura, *Udaijin* ; Nabeshima, Tokudaiji, Nakamikado, and Ogimachi Sanjo were given the rank of *Dainagon,* while Maibara, Hirosawa, Sasaki, Okuma, and Saigo Takamori were added to the list of the Sanyo.

Prince Sanjo Saneyoshi,[1] referring in 1885 to this organization of the central Government, asserted that it had been copied from the Constitution of *Tai-ho* (701-4 A.D.),[2] and there is no need to dispute the general accuracy of this statement, in so far as the details of the organization of the central Government were concerned. There was nothing more natural in the circumstances than that the model for the new Government should be sought for in the pre-feudal period of the Japanese nation, and no course could have been wiser politically than to appeal to the people for support by ascribing the new system to so ancient a national source. But, on the other hand, there was much in the eleven articles, the contents of which we have summarized above, and in the Imperial oath as well, that was not drawn from native customs, ancient or modern—for instance, the establishment of a deliberative assembly and the election of officials, which must be traced to some other and non-Asiatic origin. The mere fact that such provisions were inserted in the Constitution of June 1868 is of no great importance, for in that time changes in the principles as well as the organic institutions of the Government occurred with a frequency that was bewildering even to those directly concerned. Principles which it was impossible to apply were enunciated in grave documents and straightway forgotten. Such must have been the fate of the proposals to elect officials for terms of four

[1] *J. G. D.*, p. 91.
[2] See Murdock, J., *History of Japan*, vol. i. pp. 142-80.

years or to afford facilities to the general feudal public for discussing affairs of state with the appropriate officials. But there was one of the new ideas which seemed to impress itself upon the minds of the people, and that was the creation of a representative assembly.

Even when it is realized that this assembly was to be strictly limited to representatives of the feudal aristocracy, and that there was in 1868 no intention in any quarter to ascertain the views of the common people, the practice itself was still foreign to the traditions of the nation. It is true that the Shogun in 1866 had resorted to a general consultation upon the policy to be pursued with regard to the problem of opening the country to foreign trade ; but on that occasion the Yedo authorities had asked the clans for a written expression of opinion, not for a meeting of their representatives for public discussion of the question. So foreign to the policy of the Shogunate was the general discussion of questions of national interest that in 1867 an auditorium other than a theatre or temple was not to be found in Japan, and, moreover, it was widely believed that the Japanese language could not be used as a vehicle for public speech. Whatever the origin of this idea of creating an institution for public discussion—and it was probably an importation from Western countries—it is certain that the Government held out the prospect of an Assembly or Parliament as a measure that would be likely to disarm the suspicion of the feudal aristocracy and secure their support. It was in pursuance of this policy that the rules for the appointing of representatives were issued in February 1868 and the Assembly summoned to meet for the first time in April.

This Assembly (Kogisho) did not prove an institution of any importance. It met on several occasions, and each debate gave further proof of its incompetence ; but several reasons might be given to explain its failure. In the first place, its members were samurai, with all

The Policy of the Restoration Party

the prejudices of their caste ; and in the second, the questions sent down to them for discussion were not such as they could debate. For example, the Kogisho was asked for advice upon the policy of abolishing the feudal custom of wearing two swords. Now this practice was to all samurai the badge of their order, the sign of their superiority, and not unnaturally the vote against the proposal was unanimous. On the other hand, matters which did not concern the military class had no interest for the Kogisho. The status of the Eta (outcasts) was taken up in a series of debates, but on each occasion the House emptied : since the samurai were not in the habit of regarding the Eta as objects of any consideration whatever, they could not be brought to realize that their condition constituted a problem. For one reason or another the deliberations of the Kogisho could not be turned to any useful purpose. After attempting two or three sessions, the Government very properly allowed the institution to lapse into a moribund condition, and finally abolished it in June 1873.

Not only did the Constitution of the summer of 1868 provide for the reorganization of the central Government, but it attempted in a tentative fashion to deal with the relations between the Imperial authorities and the clans. That relationship was undoubtedly the most delicate problem of the day. As against the pretensions of the clans to sovereign powers a general claim to " supreme power and authority " in the Empire was made for the Daijokwan (Article II). This claim in itself was not startling, for the Shogunate had always issued much the same sort of *pronunciamiento*, and the feudal lords had paid attention or not as circumstances required. But the Constitution proceeded to announce the specific content of the claim to " supreme authority " made for the Daijokwan. The retinues attending the feudal lords as they moved about the country were to be reduced to insignificant proportions. Certain exercises of their sovereign powers were prohibited to the feudal magnates, such as the bestowal of honours and contracting of alliances. Tribute or taxes for the support of the Government were imposed upon the feudal nobility and the warrior class. To soften somewhat the force of these unpalatable measures, high offices in the Government were bestowed upon some of the Daimyo, and all alike were left in their hereditary positions as nominal rulers in their respective fiefs, and it was promised that the samurai should be appointed to lower offices in the State.

No definite steps for the regulation of the internal government of the clans were prescribed in June 1868, although for the Fu and Ken—formerly cities and territories belonging to the Shogun and his loyal retainers, but confiscated upon the outbreak of the civil war— a complete organization for local government was provided. Nevertheless, both before this date and afterwards, tentative measures [1] were adopted with the object of establishing the supremacy of the Tokyo authorities over the whole land. Thus as early as May 1868 the office of *Komunin* was erected in each of the daimiates, the official in charge being an intermediary between the central Government and the clan. Before the end of the year regulations were issued for the appointment in every clan of certain officials, who were subject to Imperial authority, though appointed by the Daimyo. Toward the close of 1870 the internal organization of the clans for local government was standardized upon lines almost identical with those of the Fu and Ken, and brought largely under the control of the central authorities.

In reviewing the policy of the Restoration Government no particular attempt need be made to either praise or blame the authorities. The period thus far covered was one of civil commotion and uncertainty, and there was an obvious conflict between two very different tendencies in political theory. Some of the more Radical leaders desired an infusion of

[1] *J. G. D.*, pp. 22–9.

The Policy of the Restoration Party

Western political ideas, while the Conservatives sought to copy exactly the polity of ancient Japan. This conflict explains nearly all of the inconsistencies to which we have referred. Moreover, the overshadowing menace to the new Government was feudalism, and had it not been for the continued support of the leading Western clans during these years it is difficult to see how the Restoration Government could have maintained itself, for it possessed in its own right neither prestige nor military power, except such as was derived from the Emperor's support of its policy. As befitted the circumstances of the time, its policy was cautious and tentative in its relations with feudalism, gathering boldness as its strength increased, but avoiding by every means an open break with any powerful force in the nation.

CHAPTER III

THE ABOLITION OF FEUDALISM

AFTER the fall of the Shogunate, the immediate necessity of the time was the organization of an administration to perform the functions hitherto exercised by the Yedo authorities. Under the circumstances such an undertaking was comparatively easy, so long as no attempt was made to interfere with the existing feudal régime, there being only two probable complications to make it difficult. These were, first, the possibility of friction between the Kuge and the Daimyo over the distribution of offices, and second, the hostility of the Kuge and Western Daimyo toward the Tokugawa clans. The first of these potential causes of trouble was dealt with skilfully and in the main successfully, the most important exception being the failure to placate Shimadzu Hisamitsu, the Lord of Satsuma ; the second came to a head in the civil war of 1868-9. However regrettable that struggle may have been, it at any rate disposed of a difficult situation by clearing away the claims of the Tokugawa party to any consideration in the new régime. The Western clansmen were in a position thereafter to go forward with the work of organizing the administration without regard for the former authorities.

But of much more importance than the erecting of the administrative structure, however immediate that necessity may have been, were the problems presented by the continuance of the feudal system, and the abolition of feudalism must be regarded as the most notable achievement of the Emperor's Government during the

The Abolition of Feudalism

years 1868-71. The difficulties involved were enormous, especially in view of the slender resources at the disposal of the central authority. Yet in the minds of Kido and his associates the dangers of a negative policy were greater than any which would be likely to arise in connection with the most drastic action. Moreover, the Court was desirous of abolishing the sovereign powers exercised by the territorial magnates, for without sole dominion over the people and the soil of the country the Emperor's position as an absolute monarch was as nominal as his Government's was insecure. The history of mediæval Japan, especially in the fourteenth century, furnished numerous examples of the dangers inherent in feudalism ; a new Takauji might appear and establish by force another Shogunate and set up a new dynasty of usurpers. Further, the logic of political theory proved the advisability of getting rid of the feudal aristocracy. The Japanese could point to their own ancient history as a demonstration of the fact that decentralization of authority leads to encroachments upon the sovereign powers of the throne. Every consideration pointed toward the adoption of a policy of immediate abrogation of the powers of the feudal lords. Upon the task of destroying the system the Government entered, therefore, and until 1871 most of its energies were devoted to that end.

As we have seen, the Daijokwan during 1868 and 1871 cautiously extended its influence over the internal government of the clans. In 1868 an Imperial official, appointed by the Daimyo, it is true, and therefore one of his own retainers, was nominated in every fief, and while it is probable that the interests of the central Government were lightly regarded by such appointees, still the very fact that the new offices were created and men appointed to them was significant. Here, at least, was an entering wedge. From this beginning a further advance was soon made. Later, in 1868, regulations were issued for the creation of a uniform organization for the government of all the fiefs, and two years later the assimilation of the institutions for local government in the Han to those in the Fu and Ken was completed. In the same year limits were imposed upon the size of the military force which could be maintained by any clan.

These measures directed against the clans, especially those of 1870, were taken as the result of an incident of the highest significance, which occurred early in 1869. On March 5 of that year the Lords of Satsuma, Choshu, Hizen, and Tosa proposed to give up their fiefs, and hand over to the Government the registers of their land and people. This was more than an act of magnanimity ; it was an intimation that the four great military clans of the West were prepared to participate in the central Government's efforts to abolish the feudal system.

The proposal was immediately accepted in the name of the Emperor, and as a preliminary step the Government announced in July 1869 that all those territorial lords who had not handed back the registers of their domains would be compelled to do so. At the same time, the distinction between the Court and the feudal nobility was abolished, both classes alike to be known thereafter as *Kwazoku* (" flowery families "). The feudal lords were to be retained as the governors of their respective fiefs, with the title Chi-han-ji. The final decree of abolition of the clans was not promulgated, however, for more than a year, during which period preparations were being made for the event.

The two documents [1] of greatest interest in this connection are those containing the proposal of the four Western Lords to hand back their registers and an Imperial rescript addressed to the Chihanji. The first of these was popularly attributed to Kido Takayoshi, a samurai of the Choshu clan. It contained an exposition of the political philosophy of the Restoration party, as well as a summary history of the Japanese monarchy, and concluded with the proposal

[1] *J. G. D.*, pp. 29-33.

The Abolition of Feudalism

of Shimadzu, Mori, Nabeshima, and Yamanouchi, the Lords of Sastuma, Choshu, Hizen, and Tosa, to surrender to the sovereign the registers of their fiefs. As a statement of their principles in compact form the opening paragraph may well be quoted verbatim :—

"Your servants again venture to address your Majesty with profound reverence. Two things are essential to the Emperor's administration. There must be one central body of government, and one universal authority which must be preserved intact. Since the time when your Majesty's ancestors founded this country and established a basis of government, all things in the wide expanse of heaven and all things on earth to its furthest limits have belonged to the Emperor from generation to generation. That is what is known as 'one central government.' And the sole power of giving and of taking away, which renders it impossible for the nobles to hold the people in subjection in virtue of their land, or to deal with the smallest piece of ground at their pleasure, or to seize and treat despotically any individual of the humbler classes, this is what is understood by the term 'one universal authority.'"

The fifth paragraph contained a statement of the motives which animated the signatories in making their proposal. It read as follows :—

"It is now sought to establish an entirely new [as compared with that of the Shogunate] form of government. Care must, therefore, be taken to preserve intact both one central body of government and one universal authority. The land in which your servants live is the land of the Emperor, and the people whom they govern are his subjects. Neither the one, therefore, nor the other can belong to your servants."

The Imperial Rescript on the Abolition of the Clans, which was dated August 29, 1871, is an extremely interesting document. It read, in full :—

"We are of the opinion that in a time of radical reform like the present, if we desire by its means to

75

give protection and tranquillity to the people at home, and abroad to maintain equality with foreign nations, words must be made to mean in reality what they claim to signify, and the government of the country must centre in a single authority.

" Some time ago We gave Our sanction to the scheme by which all the clans restored to Us their registers ; We appointed Chiji for the first time, each to perform the duties of his office.

" But owing to the lengthened endurance of the old system during several hundred years, there have been cases where the word only was pronounced and the reality not performed. How is it possible for Us, under such circumstances, to give protection and tranquillity to the people, and to maintain equality with foreign nations?

" Profoundly regretting this condition of affairs, We now completely abolish the Clans [Han] and convert them into Imperial Domains [Ken], with the object of diligently retrenching expenditure and of arriving at convenience of working, of getting rid of the unreality of names and of abolishing the disease of government proceeding from multiform centres.

" Do ye Our assembled servants take well to heart this Our will ! "

Compared with the previous rescripts addressed to the same body of feudal magnates, this message must have sounded ominously autocratic. Its tone is significant of the changes in the status of the Government since the spring of 1868. At that time the help of the clans was desired for the purpose of crushing the Tokugawa rebels, and the call to the Emperor's standard was couched in the following terms :—

" Do you assembled clans, therefore, assist Our imperfections, and uniting with all your heart and strength, perform the parts which have fallen to you, and zealously exert yourselves in behalf of the State."

Since the spring of 1868 the civil war had been brought to an end, four of the greatest military clans

The Abolition of Feudalism

had pledged anew their support to the throne, and their lords had even voluntarily resigned the feudal rights and powers which they had inherited from their ancestors. The leaders of the Government had been slowly acquiring experience, and with experience confidence. The sovereign's rescript to the Chihanji was virtually an impeachment of feudalism, on the ground that it stood in the way of the realization of a centralized Government, and of the feudal lords because they had been inefficient in the performance of their duties as Chihanji. For these two reasons the whole system was to be swept away and a new order created, in which the government of the whole country to its remotest boundaries was to be centralized in the Emperor.

That such a revolutionary measure should have been regarded with outward complacency by the entire feudal aristocracy has often been regarded as little short of miraculous. Yet it is not difficult to understand the situation in which the great majority of the feudal lords found themselves in 1871, for the event had been skilfully approached and every possible contingency provided against. On the one hand, the general public, in so far as it took any interest in politics, by a series of inspired articles which appeared in the limited newspaper press of the time had been instructed to regard the samurai as a parasitic class, " eating the bread of idleness," the ex-Shogun as an unholy usurper, and generally speaking the whole surviving mass of feudal arrangements as contrary to the best interests of the nation. On the other hand, the Government strengthened itself by raising an army from among all classes by means of a conscription, and, as we have seen, by securing beforehand the consent of the four Western clans to its project. Just as at the Restoration a league of the great clans had been formed to bring about the resignation of the Shogun, so in this event Satsuma, Choshu, Hizen, and Tosa were brought together into a pro-abolition party, far too powerful for any Daimyo or combination of Daimyo to resist. When the Government had thus strengthened its position it could and did act, and its action was accepted because it could not be successfully opposed by the only weapon left to the majority of the Daimyo —force of arms.

While the abolition of feudalism in 1871 was a *coup de main*, it would be unwise to accept that explanation to the exclusion of all others. Undoubtedly, in the ranks of the feudal nobility there were men imbued with a genuine loyalty to the Emperor and a liberality of outlook born of foreign intercourse, and these sentiments, wherever they existed, are by no means to be ignored. There was also a shrewd expectation of personal advantages for the Daimyo through the exchange of their revenues for the pensions promised by the Government, for it was not proposed that the lands of the fiefs should be confiscated. It is impossible to ascertain what motive or combination of motives determined each particular clan to accept its fate ; it is enough to say that the Government, while it gathered together its forces to suppress any uprising, made strong appeals to every lofty sentiment in human nature as well as to the baser passions of the members of the feudal aristocracy.

If there was anything out of the ordinary in the process by which the feudal nobility was induced to acquiesce in its own destruction, that unusual element must be sought in the means by which the four clans were persuaded to support the project, and what is more, stand ready to compel others to acquiesce in it.

Towards the end of 1870 the Government began to exhibit signs of weakness, for the support of some of the great clans was lacking in enthusiasm. Tosa had no representative whatever in the Council of State, and Satsuma only Okubo, who was known to be out of favour with both Shimadzu and Saigo. Two of the clans which had led the way in 1867 and 1869 seemed, therefore, to have more or less completely

The Abolition of Feudalism

withdrawn from the coalition which supported the Government. In the face of this danger measures of an extraordinary nature were determined upon.

Iwakura, the Udaijin, and Okubo, a Sanyo, bearing a sword as a gift from the Emperor to the shrine of the late Prince of Satsuma, were sent to Kagoshima to confer with Shimadzu Hisamitsu and his henchman, Saigo Takamori. At the same time, Kido made his way to Yamaguchi, where the two Princes of Choshu, the Mori, were residing. These two missions having successfully accomplished their purpose of conciliation, Okubo and Kido proceeded to Kochi, where they held conferences with Itagaki and Fukuoka, the two principal samurai of the Tosa clan. In the meantime Iwakura returned to Tokyo overland, visiting on his way the two Tokugawa clans Owari and Hikone and securing their allegiance. By this series of conferences the Imperial power was immensely strengthened, for it was provided that each of the three clans, Satsuma, Choshu, and Tosa, should furnish a considerable body of troops to be transferred to Tokyo and placed at the disposal of the Government as the nucleus of an Imperial army. Furthermore, Saigo Takamori and Itagaki Taisuke were to be appointed Councillors of State, and the Princes of the three clans were to take up their residence permanently in the capital.

By these *pourparlers* the four Western clans were arrayed in solid formation on the side of the Emperor. In August 1871 there was a redistribution of the offices of state to make room for Saigo and Itagaki, and almost immediately afterwards the rescript abolishing the Han was promulgated.

The apathy of the territorial nobility and the samurai in this crisis of their lives was probably more apparent than real. No open protest against the decree was made, and none was feasible. If there was no opposition, neither was there any enthusiasm for this act of violence against the long-established order. Peace was preserved for the time being, though not for long, for the compromise between the Government and the feudal aristocracy saddled the country with a burden of debt which could not be endured, and likewise could not be lifted without breaking faith with a powerful and dangerous class in the community.

After a study of the events immediately preceding the promulgation of the abolition rescript, it is evident that the disappearance of the feudal organization need not be explained by any other process than the play of forces such as are commonly at work in making the history of every country—principles, sentiments, cupidity, and fear. Neither Government nor nobility displayed on that occasion any remarkable degree of magnanimity, for behind the former the forces of the great clans were plainly visible, and in the hands of the latter were the promises of the Government to support by an elaborate pension system the various members of the privileged feudal order.

The magnitude of this pension scheme may be gathered from the number of people who were entitled to receive support. There were nearly three hundred Daimyo families and about four hundred thousand samurai households. What the Government promised to do was to support these two million people out of the revenues of the State in return for the feudal land registers. To the Daimyo the offer was extremely advantageous. For their revenues, while nominally great—in some few cases they must have been actually very large—were subject not only to the vicissitudes of the rice-harvest, but to large deductions for the maintenance of a great variety of public works and the support of their landless samurai. An offer from the Government of half their former revenues was therefore regarded as very generous and secured to them great wealth.

To take one example : A Daimyo with a nominal revenue of 100,000 *koku* of rice, which was the equivalent of £64,000 [1] sterling, would receive from

---

[1] This calculation is taken from Alcock, Sir R., *op. cit.*, vol. ii. p. 391.

the Government 50,000 *koku*, or the equivalent of £32,000; and there was one, the Prince of Kaga, with a revenue of more than a million *koku*, and three or four others with between the maximum and the figure arbitrarily chosen. The immense riches conferred upon such an individual by the pension scheme may be seen by contrasting his income with the salaries paid by the Government to the high officers of state. It was thought in the earlier days that 50 yen, £5 a month, was a suitable salary for a member of the Council of State, but that sum was raised to 500 yen, or £50 a month, when it became apparent that the foreign diplomatic representatives were making preparations to live in a state of considerable grandeur.

There could be little of a financial character, therefore, to cause hesitation on the Daimyo's part in accepting the Government's offer. His prestige as a *Kwazoku* had been ensured by the decree of 1870—though it had taken away his specific title—but his political power had existed in name only in the great majority of cases and his revenues were more or less precarious and always subject to large deductions for the support of his retainers, and it is quite probable that the abolition of the feudal system meant to the Daimyo a distinct improvement in his financial position. Moreover, the Daimyo and the yonin who ruled the clan might retain for themselves very considerable parcels of land by merely failing to insert in the registers which they handed back the whole of the lands in the fief: that this practice was resorted to to some extent is certain. Further, a number of the clans had contracted obligations which were in the nature of unfunded public debts, and in many cases it was arranged that the central Government should assume responsibility for such obligations.

As far as the samurai were concerned, the financial advantages of the pension system were not nearly so great. Their nominal and actual revenues were equal, and any diminution of their incomes, which were small, meant hardship. To them, their rights and privileges were of immense importance, however, and they were shrewd enough to see that the destruction of the feudal régime involved the disappearance of their place and purpose in society. If their vision had been less obscured by the blindness of caste, they would have perceived that the pension scheme which they were offered could not be accepted without making themselves objects of charity in the community, a class of parasites supported in idleness by the other members of society. Class prejudice, however, prevented them from recognizing the nature of the arrangement, and they acquiesced in it with general uneasiness, which increased as time went on, except in the case of those who either found service with the Government or were enterprising enough to shift for themselves in the ranks of the plebeian class as farmers, merchants, domestic servants, and the like.

As to the ultimate necessity of abolishing the feudal order as it existed in Japan at the time of the Restoration there can be no doubt. It is unnecessary, therefore, to attempt to further justify or impugn the principles which underlay the Government's policy in 1871. There remain for discussion only the means by and the time at which that policy was carried into effect. Of the measures adopted to ensure its success enough has been said. A demonstration of armed force was made in the sight of the feudal aristocracy, and at the same time an inducement involving substantial monetary advantages, to the Daimyo at least, was offered by the Government. Feudalism was thus partly driven and partly lured to its own destruction. As to the haste with which the Government carried out the scheme, the student is free to doubt its wisdom. The measure probably seemed urgent, for the samurai were becoming a source of grave danger, even to life, especially in Tokyo,[1] and only to a somewhat less

---

[1] Hirosawa, a Councillor of State, was murdered in his bed on the morning of February 27, 1871, by a two-sworded fanatic. A plot to carry the Emperor

degree in other parts of the country. That some of the ronin should have run amok in the confusion of the time was only natural, and that their fury was occasionally directed against members of the Government, instead of the common people or foreigners, did not mean that the Government itself was in danger. To any one familiar with the confusion of ideas which existed, with the samurai urged at one time to support the Emperor as against the Shogun or the "ugly barbarians," and at another vilified in the Press as parasites on society, the wonder is that so little disturbance was created by the warrior class, that so many of them were sufficiently strong-minded to keep their heads and think sensibly. Indeed, in the light of subsequent events, grave doubts may be cast on the wisdom of the authorities in bringing matters to a crisis so soon. If more time had been given, it is quite likely that the undesirable elements of feudalism would have disappeared either by the natural process of decay or under the firm disciplinary power of the Government. Nor would the authorities have suffered any serious diminution of their prestige by allowing the Chihanji to retain their offices during their active years as nominal heads of the clans, for, as has already been shown, by the end of 1870 there remained to the clans nothing but the shadow of power, so successfully had the Government encroached upon their ancient local sovereignty. Furthermore, if time had been given, the financial burden incurred in connection with the pension system might have been avoided altogether, or assumed only to an extent consistent with the resources of the country. Compensation would, of course, have had to be given to the Daimyo in return for their registers, but the great body of the samurai might easily have been merged in the common people in the course of a generation.

back to Kyoto was discovered in May, and during the first half of the year small insurrections in Bungo, Shinano, and Mikawa were suppressed by the dispatch of Government troops.

As to the manner of settlement of this great problem, while we cannot withhold admiration for the courage and dash with which it was accomplished, the Government must rest permanently under the odium which its policy engendered. Acts of violence against a proud feudal aristocracy, coupled with pledges which it was impossible to redeem, were not the materials out of which to build a stable fabric of government, and it was only natural that during the next six or seven years the Emperor's Government should have led a precarious existence, the difficulties and dangers of which culminated in 1877 in the Satsuma Rebellion.

The handing back of the clan registers had the effect of transferring all the land of the Empire to the Emperor. In the ancient Japanese polity all land was supposed to have belonged to the sovereign, and to ensure that no individual should have absolute title to land, in 645 A.D. the practice of redistributing the holdings at short intervals had been adopted. Something of this idea persisted throughout the whole feudal period, for the Shogun, when powerful enough, might remove a Daimyo from one fief to another, and within the fiefs some at least of the actual cultivators of the soil who had no title to their land were transferred periodically from one allotment to another in the same immediate neighbourhood. A system in many respects similar to the agricultural communes of Europe at the end of the seventeenth century existed in Japan at the time of the Restoration. The peasants, apart from their status as serfs, cultivated their lands, which they did not own, but which belonged to the feudal overlord, and paid taxes in kind for the privilege. Those taxes varied not only with the seasons but in the different fiefs, ranging all the way from 30 per cent. to 60 per cent. or even 70 per cent. of the produce.

Rice, being the most important crop, was used as the staple in terms of which the revenues of a fief were reckoned, the revenues, composed of the rice taxes, being handed over to the Daimyo by the peasants. The

The Abolition of Feudalism

unit of measurement for rice was the *koku*, equivalent to $5\frac{1}{4}$ bushels, and a Daimyo was said to be worth 200,000 *koku* a year, or a samurai to have a yearly allowance from his overlord of 100 *koku* of rice. The system of taxation [1] under the Tokugawa Shogunate was by no means as simple as might be inferred from the above statement, for in addition to the peasants each fief had necessarily in its population other elements of the unprivileged order—artisans, merchants, etc.—who were liable to taxation. In order to reach all the taxable persons there were imposed a number of taxes which may be roughly classified under the two headings of labour services, which fell largely upon the farming class, because they were attached to the land, and money payments, the incidence of which was felt almost entirely by the merchants and artisans, as they were imposed on the exchange of commodities and the practice of the various handicrafts. Historically, all taxation may be said to have consisted either of rice taxes or labour services, but the money payments, which were of later origin, were of considerable importance.

The abolition of the feudal system involved the transfer of all these taxes to the national treasury. It must, of course, be kept in mind that local expenses in connection with the upkeep of public works and payment of the salaries of officials who composed the local government constituted the first deduction from the revenue of each clan, or, as they were called after 1871, Ken (Prefecture). The problems of finance which faced the Imperial Treasury in those early years were therefore of the most complicated nature.

The revenues which were taken over by the Government were estimated in terms of rice, labour, and money, and the money payments were further complicated by the lack of uniformity in the currency, for silver and gold were both legal tender at a ratio of about 7 to 1, and paper money circulated within some of the fiefs and in some cases throughout a group of

[1] Wigmore, *op. cit.*, Part I, pp. 94 ff.

neighbouring fiefs. In addition to this confusion of standards there was the problem of adjusting the expenses of the Government to the total of the revenues. In the circumstances in which the Japanese Finance Department found itself, it is not difficult to imagine that even the most capable and industrious Minister would have enough worries to overwhelm him. The problem of commuting the rice and labour taxes into terms of money occupied no little time, and was solved only after an immense amount of negotiation with the agricultural classes. Furthermore, after the revenues had at last been estimated in terms of yen, the two men [1] who were at the head of the Department of Finance became convinced that the Government was bankrupt, or about to become so, and resigned their posts, having prepared a statement of their views on the matter, which was immediately published.

The successor to the headship of the Finance Department thus vacated was Okuma Shigenobu (now Count and for the second time Prime Minister). After spending a few months in familiarizing himself with the financial problems of the country, he issued a statement ridiculing the fears of his predecessors, declaring that the national finances could be easily readjusted so as to make both ends meet. He remained in the Finance Department until 1881, and during his régime justified the optimism with which he entered upon his term of office.

One of the chief financial problems of the Government was connected with the feudal pension scheme of 1871. As has been seen, that scheme involved paying to the former territorial lords about half their nominal revenues, and to the samurai varying percentages of their accustomed rice allowances. In addition the central Government had to provide for the expenses of carrying on the administration, both central and local. As a matter of fact, the expenditures of the

---

[1] Inouye, later well known as Marquis Inouye (died September 1915), was Minister, and Shibusawa (now Baron) was Vice-Minister.

The Abolition of Feudalism

State were greater after the abolition of feudalism than the combined revenues of the Daimyo had been under the old régime. There was no possibility of immediately increasing the revenues by means of indirect taxes, for the treaties with the Powers had stipulated the rates of import and export duties which were to be levied. The only devices to augment the revenues were to revise the treaties, to resort to foreign loans, or to increase the direct taxes. And about the only method for reducing expenditures was to repudiate the pension scheme.

The first of the possible devices for readjusting the finances of the nation to which the Government resorted was the revision of the treaties. An embassy, headed by Iwakura, accompanied by Kido, Okubo, and Ito as his principal advisers, was dispatched to America and Europe in December 1871. Everywhere the Japanese proposals were rejected, and it was evident that an increase of the import duties—that is, the indirect taxes—could not be resorted to as a means of making up the deficiency in the revenues. It was at this juncture that Inouye and Shibusawa resigned their offices. When Okuma turned his attention to the problems of finance he saw that it would be necessary to float loans to tide the Government over its immediate dilemma, and at the same time he determined to strike at the roots of the pension scheme, which absorbed about 20,000,000 yen annually.

In pursuance of this part of his programme, toward the end of 1873 [1] it was notified to the governors of the Ken, who were in turn to make the matter known to the samurai, that the Government would be willing to commute the pensions on the basis of the market price of rice after the next harvest for a single payment, half in cash and half in Government bonds bearing 8 per cent. interest. This privilege was extended only to samurai with annual pensions amounting to 100 *koku* or less. The commutation was to

[1] *J. G. D.*, pp. 557-62.

be made at the rate of six years' purchase for hereditary
pensions and four years' purchase for life incomes.
In defence of the six and four years' purchase it was
urged that the ordinary rate of interest in the country
ranged from 12 per cent. to 36 per cent. The object
of the Government in granting these facilities was to
enable those who were prevented from entering trade
or agriculture by lack of capital to accomplish their
desires, and in order to encourage the samurai to take
up land and work it—whether as farmers or graziers—
provision was made for the sale of Crown lands at half
their " real price " to those who surrendered their
pensions, provided they were less than 100 *koku* in
annual amount.

In this way was a beginning made in the hazardous
task of abolishing the pensions. As the regulations
summarized above were not compulsory, few of the
samurai availed themselves of the privilege offered.
Nearly three years were allowed to pass before any
further steps were taken in the matter, and then a
compulsory commutation of the pensions, whether great
or small, was decreed. The regulations [1] were issued
on August 5, 1876. For purposes of commutation
pensions were divided into three classes : first, pensions
in perpetuity ; second, life pensions ; and third,
pensions for limited terms of years. In the case of
pensions belonging to the first category, those amounting to 70,000 yen a year or over were to be capitalized
at five years' purchase, those of 25 yen or less a year at
fourteen years'. All alike were to be paid in Government bonds, which, however, bore interest at 5, 6, or
7 per cent., according to the amount of the pension in
payment of which they were issued. Thus bonds issued
for the purchase of pensions of 1,000 yen or over bore
5 per cent., of 100 to 999 yen 6 per cent., and below
100 yen 7 per cent. Life pensions were distinguished
from those in perpetuity by cutting in half the number
of years' purchase allowed, and limited term pensions

[1] *J. G. D.*, pp. 562-6.

The Abolition of Feudalism

were capitalized at rates varying from two-fifths to three-twentieths of the number of years' purchase in the case of a hereditary pension, the exact fraction being determined by the number of years for which the income had been granted.

The Daimyo whose nominal income had been 100,000 *koku* under the old régime survived the abolition of feudalism with a perpetual pension of 50,000 *koku*, valued at £32,000. By the arrangements of 1876 he would receive £160,000 or 1,600,000 yen, as the capitalized value of his pension, which at 5 per cent. would give him an income of 80,000 yen a year. The samurai whose revenue had been 1,000 *koku* under the old régime had passed into the new, let us say, with a perpetual income of 400 *koku*, approximately 2,500 yen, a year. In 1876 he was compelled to accept in lieu of his competence Government bonds to the amount of 18,125 yen, which paid him 5 per cent. a year, or 906 25 yen. Pensions of 100 *koku*, or even less, upon which a samurai and his family could barely exist, became hopelessly inadequate when capitalized according to the Government's terms.

So great was the outcry among the samurai against the measure, particularly among the Satsuma men, that a slight change in the regulations was made, by which hereditary incomes which had been purchased from the original grantees were capitalized at ten years' purchase, independent of their annual amounts. With this modification the Government carried out its plan. The issue of Government bonds required for the purchase of the pensions involved an expenditure in the form of interest of about one-third of the former cost of the pensions, which was in the neighbourhood of 20,000,000 yen. The saving of 13,000,000 yen annually—that is, the reduction of the national expenditures by about one-third—did much to relieve the necessities of the Finance Department.

Whatever may be said in justification of the Government's policy, either on the score of the necessity for relieving the overburdened national treasury or the desirability of encouraging or compelling an idle class to enter upon the more honourable and useful career of industry, the fact remained that the samurai regarded the measure as an act of injustice. Unjust it undoubtedly was, when regarded from the point of view of those directly concerned. A solemn engagement entered into by a Government ought not to be repudiated, and cannot be without a distinct breach of faith, and the case is not materially altered by admissions of inexperience or lack of foresight, nor by pleading the unfortunate consequences which had arisen for the great mass of the taxpayers in carrying out the terms of the engagement. It has already been pointed out that there had been hurriedly forced upon the country in 1871 a measure which involved, in its immediate and remote consequences, numerous changes in the lives of the feudal aristocracy, and in order to secure the acquiescence of the military class, pensions in perpetuity or for one or two lives were offered and received in good faith, to the outward satisfaction of the two parties concerned. Two years later the Government saw fit to ignore the meaning of the words " in perpetuity " [1] or " one or two lives," as applied to the pensions, which in the case of the samurai had been purposely made small because they were hereditary, or at least to run for a considerable period of years. Good faith with the samurai was broken in 1876, and the Government was soon made to feel the consequences of its temerity.

[1] Another illustration of the Japanese inability to grasp the meaning of "perpetual," especially when it is against their interest to do so, has arisen in connection with the " perpetual leases " in the former "foreign settlements."

CHAPTER IV

THE GOVERNMENT AND ITS CRITICS

THE absorbing problems of the Restoration Government until August 1871 were, on the one hand, the construction of the central and local administrative organization, and, on the other, the abolition of the feudal system. The difficulties of the former of these tasks were not great ; those of the latter were immense. The traditions, customs, and general mental attitude of a people bred for centuries in a feudal atmosphere could not be transformed by any Imperial rescript ; the outward forms of governmental institutions may be changed by such a process, but the spirit which enters into the new political body is likely to be that which animated the old. So it was in the case of Japan, for while the Han were nominally done away when the Ken were created, clanism persisted, and though it was decreed that the Government should be completely centralized, sectionalism continued. The degree of completeness with which the old habits survived varied in different parts of the country, according to the strength of the Han and their remoteness from Tokyo. Just as it had been under the Tokugawa Shogunate, so it was for some years after the Restoration ; the Government's power and influence reached its maximum intensity at the centre, gradually diminishing until at the circumference it became almost nil. In the Tokugawa period an official of the Shogun's Government entered the territory of the Shimadzu family at peril of his life, and the same was almost as true of Satsuma until after 1877. For some years after 1871 the Tokyo Government was not represented in Satsuma except by Satsuma men. The persistence of the clan *esprit de corps* throughout the country may be observed not only in various small uprisings and the great rebellion in Satsuma in 1877, but in the personnel of the central Government. The high offices of state were distributed at first among the Court and territorial nobility, while the leading clansmen of the Western fiefs, the real promoters of the Restoration, accepted offices with humbler titles. In 1871 the active members of the Council of State were nearly all samurai from the coalition of Satsuma, Choshu, Hizen, and Tosa, and when in 1873 this Satcho-Hito combination fell to pieces, Satsuma and Choshu remained in close union at the head of affairs. This combination continued to dominate the Government throughout the whole of the Meiji Era, and to retain for itself as many of the offices of state as clansmen could be found qualified to fill. In 1876 it was said by a writer in one of the most influential newspapers of the day, the *Choya Shimbun*, that four-fifths of the Government officials belonged to Satsuma, Chosu, and Tosa. This was not only the case in the civil offices, but the two military services were appropriated by Satsuma and Choshu, the former regarding the Navy as its preserve, the latter the Army.

That such a system of clan government (Hambatsu Seifu) should have grown up is not to be wondered at. Essentially similar phenomena are to be found in the history of England, in the domination of the Whigs during the first half of the eighteenth century and of the Tories during the first half of the nineteenth. Both of these great aristocratic combinations were survivals of English feudalism, whereas in Japan the connection between feudalism and clanism was immediate and not remote. Clan-government has occupied such a prominent place in the political controversies of the Meiji Era, and has brought down upon the Tokyo authorities such constant and violent criticism, that some examination into its origin is warranted ; but the consideration of this topic will be postponed to a subsequent chapter.[1]

Not only do we find one of the most powerful determinants of the political progress of Japan subsequent to 1871 in the survival of the feudal spirit, but as a consequence of the formal abolition of the old order there can be seen gradually coming into prominence two other factors—absolute monarchy and a nation of free subjects of the Emperor. Each of these new factors contributed to the reconstruction many of its characteristic features. It was the deliberate purpose of the Restoration party to re-establish the sovereign as the universal authority in the land, and as a preliminary to that end it was necessary to overthrow the Yedo Administration. The constructive and destructive objects of the movement were so indissolubly united as to form a single policy, but beyond that twofold purpose the leaders did not look, except to dream of a future expansion of the boundaries of the Empire, to include not only the neighbouring islands in the Pacific but also large sections of the continent of Asia. Being invariably members of the warrior class, to whom chauvinism is a professional instinct, they foresaw few of the ultimate consequences of the movement into which they threw their strength. That it would be necessary to disturb the existing organization of society, in which the samurai and the nobility occupied all the positions of honour and ease, probably did not occur to many of them, and centuries of habit had accustomed them to think of the sovereign as *de jure* absolute and *de facto* powerless. Hence it was inevitable that they should have overlooked the fact that the very institution they purposed to destroy, the Shogunate, had made it possible for them to reverence the Emperor as of heavenly descent, and at the same time to live in a feudal order ; and, further, that they should not have foreseen that in turning out the

G

[1] See Chapter VII, pp. 170–77.

A Political History of Japan

Shogun they were jeopardizing the existence of the whole feudal régime. However we analyse the situation, every consideration points away from the supposition that the samurai of the Restoration party were deliberately intent on political suicide, and yet in what other light can we view the great change of 1871? The monarch's cause enlisted the services of men who were willing to sacrifice the old order to the new—men like Kido, Okubo, Ito, Inouye, Goto, Itagaki, and Okuma ; and as the Emperor grew to maturity and his advisers became more ambitious the absolutism of the native theory of monarchy was gradually impressed upon the national polity. While the theory of the monarchy was thus crystallizing into autocracy, a companion process was going on in the Emperor's Government, the bureaucracy gradually hardening into an oligarchy. From 1877 forward an absolute monarchy served and ruled by an oligarchy, the two in a firm alliance, dominated the nation. In this combination of apparently incompatible elements, an absolute monarch and a ruling oligarchy, the dualism represented in pre-Meiji times by the Court and the Shogunate reappeared, the only important difference in the situations being the absence of feudalism and the presence of a free nation. The significance of that difference was not fully realized at any time in the Meiji period, nor acknowledged by the oligarchy.

Not only did the Restoration lead to the speedy exaltation of a civil oligarchy—which in time gave place to a military counterpart—to a degree of authority with which that of the Shogunate could hardly be compared, but it also gave the people a new political status as subjects of the Emperor. Under the old régime the great majority of the people had enjoyed no political rights, their only function in the State having been to furnish the taxes upon which the privileged orders lived, but with the abolition of feudalism the common people were converted into a ation, and advocates of popular rights were not want-

94

The Government and its Critics

ing to bring before the people the privileges, as well as the duties, of their new position. The struggle between the champions of popular government and the ruling oligarchy furnishes a number of the most important political incidents of this period.

Such were the purely domestic factors in the situation: clanism and oligarchy, an absolute monarchy and a free people, were the most important results of the Restoration and the main sources of the history of Meiji.

But in addition to these there must be mentioned the relations of the nation with the Treaty Powers and the continental Asiatic countries of China and Korea. We have already touched on one of the reasons which prompted a speedy revision of the treaties with European and American nations, but it should also be said here that not only were the conventional tariffs upon imports a real or fancied source of hardship to the Japanese Treasury, but the extra-territorial privileges accorded by the treaties to the foreigners resident in Japan were regarded as a reflection upon and a diminution of the nation's autonomy. How important was the part which the policy of treaty revision was to play will appear hereafter. Relations with China occupied a different place in the popular estimation, for while the Treaty Powers could hardly be made the objects of chauvinistic agitation, the neighbouring countries, especially Korea and the insular dependencies of China, could safely be allowed to serve as a safety-valve for the ultra-patriotic Imperialists of the warrior class. Expansion and aggrandizement of the Empire had formed an integral part of the teaching of the loyalist schools before the Restoration. Yoshida Shoin, the Choshu patriot, had published a book in which he had predicted, as a consequence of the Restoration of the Emperor, the conquest of Formosa, the Kurile Islands, Kamtchatka, Korea, and a large portion of Manchuria and Siberia. It was doubtless as a result of such ideas imbibed during the decade before 1867 that the samurai in the ten years immediately following proved themselves so eager to enter upon a policy of aggression against Korea and China.

The Coalition Government formed in 1871 by the four Western clans for the purpose of abolishing feudalism lasted for two years, and during that time accomplished an amount of work that seems almost incredible. The abolition rescript was issued in August 1871, and concurrently the samurai pension scheme was launched. In the closing months of the year a steady stream of ordinances poured out from the Council of State and the various administrative departments, regulating the habits and customs of the people, even their dress and the method of wearing their hair, their ceremonial manners, and the occupations they might enter, as well as announcing an elaborate programme of railway and telegraph construction and a universal public system of education. In 1872 the land-tax was made payable in money instead of grain, and the Conscription Law of 1870 was rigidly enforced. Literally speaking, hundreds of ordinances were issued, all of them having the force of law. The results of this orgy of change became apparent in 1873, when from January to June riots and disturbances of a more or less serious nature occurred in practically every thickly inhabited district throughout the country, the malcontents in nearly all cases belonged to the agricultural class, and their grievances arising from the changes in established customs which the Government had introduced. The objection of the peasants to conscription and to the payment of taxes in money showed how firmly they clung to the old customs, and with what hostility they regarded the policy of the new Government. These riots among the peasantry were quickly suppressed in the various districts, either by the local police or the samurai of the neighbourhood. The loyalty of the samurai to the Government in the first half of 1873 is noteworthy, for as yet no intimation of the contemplated change in the pension system had been made public. As we shall see, when at the end of 1873 the ordinance announcing a voluntary commutation plan for small pensions was issued, and for the first time taxes were imposed upon incomes from pensions, disturbances of a very serious nature, fomented by the samurai, became frequent.

The Coalition Government of 1871 did not confine itself to issues of purely domestic policy. It undertook to solve that problem of the nation's foreign relations which was destined to remain until 1894 the most difficult question before the Foreign Office, the revision of the treaties. In December 1871 a mission was dispatched to Europe, via America, to secure from the Governments of the various Treaty Powers a revision of the original treaties, most of which were to expire the next year. The Imperial commission given to the Plenipotentiaries at an audience granted them on December 15 made no mention whatever of the object of their mission. It ran, in part, as follows : " I now send you to several foreign countries abroad as Ambassadors. Judging from your ability and loyalty, I do not doubt that you will perform your duties with diligence, and accomplish with success the mission now entrusted to you." It was at this time, during the absence of these envoys, that the Government drifted almost to the verge of war with both China and Korea. Some of the savage tribes of the south-east coast of Formosa, a Chinese possession, had murdered the crew of a Loo-chooan fishing-boat, and as the Loo-choo Islands were dependencies of Japan, the Tokyo Government insisted that China should send a punitive expedition against the offenders. The Peking authorities declined to undertake the task at first upon the ground that Formosa was not a part of China, but later, when the dangers of such a plea were perceived, that they had no jurisdiction over the savage tribes of that island. At last, in March 1873, it was arranged by Soyejima, the Japanese Minister of Foreign Affairs, that his Government should dispatch the expedition at its own expense. Friendly relations with Korea had been jeopardized by what was considered an act of war, Korea's refusal to pay the usual tribute to Japan.

It is not difficult to state the reasons for the Government's hostile attitude toward the neighbouring countries. The samurai of the Western clans had been diligently coached for some years in the advantages of a strong policy toward China and Korea. Since 1869 there had been no opportunity in Japan for them to display their military prowess, and they chafed under the enforced inactivity. They openly criticized the Government for its weakness in hesitating to enter upon the course of expansion which they had been taught to expect would immediately follow the Restoration. It was this pressure by the samurai which drove the Government into taking up the above-mentioned questions with the Chinese and Korean authorities. Further, it must be pointed out that among the Ambassadors sent to foreign countries in 1871 there were at least two of the three men who had dominated the Japanese Government from 1869 to 1873, Kido and Okubo, the third of that all-powerful triumvirate being Saigo Takamori. Associated with Saigo in the Council of State in 1872 and the first half of 1873 were Itagaki and Eto, representing Tosa and Saga, while at the head of the Departments of Foreign Affairs, Finance, and Public Works were Soyejima, Inouye, and Okuma, of Saga, Choshu, and Hizen respectively. Apart from Inouye, it is doubtful if any of the members of the Government in 1872 were in sympathy with the policy of peaceful progress which was in the minds of Kido and Okubo. The personnel of the Government, when taken in connection with the pronounced nationalism of the samurai, is sufficient to explain the Chinese and Korean policy of the Tokyo authorities.

When the news of these developments reached the envoys in Europe it brought them hurrying home.

The Government and its Critics

Their mission was a failure. Everywhere they had been received courteously and royally fêted, but in none of the capitals of the Treaty Powers had their plea been entertained for an instant. What the members of the mission saw in America and Europe was enough to confirm them in certain ideas, already entertained, as to the policy to be pursued in Japan. Each was doubtless impressed in varying degrees by different phases of the history and life of the countries visited. Kido, who gave public expression to his opinions [1] upon his return to Japan, declared that the most urgent need of the country was to " establish the Constitution and the laws." That views essentially similar were held by the other envoys is plain enough from their subsequent actions.

All of the " Ambassadors to different foreign countries " having returned to Tokyo by September 1873, the inevitable clash between the two parties in the Government immediately occurred. The failure of the mission naturally caused great dissatisfaction among the people, and to a certain extent diminished the prestige of the envoys. Persistent rumours of dissension, while in Europe, between Kido and Okubo were disseminated in Tokyo by the Press. On the other hand, Iwakura, Kido, Okubo, and Ito were not slow with their *tu quoque*, for they could point to the mistakes of the stay-at-home section of the Administration, which had not only stirred up an almost universal discontent among the lower classes, but had been led by the clamour of the samurai into destroying the country's long-standing friendly relations with China and Korea. This unseemly dispute within the ranks of the Coalition was, however, only the outward manifestation of the difficulties of the times ; beneath the surface issues of a fundamental nature were hidden, and upon their outcome depended the future policy of the country.

The issue between the opposing parties in the

[1] *J. G. D.*, pp. 567–77.

A Political History of Japan

Coalition was one of policy : Was Japan to enter upon a course of military expansion in Asia or to employ all her energies in the work of internal reconstruction? The arguments of the advocates of peaceful progress were, as stated in Kido's Memorial, in the first place that Japan was not prepared for war, her wealth and population not being great enough and her military establishments insignificant ; and in the second place that if Japan was to continue to exist as an independent State and develop into a great modern country she must establish a Constitution and laws. Opposed to these views were the teachings of the pre-Meiji " patriotic schools " and the professional chauvinism of the warrior class. It is interesting to note that Kido, Okubo, and Ito had all alike been educated in the very ideas which now animated the great body of the samurai, and that they had divested themselves of the last shreds of their early militarist prejudices was a tribute to their shrewdness in recognizing the changing needs of their country.

By what arguments or influences the peace party secured the adoption of their policy it is unnecessary to inquire, but the influence of Iwakura, Kido, and Okubo would have been likely to carry the day for any policy they chose to espouse. The immediate outcome of the triumph of the peace party was the break-up of the coalition of the four Western clans. Soyejima resigned his office as Minister of Foreign Affairs, and Saigo, Itagaki, Eto, and Goto Shojiro withdrew from the Council of State, though Saigo retained his position as Commander-in-Chief of the Army. To fill the vacancies, Kido, Okubo, Ito, and Katsu Awa were appointed to the Daijokwan. In the reconstructed Government Terashima became Minister of Foreign Affairs, Katsu Awa and Ito Ministers of the Navy and Public Works respectively. Okuma and Oki retained their places in the Departments of Finance and Education, and Sanjo and Iwakura remained in the offices of Daijodaijin and Udaijin. A Sadaijin was not appointed.

The Government and its Critics

The triumph of the peace party threw the advocates of immediate hostilities against Korea and China into a frenzy of discontent, and their anger was increased, not diminished, by the very first acts of the reconstructed Government, especially by the ordinance which foreshadowed the repudiation of the samurai pension scheme. The nature of this measure has already been given in detail ; only its consequences remain to be described. In January 1874 an attempt to assassinate Iwakura was made by nine samurai of the Tosa clan. The assailants were subsequently arrested and sentenced to death to expiate " the crime of conspiring together in a band of nine persons and wounding Iwakura Udaijin, in the hope that by his murder the counsels of the Government might be shaken." The following month rebellion broke out in Hizen, under the leadership of Eto Shimpei, the former Councillor of State. For participation in this revolt twelve samurai, among them Eto, were executed, and many others were sentenced to imprisonment for varying terms of years. At about the same time Maibara, a Choshu samurai, who had been taken into the Government in 1869 and subsequently dismissed, fomented a rebellion in his native province and forfeited his life. Practically all of these disturbances were created by former samurai, and, judging by the written decisions of the law-courts, their treason was in all cases animated by either an intense desire to preserve the honour of the country against the fancied insults of the Koreans or Chinese, or to restore the feudal institutions of pre-Meiji days.

These disturbances were of sufficient magnitude to induce the Government to compromise with the agitated military class to the extent of permitting the dispatch, in 1874, of the expedition against the savages of South Formosa. The acquiescence of the Peking authorities in such a course had been obtained the year before by Soyejima, and so no complications were to be feared in that direction. A force of three thousand men, under the command of Saigo Yorimichi, a younger brother of Takamori, set out in May, and for the time being the Government had rid itself and the country of a number of the most violent partisans of aggression. The expedition cost the Government 5,400,000 yen and the co-operation of Kido, who resigned his position in the Council of State rather than endorse the policy.

Of essentially the same nature as the above-mentioned protests against the policy of the Government was the great rebellion in Satsuma three years later. How influential in causing that rebellion was the compulsory pension capitalization ordinance of 1876 may in part be judged by the energy of Satsuma's protests against it. But whatever the immediate cause of the outbreak, the struggle between Satsuma and the Imperial Government was wellnigh inevitable. It is difficult to come to any other conclusion than the obvious one, that treason on a huge scale, animated by loyalty to the Emperor, paradoxical as it may sound, was deliberately planned and carried out. After 1874 Saigo Takamori was in and out of the Government by turns, and Shimadzu Hisamitsu occupied the office of Sadaijin for a short period ; but at no time did the Satsuma leaders whole-heartedly support the Administration policy of domestic reconstruction. Saigo, during the three years after the break-up of the Coalition in 1873, had maintained in Satsuma his so-called " schools," which turned the whole clan into a military camp. Shimadzu had grown more and more reactionary, and demanded among other things the restoration of the feudal régime.

Satsuma had been the foremost of the clans which had brought about the Restoration, and its services to the Imperial cause on that occasion were such as could never be forgotten. Saigo had received a personal letter of thanks from the Emperor and a pension of 2,000 *koku* a year. In 1869 Shimadzu was the first of the signatories of the proposal to return

The Government and its Critics

their registers to the Emperor, and in 1871 he joined the Coalition to destroy feudalism. During 1872 and until September 1873 Saigo had been one of the leading figures in the Government. Nevertheless, the Satsuma samurai remained true to their clan interests and their feudal traditions. Though their fief was turned into a Ken, they continued to administer its affairs. Its leaders, Saigo and Shimadzu, blew hot and cold, and after 1873 permitted and encouraged flagrant treason against the central authorities.

Situated at the south-western extremity of the Empire, Satsuma was so slightly affected by the changes which were taking place that when Shimadzu, the ex-Daimyo of the clan, came up to Tokyo in 1874 with four hundred of his men, their fierce appearance fairly terrified the citizens of the more peaceful capital. It was evident from that significant display that Satsuma had preserved all the customs and traditions of the past, even though it had submitted to, nay, abetted, the inception of the new régime. Furthermore, Shimadzu disagreed with the Government in everything except the maintenance of the Imperial house. Not only so, but his clan claimed for itself the privilege, accepted as legitimate throughout the mediæval period, of regarding the Government of the day as a conspiracy against the true interests of the people, an oligarchy which used the Imperial name and prestige as a justification of its despotic rule. Criticism of any established government for usurping the power of the throne was always considered valid among the opponents of an administration, since in the feudal period the Emperor himself was never regarded as a part of the Government. Hence it was always possible to hatch treason against the authorities and at the same time claim loyalty to the throne. Such was the reasoning of Choshu in 1864, when the clan tried to carry off the Emperor Komei Tenno and in his name dispute the title of the Shogunate, and a precisely similar attitude was adopted by Satsuma after

A Political History of Japan

the Restoration. The clan desired the destruction of the Government and the release of the Emperor from what they chose to regard as his bondage, in order that they might themselves control his policy and in his name reform the administration to make it conform to their own views of what was wise and necessary.

If this reading of the Japanese mind is correct—and there are numerous incidents in the history of the nation to support it—the Satsuma Rebellion takes on the semblance of a mistaken though loyal movement, a view which explains not only the still existing admiration with which the nation regards the spirit of the clan and the veneration shown the memory of its leader, Saigo, but the attitude of the Government in suppressing the revolt.

The late Count Hayashi Tadasu, diplomat and Minister of Foreign Affairs, whose *Mémoires* have been published recently, has left an account in a series of *Reminiscences*, printed some years ago by the *Jiji Shimpo*, of the way in which Okubo, the Home Minister, arranged for the suppression of the Satsuma rebellion. When the first news of the outbreak reached Kyoto, in February 1877, the Emperor and his Court were temporarily established in the ancient capital. The Government was thrown into a panic. Ito and Hayashi set out for Kobe to meet Okubo and convey the news to him. As they all journeyed back to Kyoto in the evening, Okubo is described as apparently unimpressed by the crisis and as saying nothing to indicate the train of his thoughts. To their astonishment, however, Ito and Hayashi awoke the next morning to find the city placarded with edicts depriving Saigo of his titles and rank, proscribing him as a rebel, appointing Prince Arisugawa the Commander-in-Chief of an expedition against Satsuma, and summoning the Council of State to a meeting that very day. This story is told by Hayashi as illustrative of Okubo's methods : overnight he had formulated the plans which in his mind were required by the occasion, and without consulting any

The Government and its Critics

of his official colleagues he had caused the necessary proclamations to be issued.

The importance of the Satsuma Rebellion, which was suppressed after a six months' campaign, was not in the expense entailed upon the Government nor in the loss of life so much as in its effects upon the general political situation. In political theory it was to be no longer possible to separate the throne and the Imperial Government, or to claim loyalty to the former as a pretext for an armed attack upon the latter. Likewise, the suppression of the rebellion demonstrated that the feudal pretensions of a clan were powerless against the new central Government. The fact that the revolutionary spirit did not spread [1] beyond the limits of Satsuma, even at a time when the whole samurai class was in a state of profound discontent, showed how thoroughly the feudal aristocracy had comprehended the main political ideas of the Restoration movement. It was amply proved that any criticism of the Government must follow a peaceful course, under the guidance of educated public opinion, not the desperate counsel of military fanaticism.

Since 1877 there have been in Japanese history no armed risings on a great scale against the policy of the Government. But political assassinations have been frequent. In 1878 Okubo was murdered by six samurai of Ishikawa and Shimane Ken, and attempts were made upon the lives of Itagaki and Okuma a few years later. Even the enlightened Government of Meiji cannot be said to have unqualifiedly condemned the practice, for a celebration in honour of the Mito clansmen who slew the Regent Ii Naosuke (Ii Kamon-no-Kami) in 1860 is held each year in Tokyo, and has been attended in recent times by high military officials, and even by Cabinet Ministers and Princes of the Blood. There is something in the taking of the life of a fancied enemy of the country, no matter how

[1] The armed neutrality of Tosa might perhaps be cited as an exception to this statement.

highly placed, as a protest against or criticism of his actions, that appeals to the Japanese mind, and the nation looks upon such conduct with a leniency that is only to be explained by the defects of the military despotism under which they lived for centuries.

If the policy of the peace party in placing the development of the national resources, the increase of wealth and armaments, and the establishment of laws, before and above a career of aggression, met with a veritable storm of protest in the form of revolution, it also seems to have given rise to a very different and much more significant form of criticism. Among the early events of 1874 was the launching of a campaign for an elective assembly by the four ex-Councillors of State, Soyejima, Itagaki, Goto, and Eto, and their friends. The movement was initiated by a Memorial [1] addressed to the Government and signed by nine samurai. The document is said to have been written by two Tosa men, Komuro and Furusawa, who had just returned from Europe, where they had been greatly impressed by the representative assemblies of the various countries they had visited, especially by the English Parliament. In the accompanying letter it was stated that some of the memorialists, while in office, had repeatedly advocated the establishment of a representative assembly, but had been put off with promises. The determination to wait no longer before beginning a public agitation for an assembly had been reached in view of the fact that " the popular mind has been agitated and mutual distrust has sprung up between the governors and the governed, and a state of things has arrived in which it cannot be denied that there are signs of destruction and ruin ready to break forth at any moment." This action of the memorialists was entirely justified in their own minds by the conviction that " the cause of this discontent is the suppression of the general opinion of the Empire as ascertained by public discussion." The Memorial began

The Government and its Critics

by setting forth the complaint, so often heard in Japan, that the governing power lay not with the Crown nor the people, but with the officials. Such a form of government could not possibly conduct the affairs of the Empire successfully; " an infant knows that it cannot be done." To rescue the country from the ruin which impended it was necessary to establish a " council chamber chosen by the people," for by that means a " limit will be placed to the power of the officials and both the governors and the governed will obtain peace and prosperity."

The general political principle of democracy was then stated : " The people, whose duty it is to pay taxes to the Government, possess the right of sharing in the Government affairs and of approving and condemning." This philosophy of democracy was about as foreign to the Japanese mind as it could well be, for during the whole of the feudal period the tax-paying classes were considered to have performed their whole political duty when they contributed a share of each harvest or of the gains of trade and handicraft to the support of the governing class. Chinese political philosophy, which had been adopted by the Japanese along with so much else that was Chinese, can be summarized in a sentence—it is the duty of the governors to rule, and of the governed to obey. But after 1867, and especially in view of one of the paragraphs of the Imperial oath, the mediæval expression of that dogma had been modified, and the Government had justified its failure to consult " public opinion " by saying that the people were as yet " wanting in culture and intelligence " and could not comprehend questions of state. There was undoubtedly some justification for the official view of the matter in the failure of the Kogisho as a body of representatives of the clans. Nevertheless, this official argument was combated by the memorialists on the ground that it was false and displayed in the Government " a shocking self-conceit and arrogant contempt of the people."

A Political History of Japan

" No representation no taxation " was the main argument set forth in the Memorial. There was much else in it which was designed to offset the official arguments in favour of a conservative policy of slow and steady progress toward constitutional government.

The answer given by the Sa-in, the department of the Government to which such memorials were sent, was interesting as an example either of the confusion within the Government or of its disingenuousness. The principle of the Memorial was admitted by the Sa-in to be " an excellent one," and the adoption of the suggestion was promised. An announcement was made that for the immediate future " local assemblies " only would be established and the " question of a council chamber chosen by the people " would be taken up subsequently.

But the agitation for a national elective assembly was not allowed to rest with this equivocal pronouncement from one of the Government departments. Kato Hiroyuki, the head of the Daigaku (Government University) in Tokyo, was delegated to reply to the Memorial. Kato was a profound Chinese scholar, as well as a student of Western learning, and in his reply voiced the opinions of the conservative element in the ruling class. What is more interesting still, his arguments were mainly based on analogies which he found in the history of Prussia. He was a staunch believer in despotic government, and did much to influence other members of his class in the same direction. The views in his first reply [1] were mainly an amplification of the idea that national institutions must bear a close relation to the stage of progress reached by the people ; the Japanese, being unenlightened and narrow-minded, were not fitted for public discussion, and therefore must continue to be ruled by a body of officials acting despotically and arbitrarily, but on the whole in the best interests of the nation.

The controversy thus begun continued, the petitions [2]

[1] *J. G. D.* pp. 433-9.   [2] *Idem*, pp. 440-95.

for a council chamber elected by the people and the arguments against such an institution being by no means confined to the original memorialists and Kato. So great was the interest taken in the question that it would be impossible to give in detail even a tithe of the opinions which found their way into print. The newspapers of the day took sides, the *Choya Shimbun* being the foremost of the champions of Soyejima and his party, the *Nichi Nichi Shimbun* of the opponents. The latter paper advocated patience and slow advancement, though it often attacked the agitators for an assembly and impugned their motives. In 1875 an assembly was said to be necessary in order to determine whether or not the nation wanted war with Korea, and in 1880 in order to induce the foreign Powers to revise the treaties. All through this period it was argued and reiterated by the friends of the cause that a representative assembly would reform the administration, reduce the expenditures of the Government and the burden of taxation, and the like, and, moreover, that such an assembly was the natural and necessary counterpart of the system of taxation.

After 1877 the propaganda began to assume a new and important form. Political societies were formed, and for a period of years conducted an organized campaign against the Government. The nature of these organizations and their influence will be described later.

The criticism involved in this agitation was not directed so much against any particular items of policy as the form of government itself. It was held to be despotic and arbitrary, and consequently inept and impossible. There is no particular reason for supposing that the agitators were merely bent on venting their spite against the ruling clique which had ousted Soyejima, Itagaki, Goto, and Eto from office in September 1873, yet the coincidence between that event and the initiation of the agitation is striking.

The first article of the Imperial oath taken by the

A Political History of Japan

Emperor at the time of his accession to the throne intimated that much stress would be laid upon the wishes of the people in determining the policy of the Government. The " people " thus referred to was the feudal aristocracy, especially the samurai, and to give the term a wider connotation would be to misinterpret the whole movement which culminated in the Restoration. A further proof of this point might be found in the constitution of the first assembly of the representatives of the people, when the *Koshi* nominated by the clan lords from among the samurai came together to form the Kogisho. But when the clans were abolished in 1871, one of the consequences of that change was to enlarge the meaning of the term " public opinion " to make it include the masses. At that time the Administration gave no indication that the terms of the Imperial oath were to be changed, consequently it was a correct interpretation of the meaning of the oath to claim thereafter that it referred to the opinions of the whole people as having weight with the Government. Those signatories of the original Memorial who had held office in the Council of State had evidently brought the matter to the attention of their colleagues, who quite naturally refused to reissue the oath in a revised form, adopting rather a policy of postponing the fulfilment of the first article. It was, therefore, open to Soyejima and Itagaki and their friends to continue to insist upon the carrying out of the promises made at the beginning of Meiji to call together the elected representatives of the people and to give them a share in the government of the nation. Doubtless the embarrassment of the Government which resulted from their action was not unwelcome to the Opposition. They were only human, after all, and to take pleasure in the discomfiture of political opponents is a universal weakness. But to say that factious opposition to an already overburdened Government was their main object is to completely misrepresent the case. The subsequent action of Eto, one of the original group

The Government and its Critics

of memorialists, in heading a rebellion in Saga, for which treason he forfeited his life, was to the Japanese way of thinking clear proof of the sincerity of his protest against the failure to carry out the terms of the Emperor's oath. Likewise, Itagaki's subsequent re-entry into the Government, on the basis of the compromise arrived at in the Osaka Conference in 1874, proved that his purpose was to secure the fulfilment of the Imperial oath as announced at the coronation. There is little doubt also that the leaders of the Opposition, who were advocates of a policy of expansion in Asia from habit rather than conviction, felt that if a vote of the people upon the question of war with Korea or the punishment of the South Formosan savages were taken the war party would be in the majority.

One of the extraordinary features of the whole controversy over the part public opinion was to play in determining the policy of the Government was the prominence given to the first article of the coronation oath. The Emperor himself was too young to have taken any part in the preparation of that document, which represented the ideas of Kido and his colleagues, and must have been written by some one in that group. What was actually meant by the clause " all measures shall be decided by public argument " it is now impossible to determine, but it is certain that to those present when the oath was read the impression conveyed was that " public argument " referred to such argument as might be advanced by the clan leaders. Yet the oath when once uttered by the Emperor immediately took on a sanctity and importance out of all proportion to its origin, and it was adopted seven years later as the shibboleth of a cause the very nature of which was inconceivable in 1867.

CHAPTER V

THE RECONSTRUCTION OF THE CENTRAL AND LOCAL GOVERNMENTS

THE task of reconstructing the institutions of the central and local governments was entered upon immediately after the abolition of the feudal system. Before that event all measures involving changes in institutions may be regarded as provisional, for as long as feudalism persisted no real beginning could be made on a permanent basis.

In 1871 a Commission was established and charged with the re-organization of the central Government. Kido was appointed President and Saigo Takamori Vice-President, and among the members of the Commission were Itagaki, Goto, Ito, Inouye, Okuma, Terashima, and others of the advanced Liberal group. As a result of their deliberations the Daijokwan was divided into three Boards or Colleges—the Central Board (Sei-in), the Left Board (Sa-in), and the Right Board (U-in)—and at the same time the office of Councillor (Sangi) was created.

The administrative departments created in 1868 had received two additions—the Department of Civil Affairs in 1869 and the Department of Public Works in 1870. The former of these additions was abolished, but the others, both original and additional, were taken over as an integral part of the new system of government. By this means the complicated arrangements of 1868 were simplified. The first two offices of the system established at that time, the " Deliberative Assembly " and the " Lords President of the

The Reconstruction of Governments

Council," were abolished and their functions handed over to the three Boards. The powers exercised by the " Upper House of the Deliberative Assembly " and by the " Lords President of the Council " devolved upon the Sei-in and U-in, while those of the Lower House were given over to the Sa-in.

Simple as this reorganization may seem, it was not without its difficulties, which arose mainly out of the desire for extreme centralization of authority coupled with an appearance of decentralization. Thus the U-in was composed of the departmental Ministers, who were no longer ex-Kuge or Daimyo, but members of the former ruling coterie of samurai. With the abolition of the clans in 1871, the policy of appointing to high offices the members of the Court or territorial nobility, which had been announced in 1868, was discarded, and the real promoters of the Restoration stepped forward and assumed the high offices of the Administration. But it was not enough that these samurai should be members of the U-in ; some of them were appointed Sangi and thus took their places in the Sei-in, which exercised supreme executive authority. The U-in was therefore composed of the heads of the administrative departments, some of whom in turn served the purposes of centralization by being appointed to the Sei-in—that is, combined administrative and executive powers. But the problem of greatest difficulty concerned the composition and powers of the Sa-in. In 1868 the " Lower House," commonly called the Kogisho, was made up of *Koshi*, representatives of the clans, but after 1871 the Lower House ceased to have any active existence, though its name remained in the calendar until 1873. The difficulty in disposing of this body, which ostensibly represented public opinion, was connected with the promise made in the Imperial oath that " all measures " should " be decided by public argument." The Government not feeling secure enough in its power to openly repudiate the terms of the oath and announce its determination to rule the country without consulting the people, the Sa-in was therefore created with advisory powers, and its members were appointed by the Emperor for the purpose of representing public opinion, but, lest it should by any chance attempt an independent course, its functions were strictly limited to giving advice upon projects of law proposed by the Sei-in. This device of appointing men who were regarded as staunch adherents of the ruling oligarchy to represent the people made its appearance from time to time. There was a sufficient element of reality about it to satisfy the majority, whose custom it had always been to permit their superiors to do their political thinking. As we shall see, in five or six years the newspaper-reading element of the public was made aware of the essential difference between being represented by officials chosen by the Government and by members elected by the community at large.

Under the system of government established in 1871, as in 1868, the supreme power in the State rested in the Daijokwan. The Sei-in and U-in divided between them all the substantive powers of the Government, the former controlling general policy and supervising the administration, the latter carrying out administrative measures. The Sa-in was a shadow, with neither influence nor authority. In creating such a body it is evident that the Government gave up all thought of consulting or being guided by the wishes of feudal public opinion, and was not willing to admit to a share in the government the great mass of the people. Nevertheless, the oligarchy was not unwilling to have a so-called representative body in existence, to which they could point in order to satisfy such demand as existed for popular government.

When some fourteen years later the Daijokwan was about to be abolished, the Prime Minister, Sanjo Saneyoshi, in a memorial [1] to the throne referred to

---

[1] *J. G. D.*, pp. 90-3.

The Reconstruction of Governments

this organization of the Government and offered a variety of criticism. " The system, although suited as a temporary expedient to the exigencies of the time, is opposed to the principle of personal government by your Majesty ; it has tended, moreover, to lessen unduly the responsibilities of the Ministers of departments, and has caused obstruction in the public business." The meaning of these objections becomes apparent only in the light of some further commentary. The Daijokwan had been set up during the Emperor's minority, and had therefore assumed practically Imperial powers. It was a Regency put into commission because the active promoters of the Restoration were unwilling to hand over the Imperial power to any one individual, a fact which throws light upon their early ambitions. In 1885, after the Emperor had arrived at the age of discretion—he was thirty-three years old—the Government came to the conclusion that it was time to abolish the virtual Regency, hence Sanjo's criticism of the Daijokwan as " opposed to the principle of personal government by your Majesty." The second objection to the Daijokwan lay in the fact that it tended " to lessen unduly the responsibilities of the Ministers of departments." What had actually happened was that the commanding figures in the Government who were both heads of departments and Sangi had formed the habit of proceeding with such departmental measures as they chose to adopt, subsequently notifying the Daijokwan of the action they had taken, whereas men of little influence in the Sei-in, who were notwithstanding Ministers of departments, took little interest in their proper administrative functions because they were not powerful enough to obtain the Sei-in's sanction to such measures as their departmental subordinates proposed. This condition of affairs became so scandalous that the Government finally undertook to remove the abuse by providing that Ministers of departments should not be members of the Sei-in, and that they should be strictly guided by that body in the performance of their duties. But as this change had the effect of retarding the business of the departments, it was given up after about a year's experience, and the old system was reverted to. The third of Sanjo's objections to the Daijokwan was the obstruction which it caused in the prompt dispatch of public business. As the Council of State had the supervision of all public business, it was impossible for its members to attend to all the matters that were brought before them, for not only were the administrative departments supposed to apply to and receive their instructions from the Daijokwan, but all memorials to the throne and all questions of policy, whether affecting domestic or foreign relations, had to be considered and decided upon by this body. In plain terms, the Council of State was so choked with business that it could not possibly transact it with speed.

It took more than a decade of experience to make these defects of the system apparent, but in 1871 the members of the Commission probably took no small pride in the organization they devised. As to the personnel of the reorganized Government, Sanjo Saneyoshi, a Kuge, and Iwakura Tomomi were appointed respectively Daijodaijin and Udaijin, while Kido, Saigo, Itagaki, and Okuma were made Sangi. The changes in the holders of the offices were frequent, and only a few of them are of any interest. In the early part of 1872 Okuma was transferred from the Department of Public Works to the Finance Office upon Inouye's resignation, and a little later Goto and Eto were created Sangi, Soyejima becoming Minister of Foreign Affairs and Oki Minister of Education. In September of 1873, as a result of the triumph of the peace party, Saigo, Itagaki, Goto, and Eto resigned from the Council of State and Soyejima from the Foreign Office, and the Government was left in the hands of Sanjo, Iwakura, Kido, Okubo, Ito, Okuma, Terashima, Kuroda, Ichiji, Yamagata, and Katsu Awa. In 1874 Kido resigned because of the Formosan expe-

The Reconstruction of Governments

dition, but along with Itagaki and Saigo he was re-appointed Sangi after the Osaka compromise, and later in the year Shimadzu Hisamitsu joined the Government as Sadaijin, a post from which he soon retired. Kido,[1] Itagaki, and Saigo soon afterwards withdrew.

During the three years and a half which followed, the system of government established in 1871 persisted, though from time to time changes were made in the number of administrative departments. In 1872 the Department of War was abolished, and in its place two departments, those of the Army and the Navy, were created. In 1873 the Department of Home Affairs was set up, and complete powers of control over internal administration bestowed upon it. The importance of this department we shall point out in connection with the system of local administration ; at this juncture it is sufficient to say that Okubo held the office practically from the time of its inception until his assassination in 1878.

The next important reorganization of the central Government occurred in 1875. The name " Daijo-kwan " was retained, no longer as the " Council of State " but as a " Privy Council," and in place of the three Boards, which were abolished, two new bodies were created, the Senate (Genro-in) and a Supreme Court (Daishin-in). The ostensible object of these changes was to divide the Government into executive, legislative, and judicial bodies. That the little group of oligarchs which ruled had no intention of setting up independent legislative or judicial authorities in the Genro-in and Daishin-in may be seen from an examina-

---

[1] By 1875 Kido's services to the State ended, and two years later he died. His official career was in many respects disappointing. Till 1873 he was undoubtedly the foremost of the Meiji reformers, the philosopher of the Restoration, but as a practical politician he was lacking in the requisite ability to get along with his colleagues, especially with Okubo, whose imperious temperament permitted little opposition. Nevertheless, with Kido's death Japan lost one of its very greatest men, whose wisdom might have saved the nation in the following decade from Ito's deplorable blunder in the matter of the Constitution.

tion of the powers conferred on both, and that they had any idea of establishing personal rule by the Emperor, as might be inferred from the title " Privy Council," may be positively denied. The Senate was so hedged about that it could accomplish nothing more than had the Sa-in, which, as we have seen, had no substantive powers in legislation. Nevertheless, the composition of the Senate and its legislative powers are interesting in two respects. In the first place, its members were to be appointed by the Emperor from among the following classes : " (1) nobles ; or (2) persons at present or formerly of official position in the first or second grades ; or (3) persons who have rendered meritorious services to the State ; or (4) persons of political or legal knowledge and experience." With a few additions these are the classes from which the House of Peers was afterwards constituted. In the second place, the regulations governing the deliberations of the Genro-in and determining its powers were in nearly all cases adumbrations of the present rules of procedure and powers of the Diet, especially of the Lower House. Likewise, the rules drawn up for the guidance of the Supreme Court were such as to make that body subject to the control of the Daijokwan through the Department of Justice. It may be doubted whether even at the present day there is in Japan any real separation between the judiciary and the Government.

These changes were deemed of sufficient importance to warrant the issue of an Imperial rescript,[1] on April 14th, to announce them. The Emperor was made to say, in part :—

" It is Our desire not to restrict Ourselves to the maintenance of the five principles which We swore to preserve, but to go still further and enlarge the circle of domestic reforms.

" With this in view We now establish the Genro-in to enact laws for the Empire, and the Daishin-in to

[1] *J. G. D.*, pp. 41–2.

consolidate the judicial authority of the courts. By also assembling representatives from the various provinces of the Empire, the public mind will be best known, and the public interest best consulted, and in this manner the wisest system of administration will be determined.

" We hope by these means to secure the happiness of Our subjects and Our own. And while they must necessarily abandon many of their former customs, yet must they not, on the other hand, yield too impulsively to a rash desire for reform."

For effrontery and sheer contempt of the nation's intelligence it would be difficult to find a parallel to this rescript even in Japanese annals. The Government chose to call a body which could advise upon certain projects submitted to it by the Privy Council, and could only give assent to others, a legislative body. What was meant by the words "to consolidate the judicial authority of the courts" it is not possible to say precisely, but if an independent judiciary were meant, then the regulations subsequently issued completely stultified the promise. To describe the assembling of the local officials [1] from the various provinces of the Empire as the best method of consulting the public interest, knowing the public mind, or devising the wisest system of administration, must have seemed to the champions of popular government a gratuitous insult. That such was the case is to be inferred from Itagaki's action in resigning his office in 1876, as soon as the regulations governing the Daijokwan, Genro-in, and Daishin-in were published. From these various considerations we are forced to the conclusion that the changes were undertaken to satisfy a demand for a less autocratic form of government, and that while new forms were created the old principle of absolutism was retained by the oligarchs.

[1] The name given to this quasi-representative body was Chihokwan-Kwaigi. An extended notice of this assembly will be found below in Chapter VI, pp. 133-41.

A Political History of Japan

The explanation of this reorganization of the central Government institutions is to be found partly in the unrest which existed among the ex-samurai in 1874, and partly in the dissensions among the members of the Government. When in 1873 the peace party imposed its will upon the Administration there was intense discontent among the samurai and a serious split within the ranks of the Government itself. In the first months of 1874 the hostility to the Administration broke out into open rebellion, and the Government, as a means of calming the excitement among the samurai and placating Saigo Takamori, sanctioned the Formosan expedition, though this very measure caused Kido to resign his office in the Council of State. The position of the Government was further weakened by the action of Itagaki and his followers in launching, in January 1874, their campaign for the establishment of a representative assembly. To discuss the situation, and if possible effect a compromise which would reunite the broken ranks of the Administration, a conference was arranged by Ito, it is said, at Osaka. The Government was represented by Okubo and Ito, and the Opposition by Kido and Itagaki. The arrangements arrived at in that conference were embodied in the changes in the institutions of the central Government described above. Kido gave an *ex post facto* consent to the Formosan expedition, and while Itagaki was not altogether satisfied with the provisions made for representing public opinion, still he consented to enter the Government after an Imperial order to that effect had been addressed to him.

As the outcome of the conference most of the difficulties of the times seemed to have been smoothed away. But it was only the appearance of harmony that had been achieved, for both Kido and Itagaki soon resigned on the ground that the terms of the compromise had not been carried out by the Government.

The arrangements made in 1875 for carrying on

The Reconstruction of Governments

the government of the nation remained almost un-
touched for a decade. During those ten years a
number of important political changes in the country
took place. The agitation for a Parliament went on
almost without interruption, and so successful had it
been that in 1881 the Government actually promised
to set up the Imperial Diet in 1889. It was partly
as a preparation for the latter event, and partly as a
fulfilment of Ito's designs to create in Japan an imitation of the Prussian oligarchy, that the changes of
1885 have to be interpreted. In that year the
Daijokwan was abolished and a Cabinet (Naikaku)
created in its place. The functions hitherto exercised
by the Daijokwan were transferred to the Naikaku,
which was composed of the various departmental
Ministers and presided over by the Minister President
of State. The offices of Udaijin, Sadaijin, and Sangi
were abolished. Of the then existing institutions only
the Genro-in and Daishin-in survived, as they performed the useful function of giving an oligarchic
government the appearance of harbouring a popular
element and fostering an independent administration
of justice.

The change from the Daijokwan to the Naikaku was
explained as a return to the ancient Japanese polity, in
which the Emperor personally ruled, receiving reports
from his Ministers of State, and deciding all matters
by and with his Ministers' advice ; the reason for
making the change in 1885 was stated to be the
Emperor's arrival at a stage in his development which
made his personal rule possible. It was also claimed
that the establishment of the Cabinet would facilitate
the conduct of business and get rid of the abuses
which had crept into the old system.

It is permissible to doubt, at least, the first two of
these statements. The oligarchy had no intention of
handing over its power to the Emperor, any more than
had the Emperor developed the capacity to exercise
such powers. The changes were dictated by a desire

to get rid of the Daijokwan and the abuses connected with it. Ito, who had been the leading figure in the Government since Okubo's assassination in 1878, was well aware that a system of government borrowed from China and dating from the eighth century was an anomaly in the nineteenth. The adoption of such antiquated arrangements in 1868 had been expedient, but their perpetuation till the promulgation of the Constitution would have had the effect of leaving the oligarchy in a difficult position. Ito desired that the Government should have the start of the people by at least four years, in which time their necessary training in the Bismarckian methods which he already had in mind could be completed. It might easily be imagined, too, that Ito and his colleagues in the Administration chafed at the nominal leadership of Sanjo and wished to be rid of him, and with him of every remaining element of Kuge influence. This supposition is in part justified by the personnel of the newly created Naikaku : Ito, Inouye, Yamagata, Matsukata, Oyama, Saigo Yorimichi, Yamada, Mori, Tani, and Enomoto. In this list there are the names of four Choshu and four Satsuma men, and only two outsiders. The Naikaku might be pointed to as an example of what is meant by clan government.

Immediately after the formation of the Naikaku under Ito as Minister President there were issued a variety of instructions and ordinances [1] intended to enlighten the Ministers of State on the nature of their functions under the new order. By this means Ito made his preparations for the approach of the constitutional régime, in which he and his fellow-oligarchs purposed playing the leading rôles, just as they had in the past.

The only other institutional change of any importance previous to 1899 was the setting up of the Privy Council [2] (Sumitsu-in) in 1888. This Council was created for the purpose of sanctioning the final draft

---

[1] *J. G. D.*, pp. 99–127.　　　　[2] *Idem*, pp. 127–33.

The Reconstruction of Governments

of the Constitution, and thereafter it was intended to discharge the function of advising the Emperor upon matters of great concern in the State.

In 1889 the central Government was finally organized upon the basis on which it has continued to stand ever since. Under the supreme direction of the Emperor, the administration is carried on by the Cabinet with the advice of the Privy Council and the consent of the Imperial Diet. Outside of these legally constituted bodies there is a powerful extra-legal committee, the members being popularly known as the Elder Statesmen (Genro), which upon occasions both political and non-political is consulted by the Emperor. The Constitution of 1889, in addition to certain claims which it made regarding the nature of the sovereignty, guaranteed that the various institutions composing the Government should be operated in accordance with the provisions of law. The importance of the instrument lies not so much in any of its specific provisions as in the fact that for the first time in Japanese history, if we except perhaps the Tokugawa laws referring to the Court nobles, feudal lords, samurai, and peasants, an attempt was made to define the channels through which the Imperial prerogatives should be exercised. It places no limitations upon the absolute powers of the Emperor, but promises that those absolute powers shall be exercised in accordance with the law of the land.

The only new institution [1] created by the laws which were promulgated on the same day as the Constitution was the Imperial Diet, consisting of Upper and Lower Houses. The Upper House was to be composed of the Princes of the Blood, hereditary and representative peers, Imperial nominees, and a representative of the fifteen highest taxpayers in each Fu and Ken ; the Lower House, of the representatives of the people chosen in accordance with the provisions of the law of election. The functions of the Diet were enumerated

[1] For the text of the Constitution and of all the other laws referred to in these paragraphs consult *J. G. D.*, pp. 133–231.

in the Constitution, and the procedure and powers were stated *in extenso* in the law of the Houses. Independent powers of legislation were not granted to the Diet, and could not have been, considering the theory of monarchy which was set forth in the Constitution and the ambitions of the ruling clan oligarchy. It would be easy, therefore, to criticize the Diet as lacking substantive powers, but such an objection would be beside the point, for the authorities had no intention of setting up a democratic form of government, or any system remotely resembling it. In so far as it was possible, the oligarchy prevented the people's representatives from controlling either the legislative or executive branches of the Administration, and inserted in the Constitution and the organic laws disabling provisions.

Having followed in brief outline the various changes which were made in the organization for central government in the period between 1871 and 1889, there remains to be surveyed the field of local government.[1] At the outset, it will be remembered that previous to 1871 the Restoration Government contented itself with insisting that the feudal clans (Han) should standardize the official organizations of their various governments. Thus standardized, at the head of each clan government was the Chihanji, the former feudal lord, and under him, arranged in a descending scale of importance, was a list of officials with their corresponding offices. Each clan's government was nominally directly under the control of the Daijokwan, but enjoyed a large degree of independence, the only limitations imposed being such as were necessary to avoid the most obvious conflicts of jurisdiction. Thus the clans were forbidden to contract alliances with foreign countries, or to coin money or bestow honours, as such powers inhered solely in the central Government. Generally speaking, the system of local government in force until 1871 was practically the pre-Meiji

[1] For the essential documents relating to the organization of local government institutions see *J. G. D.*, pp. 22–9 and 250–425.

The Reconstruction of Governments

feudal government, the sovereign powers of the clans in the cases of the more powerful daimiates being but slightly diminished by their nominal subordination to the Daijokwan.

In the case of the former Tokugawa domains a somewhat different régime existed after 1868. At the outbreak of the wars of the Restoration the Tokugawa lands were confiscated, and in many cases the local representatives of the Shogun fled from their posts. This situation was dealt with immediately by appointing loyalists to the vacated offices. The chief seaports, which had been under the direct control of the Shogun, were named Fu, and the fiefs Ken, and the highest of the newly appointed officials were called Governors of Fu (Chifuji) or Governors of Ken (Chikenji). Not only was the official organization of these Fu and Ken governments prescribed, but a brief statement was made of the objects which the local administration should keep in mind. Thus the policy of local government, in so far as the Fu and Ken were concerned, was more or less completely controlled by the central Government. In this respect, and this only, did the local government of the Ken and the Han differ after 1868.

When all the remaining Han were abolished in 1871 and turned into Ken, the organization which had been established in the ex-Shogun's domains in 1868 was extended over the whole country. The number of the Fu in 1869 had been reduced from nine to three—Tokyo, Osaka, and Kyoto—and these three cities have had a special form of local government ever since. But apart from this exception, the abolition of feudalism resulted ultimately, if not immediately, in standardizing the local government institutions. In September 1871 there were some 302 Ken, varying in size and importance, and one of the first reforms introduced was the rearrangement of these areas by splitting up or regrouping, with the result that the number was reduced to seventy-two. Subsequently the process of

I

realigning the boundaries of the Ken was continued, and by 1890 the Empire, with the exception of the Hokkaido, had been divided into forty-five Ken. In 1872 these areas were subdivided into Districts (Gun), for purely administrative purposes, and the Gun were further subdivided into Cities (Ku), Towns (Cho), and Villages (Son). By these reforms uniformity was introduced into the arrangements for local government. The bureaucracy was composed of the officials attached to the offices of the Ken, Gun, Ku, Cho, and Son. The Ken officials, under the Kenchiji (or Kenrei), the representative of the Daijokwan in the prefecture, determined the main outlines of local policy and supervised the execution of measures adopted ; the Gun officials' function was to administer within their jurisdiction the policy outlined by the Kenchiji. The Ku, Cho, and Son officers were responsible for the execution of the orders of the Kenchiji within their areas, and in addition performed a multitude of local services, which from time out of mind had been delegated to village and town officials, such as the compilation of registers, lists of taxpayers, and the amounts of taxes.

In 1874 a change of the greatest importance was made in the relations between the local government bodies and the central Government. In 1873 the Department of Home Affairs (Naimusho) had been created, and in the following year it was given control over the entire local government system. In the rules for the conduct of the business of the Naimusho [1] the following powers were specified and granted : to regulate the processes of taking the census ; to establish poorhouses and hospitals; to encourage good behaviour among the people ; to establish agricultural schools and societies ; to delimit the boundaries of Ken and Gun ; to establish, remove, or abolish local government offices ; to increase or decrease the expenses of the local government offices and the burden of local taxation ; to make roads, embankments, and

[1] *J. G. D.*, pp. 36–41.

The Reconstruction of Governments

bridges ; to regulate the postal service and merchant ships ; to make loans or give charity ; to increase or decrease the number of officials ; to preserve the records from all parts of the country, as well as places and buildings of historical importance ; to investigate the boundaries of towns and villages ; to conduct a survey of the land ; to revise the organization of towns and villages and change their names, etc. The Minister of Home Affairs had power to rearrange the boundaries of the Ken and all other local government areas, and he had similarly complete control of the local government organization, the expenditures of any area, and the taxes to be collected from the local people.

The establishment of the Ministry of Home Affairs, which was subject to the control of the Daijokwan in precisely the same degree as any other department of state, although given complete jurisdiction over all local government affairs, helps to account for the peculiarly centralized nature of the Japanese Government. From that time till the present every matter of importance which concerns a locality has to be brought before the Home Office by the local authorities, and the action to be taken is decided virtually by the central Government. Thus, if a city wishes to bestow a franchise upon a street-railway company or a gas company, the consent of the Home Minister must be obtained before any action can be taken by the city authorities.

The newly created Department of Home Affairs under the leadership of Okubo, who was a man of extremely dictatorial methods and believed little in consulting the wishes of the people, began the process of building up the local bureaucracy. As far as local official organization was concerned no sweeping changes were ever made, but in the matter of the discretionary powers of local officials more and more detailed and stringent rules were issued. Thus in 1875 the laws of the Fu and Ken were completely revised, and instead of the old grants of power to the local authorities couched in general terms, such as " taxes shall be moderately and impartially levied," there appeared a list of sixty-two specific grants of power, a little more than half of which were to be exercised without consulting the Home Office. In one respect the authority of the Kenchiji was immensely increased : in 1874 the local police were made subject to his control.

To secure efficiency in the local government offices was one of the main problems of the day. Under the old régime every Han had a system of local government which served its purposes and officials with offices which were usually hereditary. Moreover, in the Han the relations between lord and vassal on the one hand, and the privileged class and the common people on the other, were feudal in character and unchanging. Under these circumstances local traditions and customs were so powerful that the governing officials, whatever their offices, had no serious difficulty, in co-operation with the people, in performing their duties. But after 1871 the old order changed, and it was supposed that a considerable period of time would be required to train the bureaucracy in the performance of their functions. Another factor which obstructed the transition from the old to the new system of local government was the nature of the men appointed to office. The office-seekers of that day were practically all ex-samurai, who by training and tradition were not suited to the transaction of the routine business of an office. Most of them were educated in the Chinese and Japanese classics and steeped in the teaching of the " patriotic schools." However, this was the only material which was available for the minor offices in the Government, for the common people were too little removed from their former serfdom to be eligible. The samurai in office was likely to be overbearing to his inferiors, impatient of routine, and visionary in his choice of projects. To correct these failings two measures [1] of a very different nature were adopted in 1876. The first was intended to discourage inefficiency, and con-

[1] *J. G. D.*, pp. 264–70.

The Reconstruction of Governments

sisted of a series of disciplinary punishments ; the second, to encourage efficiency by providing reward for faithful service.

Still another defect of the local government of the time arose from the dishonesty of the higher officials, especially the Governors. The opportunities for corruption were many, and a considerable proportion of the Kenchiji were incapable of resisting the temptation to enrich themselves while in office. One of the curious taxes of the time—for that matter still in existence—was a levy imposed upon licensed prostitutes. The funds raised in this manner were evidently regarded by the authorities as tainted, and were turned over under the head of miscellaneous taxes to constitute a secret fund in the possession of the Governor to be used in cases of emergency. As no strict accounting was ever made of the funds acquired in this way, the Governors usually pocketed a large part of them. As in large cities the revenues from this source were often very great—in some cases over half a million yen a year—the Governors of some of the Ken grew rich apace. Another fruitful device for corrupting the officials was plain bribery. A company which desired the privilege of building a light railway would enlist the services of the local Governor by an offer of money, or the Governor, having official knowledge of where the road was to be built, would buy up the land and sell it to the company at an increased price. Corruption of this kind was, however, easily enough dealt with when the central Government chose to suppress it, and after a few years it had practically disappeared.

With the death of Okubo in 1878, as the main part of the Government's policy of conciliating its opponents, regulations [1] for the establishment of assemblies in the Fu and Ken were issued, and before any of the assemblies were actually elected certain changes [2] in the powers of the Governors were made to enable them to deal with the local representa-

[1] *J. G. D.*, pp. 272-6.   [2] *Idem*, pp. 276-85.

tive bodies. The assemblies were strictly limited in
their powers and in the means of exercising them.
The Governor was the presiding officer, and he submitted such subjects as were to be debated, and was
empowered to veto all decisions which seemed contrary
to the welfare of the community. The assemblies
proved troublesome bodies, so much so that in 1881
a Board was created in the Daijokwan called the Board
of Adjudication,[1] the purpose of which was to settle
disputes between the local Governors and the
assemblies.

In 1880 the principle of taking into consideration
the wishes of the local people in matters of local
interest was extended, and assemblies were granted
to cities, towns, and villages. The development of
this system of local representation continued through a
period which lasted till 1888, when the local government
Code was issued, a huge body of rules and regulations,
a digest of which will be given in a succeeding
chapter.[2]

The interest which attaches to the building up of
the institutions for local government during this period
is centred in two diverse but closely related processes
which were going on synchronously, the organization
and training of the local bureaucracy and the creation
of the elected assemblies. In 1878 it would appear
that the central Government, upon the advice of the
Chihokwan-kwaigi, deliberately set up the provincial
(Fu and Ken) assemblies as an experiment in representative government in Japan. The local assembly
was the forerunner of the national assembly, not only
in time but in its constitution and powers also. This
method of procedure has often been referred to as a
proof of the wisdom of the Japanese statesmen of
the day, especially Ito, but the lesson furnished by
the Ken assemblies was far from encouraging. In
many of the local areas so little interest was taken in
the assembly that some years elapsed before the people

[1] *J. G. D.*, pp. 76–8.   [2] See Chapter VI, pp 145–7.

could be got to form one, while in other cases educated
men would not consent to sit after their election. Also,
the assemblies which were created in 1878 and the
years immediately following were extremely contentious
bodies, in almost constant conflict with the authorities.
If any lesson was to be learned from this experiment
in democracy, it certainly was not to the effect that the
nation was ready for representative institutions, at any
rate when coupled with a bureaucracy which was able
to thwart the people's wishes at every turn.

Yet it was in 1881 that the Parliamentary Rescript
was issued, promising the establishment of a national
assembly in 1889. The very fact that the clamour
in 1881 was for the immediate establishment of a
national Parliament, whereas the Government's promise
placed the date eight years later, is sufficient indication
of the opinion of the authorities upon the advisability
of representative government.

It would be a much truer reading of history to say
that the oligarchy in 1878, and again in 1881, yielded
to pressure which could no longer be safely resisted.
The Satsuma Rebellion had been an experience which
it was difficult to forget. Okubo's assassination in May
1878,—an even more forcible illustration of the
animosity in certain quarters against the Government,
—the growth to really formidable dimensions of
political societies, the failure of the Chihokwan-kwaigi
to satisfy the popular demand for representation, were
among the most important signs of the times, written
so large that even the oligarchs, however preoccupied
with their own affairs, could not fail to read them.
Their action was characteristic. Ken assemblies were
granted instead of a national assembly, on the plea
that it was wiser to make haste slowly. When the
popular excitement had abated, regulations governing
the assemblies were issued in such form as to make the
local representatives powerless as against the Governor
of the Ken, who submitted the subjects for debate,
vetoed the decisions if they seemed contrary to public

interest, or dissolved the assembly altogether if it became unmanageable. In 1881 the Parliamentary Rescript had to be issued to quell a disturbance in Tokyo, but the oligarchs provided for ample time in which to adjust themselves to the promised régime. How thoroughly they prepared for the establishment of representative institutions we shall see.

The companion process relates to the development of the local bureaucracy. In 1874 the Home Ministry became the centre of authority for local government ; from that time the efforts of the new department were directed to the creation of an official organization in the provinces, and the bestowal of such powers upon its members as would enable the Home Minister to dominate local administration, even to its minutest details. By a system of inspection, by frequent reports, by strict limitations upon the provincial Governor's discretion, by the power of appointment and dismissal of high local officials or removal of Governors from one province to another, the central Government provided that its will should prevail. As against the people, even as represented in an assembly, the local officials were given ample powers, and the Governor's control of the police of the Ken assured him of protection in any ordinary local disturbance.

If the two processes—the erection of a highly centralized local bureaucracy and the creation of local assemblies—be combined, as they must be in any attempt to understand the period between 1874 and 1885, we can see plainly the policy of the central Government. The main purpose of the ruling oligarchy was to extend and consolidate its control over local affairs, and its secondary object was to enfranchise the people in as small a degree as possible—sufficiently to satisfy the popular demand for representation while at the same time not endangering its own supremacy.

CHAPTER VI

THE GROWTH OF REPRESENTATIVE INSTITUTIONS

THERE are four clearly marked stages in the growth of representative institutions in Japan, which may be indicated in their chronological order by the names of the assemblies involved—first, the National Deliberative Assembly (Kogisho), created in 1869 ; second, the Assembly of Local Governors (Chihokwan-kwaigi), in 1875; third, the Local Assemblies (Fuken-kwai), in 1878 ; fourth, the National Assembly (Gi-kwai), in 1890.

The first of these assemblies, the Kogisho, calls for no further comment, for its origin and history have been fully described above. It was nothing more than a feudal Council, strictly analogous to that provided for in England by Magna Charta (Section 14). Its deliberations were productive of neither light nor encouragement to the Government of the day, which was contemplating many radical changes in the customs and traditions of the people.

The Chihokwan-kwaigi was likewise not an assembly of the elected representatives of the people, but an arbitrarily convened college of the Fu and Ken Governors, a council of the bureaucrats called together to advise with one another upon questions of local interest, and on one occasion, in 1878, to deliberate upon a matter of national concern, the establishment of the Fuken-kwai.

The political considerations which produced this assembly have already been adverted to ; in this chapter it is necessary only to give some of the more interesting details of the organization and powers of this body and to state the results of its earlier meetings. To this day a convocation of the Governors of the Fu and Ken is held annually in Tokyo, immediately after the close of the session of the Imperial Diet, but never since 1878 has it been asserted by the Government that the meeting has any popular significance. The true status of the assemblage, long openly acknowledged, is that of a meeting of the local bureaucrats to hear a report upon the administrative and legislative activities of the year, and to listen to a homily delivered by the Home Minister upon the duties and proper conduct of the Governors of the Fu and Ken.

In March 1874 an Imperial decree had been issued announcing the Emperor's intention of setting up the Chihokwan-kwaigi, and two months later the rules and regulations governing its constitution and conduct of business were promulgated.[1] The object of the assembly was explained in a preamble to its constitution, in the form of an Imperial address, in the following terms : " In accordance with the meaning of the Oath taken by Me at the commencement of My reign, and as a gradual development of its policy, I am convening an assembly of the representatives of the whole nation, so as by the help of public discussion to ordain laws, thus opening up the way to harmony between the governors and the governed and of the accomplishment of national desires. . . . I have therefore issued this constitution of a Deliberative Assembly providing for the convening of the chief officials of the different local jurisdictions and for their meeting and deliberating as the representatives of the people." Such was the official statement as to the nature and purpose of the assembly.

From the rules embodied in this document, called " The Constitution of the Assembly," the reader may discover the following facts : Governors of Fu and

[1] *J. G. D.*, pp. 505-12.

Growth of Representative Institutions

Ken or their deputies were to constitute the assembly ; the assembly was to be convened ordinarily once a year and its sessions were to be opened and closed by the Emperor in person ; the Ministers of state or their delegates might attend the sittings and speak, but not vote ; all Bills were to be laid before the assembly by its President, and when a decision had been arrived at it was to be reported to the Emperor, " who will himself decide whether or not it shall be put into execution " ; Bills sent down to the assembly by the Emperor might be withdrawn if the discussion proved " unsuitable " ; decisions arrived at upon Bills initiated by the assembly were to be subject to the Emperor's veto ; in all divisions the majority ruled, and in case of a tie the President cast the deciding vote ; the President for the time being was to be nominated by the Emperor.

The prominence of the Emperor's connection with this institution is interesting. His attendance at the formal opening and closing of the sessions was a natural and obvious device for magnifying the importance of the assembly, and no objection can be taken to such a proceeding. But that the Daijokwan, which in 1874 and for eleven years thereafter exercised the powers of a Regency, should have tried to make it appear that the Emperor was to exercise his personal prerogative of veto upon the decisions of the assembly was surely a huge piece of deception. In 1885, when the Daijokwan was abolished, it was intimated in various contemporary official documents that the Emperor had at last arrived at such a complete understanding of national affairs that it was possible for him to personally conduct the government. Yet in 1874 the personal rule of the Emperor was described as being already in existence. This sheltering of the oligarchy behind the person of the Emperor was probably resorted to on account of the dangers of the time, but whatever explanation be adopted, the action was quite consonant with the deception involved

in describing the Chihokwan-kwaigi as an assembly
of the representatives of the people.

In the accompanying " Rules of the Assembly " provision was made for the establishment of a committee
of the whole and various standing and select committees ; for the appointment of the necessary officials,
chairmen, secretaries, and treasurers ; for the division
of the members into *sections*, the membership of which
was to be determined by the President ; for the duration of the session and the etiquette to be observed
by the members during the sittings ; for the main
outlines of procedure in respect to Bills, debates,
divisions, quorum, and discipline. The only item in
this list which is peculiarly Japanese is that which
empowered the President to divide the assembly into
sections. The sections and the committees were entirely
different, and what gives the former their interest is
the fact that both Houses of the National Diet from
the time of their establishment have been divided into
sections by lot. The origin of this peculiar institution was probably the old feudal *Gonin-kumi*, or group
of five men, and it was probably resorted to in this
assembly in order to secure a greater degree of com-
pliance by distributing the more Radical members
among sections the majority of whose members were
staunchly Conservative.

A revised edition of the constitution and rules for
the conduct of business of the Chihokwan-kwaigi was
issued in March 1878,[1] and while a number of additions were made, mainly in the direction of simplifying
the rules of procedure, no new powers were accorded,
and no changes of any significance were made in the
original scheme.

The assembly was not convened in 1874, although
a meeting was called for September 10. In August
an announcement was made that " for reasons of ex-
pediency " the convocation was indefinitely postponed.
But the following year, on June 20, the first session

[1] *J. G. D.*, pp. 521–9.

of the Chihokwan-kwaigi was formally opened, amid
great rejoicings and demonstrations. An elaborate
ceremonial was carried out in the Monzeki Temple
in Asakusa, a ward of Tokyo, at which were present
all the high officials of the Government and the Court
and the diplomatic corps. The Emperor opened the
proceedings in person, and read the Speech from the
Throne, which ran, in part, as follows :—

" Our object in opening in person this the provincial parliament has been by its means to secure the
thorough discussion of all matters affecting the interior
economy of Our Empire, and of securing to the
provinces adequate representation. You have been
convoked for this purpose in order that your knowledge of the condition and feeling of the people of
your several districts may aid you in discussing their
requirements and introducing such reforms and changes
as may seem to you to be most urgently demanded."

The session in 1875 lasted twenty-seven days and
was terminated on July 17 by the following Imperial
message : " We are glad that your deliberations have
been conducted conscientiously. We shall in due
course, and after consulting with the Genro-in, consider
the recommendations which you have drawn up for Our
information and approval, and will take action thereon.

" Return, now, to your respective offices and discharge your duties to the State industriously."

The President of the assembly during this first
session was Kido Takayoshi, and there were about
seventy members, including not only the Governors of
the Fu and Ken, but a few members chosen from
among the people. The inclusion of this latter
element had not been provided for in the regulations as
originally issued, but a suggestion to that effect made
by certain of the local officials in a memorial [1] to the
Daijokwan in July 1874 was adopted, and the
Governors notified privately. Portions of twenty days
were occupied by the sittings, and the debates centred

around five subjects, the most important of which were roads and other local public works, local taxes, and local assemblies.

The most diverse estimations of the importance of this assembly were current at the time, but, generally speaking, the tone of the Press and the people was hostile. Even papers like the *Nichi Nichi*, a staunch pro-Government organ, admitted that the Chihokwan-kwaigi was in no sense a " popular assembly." The Opposition Press was outspoken in its denunciation. The *Akebono* said : " It is probable that it will leave behind it, except for its name and its forms, no vestige by which it may be remembered." That the news-paper Press should have been critical was to be expected, for the Government made the mistake of excluding reporters from the meetings. This decision to hold the debates *in camera* was only arrived at and announced as the time was at hand for the session to begin, and the reason offered, an obvious subter-fuge, was that there was no room in the Monzeki Temple for the newspaper men. As a substitute for daily reports of the proceedings the Government announced that it would compile an official account of the debates and publish it at the close of the session. This action was violently criticized, the *Nichi Nichi* even going to the length of explaining it as a device to " screen inexperience " and save the members of the assembly from incurring " the ridicule of the country " and the " dissatisfaction of the people," and other papers were even more outspoken in their anger at being excluded. The Government had probably been moved to keep out the Press representatives owing to the extraordinary interest which the assembly created, and hoped that by keeping the people in ignorance of its proceedings it might preserve in the public mind the mistaken impressions which had been created. The result was just the reverse and the assembly stood condemned in the public mind as soon as its first meeting took place.

Growth of Representative Institutions

Not only was the criticism of the assembly voiced by the Press, but an attack was made upon its constitution and procedure by some of the local officials themselves, in a series of memorials [1] addressed to the Daijodaijin. The first of these documents intimated that the memorialists were looking forward anxiously to the time when the assembly should meet, in the hope that as a result of its debates the powers of the Daijokwan and the Department of Home Affairs would be limited and the confusion in the minds of the local officials as to their proper functions removed.

The second memorial offered a number of amendments to the proposed constitution and rules as announced by the Government, and recommended several additional regulations which seemed desirable. The memorialists suggested by way of amendments that the assembly should be convened in March and April ; that in case any Bill accepted by the assembly was vetoed by the Emperor the members should be fully informed of the objections against it, and the Bill be referred a second time to the Emperor by a two-thirds majority of the members ; that all new laws should be submitted to the assembly and that decisions thereon arrived at after free discussion and debate should be carried into effect ; that in case a Bill submitted by the Emperor was withdrawn from discussion, the reason for so doing should be explained ; that the President should be elected by the members of the assembly from among their own number. Among the additional articles proposed were the following : " Draft-bills, when laid before the assembly for discussion, should contain a distinct recital of the clauses, rules, and arrangements by which their practical working is to be carried out," and not merely a general outline of the measure ; that the assembly should have the right to inspect the records and documents of the various departments of state, if such examination were essential for a clear understanding of the subject to be

---

[1] *J. G. D.*, pp. 513–19, for two of the series.

discussed ; that the public should be freely admitted to the debates except when Government secrets were being discussed ; that the members of the assembly should be released from all responsibility in respect to the duties of their proper offices, be free from arrest, except by consent of their peers, during the session, and be allowed to bring with them to the assembly such persons as they thought fit to be appointed as representatives from their jurisdictions.

The memorialists whose views are here summarized represented fourteen different Ken, scattered over the whole country, but apart from the admission of the public to the debates and of non-official people to membership in the assembly, none of their ideas was embodied in the revised regulations issued in 1878.

The next meeting of the Chihokwan-kwaigi was not convened until 1878, the Emperor's tour of the northern provinces in 1876 and the Satsuma Rebellion in the following year having precluded holding a session. As on the former occasion, the opening ceremony was attended by the Emperor amid a great display of pomp and splendour, but there was little popular enthusiasm. The debates were again held *in camera*, and as in 1875 the Press took revenge by ridiculing the assembly and abusing the Government. The session lasted from April 11th until May 3rd, and the main subject of discussion was the establishment of local assemblies. Ito presided at the sittings, for the Government was no more willing to allow the assembly to choose its own President in 1878 than it had been three years before.

The *Akebono* expressed the views of the populace of Tokyo and of the members of the political societies when it said : " Till the present moment the public has been nursing the idea that the Chihokwan-kwaigi was to be the stepping-stone to a great national assembly, but they now begin to see that a national assembly can only be obtained by a union of minds ; and the time for such an institution can only arrive when the many difficulties in the way have been swept aside by united popular feeling."

Other meetings of this assembly were held in subsequent years, but they attracted little public interest, mainly because it was generally recognized that no attempt to represent public opinion in the assembly had been made.

The year 1878 witnessed not only the complete discrediting of the Chihokwan-kwaigi as a representative assembly, but also the birth of the Fuken-kwai. From a nominally popular assembly which was actually a bureaucratic council, the Government turned to establish a *bona fide* elective assembly in each Fu and Ken. This change of policy marked a genuine departure from the complete bureaucratic despotism of the past. The significance of the change might be easily overestimated, however, for after nearly thirty years of participation in local government, at present the people's representatives still remain an advisory or consultative body, with no positive powers which can be exercised in the control of the bureaucracy. The Home Minister is still the apex of the system of local government, and to him the whole permanent official body is responsible ; executive authority is still the monopoly of the bureaucracy. In such a system the influence of the elective assembly has remained of minor importance.

The regulations [1] for the Fuken-kwai were issued in July 1878. The main business of the new assemblies was to " consult upon the budget of the expenditures which are to be defrayed out of the local taxes, and upon the means of raising the local taxes." Each assembly was to be called together for certain statutory meetings, and the Governor of the Fu or Ken was to initiate all Bills. Subject to the approval of the Governor, the assembly was to draft its own rules of procedure. The quorum at all meetings was to be 50 per cent. of the members. The Governor was to

[1] *J. G. D.*, pp. 272-6.

exercise his veto upon the decisions of the assembly in cases where such action seemed wise. If the debates, which were open to the public, seemed such as to disturb the peace, the meeting was to be suspended by the Governor, and if the members proved intractable the Home Minister was to dissolve the assembly, whereupon a new election was to be held. The members of the assembly were to be elected in groups of five from each Gun or Ku in the Ken, and were to hold office for terms of four years, one-half retiring every two years. The electorate was to consist of males of twenty-five years of age, who were domiciled in the Gun or Ku and paid land taxes of at least five yen in annual amount. Lunatics and idiots, bankrupts, and persons who had been sentenced at any time to imprisonment with hard labour for a year or for a longer term were ineligible. Qualifications for membership in the assembly were age, residence in the Ken for three years, and the payment of at least ten yen a year in land taxes. In addition to the disqualifications mentioned above in connection with the electorate, officials and primary school teachers were ineligible. Polling took place on a day set by the Governor at the Gun or Ku offices, and a vote in order to be counted had to contain in addition to the names of the candidates the name, age, and residence of the elector. A plurality of votes elected. If a successful candidate refused to sit, or was disqualified for any reason, the candidate with the next highest number of votes was declared elected. The chairman and vice-chairman of the assembly were to be elected by the members from their own number. Essentially similar principles were embodied in the regulations of 1880 [1] which set up elective assemblies in the Ku (city), Cho (town), and Son (village).

Experience in the working of these regulations, as the Fuken-kwai were established in the provinces, led to their frequent revision by the Government. In the

[1] *J. G. D.*, pp. 296–7.

Growth of Representative Institutions

revision [1] of 1880 there were no essential changes in principle, but a noticeable effort was made to prevent controversies from arising between the Governor and the assembly by introducing some modifications of the Governor's arbitrary powers, and many subsequent changes were made with the same end in view. Thus in 1881 it was provided that the Governor, if he objected to a resolution of the assembly, should send it back for reconsideration, and if the measure thereafter should still be unacceptable he was to forward it to the Home Minister for decision.

Other amendments of the regulations bear testimony to the continually strained relations between the assemblies and the bureaucracy: for example, in 1881 the following provisions were added: " In the event of the assembly refusing to deliberate upon Bills, the Governor, having obtained permission from the Home Minister, may put the measure in force without the decision of the assembly," or " in case more than half of the members of the assembly absent themselves from the meeting, and the deliberations cannot go on, the Governor shall report the matter to the Home Minister for instructions," or, further, " in case the assembly acts in such a way as to disturb the peace of the State, or passes resolutions which are contradictory of laws or regulations, the Governor may at any time dissolve it."

In the years 1880 and 1881 two institutional [2] changes occurred in the system of local government which are worth noting. The first was the creation of a Standing Committee in connection with the Fukenkwai. The purpose of this Committee, which was composed of from five to seven members elected by the assembly from among their own number, was to form an advisory council for the Governor, through which the representatives of the people might be admitted to a share in the executive power. Subsequently, in 1888, the Standing Committee developed into the Executive Council, but for a variety of reasons the

[1] *J. G. D.*, pp. 289–95 and 297–8.   [2] *Idem*, pp. 297–8 and 303–4.

143

Council fell into disrepute in the cities, and was abolished about five or six years ago. The second new institution was the result of the division of the Fuken-kwai into urban and rural sections, each of which was to deliberate upon those questions which directly concerned the interests of their constituents. The purpose of this change was to obviate the danger of conflicts within the assembly between city and country members. For example, the area known as Tokyo-Fu contains not only the city of Tokyo, but twenty-two contiguous towns and 156 villages, as well as hundreds of small islands scattered all over the Empire, and it is obvious that the question of extending the water supply to a suburb of Tokyo city is not a matter of any interest to those members who represent the 156 villages; more than that, they might naturally be disposed to object to the expenditure of taxes collected in their villages on works necessary to supply a Tokyo suburb with water. To prevent obstruction and dissension of this sort, the Fuken-kwai were divided into urban and rural groups, and the taxes likewise, specific amounts being allotted for disbursement in each area and collected therefrom.

Such was the system of local government, so far as the provincial assemblies were concerned, with which the Japanese entered upon the constitutional régime in 1889. No changes in principle have been made since 1881, though many minor amendments have been introduced. The larger local areas have continued under the domination of the local bureaucracy, at the head of which stand the Fu and Ken Chiji, and below them, in their respective ranks, the members of the official executive body. Side by side with the bureaucracy are arranged the representatives of the people in their assemblies, powerless to control their official colleagues, exercising their right of consenting to the proposals of the bureaucracy or of not consenting. Doubtless the elective assemblies have acted as a check upon the Governors, for, after all, the bureaucrats must live more or less in harmony with the people over whom they rule, but in a larger sense the assemblies have not succeeded in obtaining the reality of home rule for the provinces, for it is still with the Home Minister and the central Government that the final decision of all important local matters rests.

In 1880 elective assemblies were established by the central Government in cities, towns, and villages upon the basis of the regulations issued two years earlier for the Fu and Ken. From that beginning the system grew, and in 1888 two large bodies of laws,[1] jointly known as the Municipal Code, were promulgated. These two laws, containing some 130 articles each, form the basis of the government of cities, towns, and villages at the present time. The personnel of the government of the various urban areas is substantially similar in all—an executive official, known in the cities as *Shi-cho* or Mayor, in the towns as *Cho-cho* or Headman, in the villages as *Son-cho* or Headman ; the deputy mayors and headmen ; a council (originally in the cities only and recently abolished) ; and an assembly. All these officials are elective, but according to very different methods : the members of the assembly directly by the citizens of the respective areas ; the council indirectly by the members of the assembly from among their own members ; the headmen of towns and villages by the members of the assembly from among the resident citizens of thirty years of age or over, the choice to be ratified by the Governor of the Ken ; the mayors of the cities indirectly by the members of the assembly from among the citizens of the Empire. The election of the mayor is doubly indirect, for the city assembly nominates three candidates and the Emperor, acting upon the advice of the Home Minister, appoints one of the three or declines to appoint any of them and calls for a further selection of candidates. The electorate consists of the citizens of the respective areas, and the qualifications for citizenship are, in the

[1] *J. G. D.*, pp. 331–404.

main, residence and possession of landed property. Elegibility for membership in the assembly, whether of a city, town, or village, is obtained by qualifying as to age, residence, and the payment of national taxes. Elections are conducted in the cities on the Prussian three-class system, in towns and villages on a two-class system. The basis of classification in all cases is tax-paying ability. Members of the city assemblies sit for terms of six years, one-half retiring every three years, and members of the council for four years, one-half retiring every two years. Deputy mayors are elected for terms of six years, but the mayor of a city enjoys an indefinite term of office. The headmen of towns and villages hold office for four years.

The competency of the various assemblies is defined in general terms : " The assembly of a city shall represent the city and decide on all subjects relating to city affairs, in conformity with the provisions of the law, and also on those matters which have already been entrusted to its management, or which may hereafter be so entrusted by law or Imperial ordinances." In addition to these general terms, the law proceeds [1] to enumerate specifically those subjects with which the assembly may deal, chiefly matters concerning the city budget, taxes, loans, and property. Of the same general import is the competency of the town and village assemblies.[2]

The city council, composed of the mayor and his deputies and elected members, constitutes the local administrative authority. Its competence is defined in specific terms,[3] whereas that of the mayor is covered by the general provision [4] : " The *Shi-cho* shall direct and superintend all the administrative affairs of the city," including police affairs. In the towns and villages the headmen and their deputies conduct the administration.

---

[1] *J. G. D.*, p. 341, Organization of the Government of Cities, Article XXX.
[2] *Idem*, pp. 377-8, Organization of the Government of Towns and Villages Articles XXXII-XXXV.
[3] *Idem*, pp. 349-50.　　　　　　[4] *Idem*, p. 350.

Growth of Representative Institutions

Above and as the controlling power over the machinery for local government in the urban areas are placed the Governors of the Ken, and in the last resort the Home Minister. In certain matters specified—the issuing of bylaws, raising of loans, imposition of special city taxes, etc.—the Home Minister's consent is necessary, and in other matters—the alienation of city property and the imposition of special burdens on any class of the people, whether in the form of taxes or services—that of the Governor of the Ken must be obtained before the assembly's decisions can be enforced. Generally speaking, the Governor of the Ken exercises supervision over the administration of the affairs of every urban area within his jurisdiction. The mayors of cities and the headmen of towns and villages are the representatives in the local areas of the Home Minister or the Governor of the Ken. The power to dissolve an assembly is reserved to the Home Minister.

The development of the representative institutions, as exemplified in the Fuken-kwai and Shi-cho-son-kwai, was significant in the highest degree as illustrating the lines upon which Japanese polity was being gradually reconstructed. There was not the slightest indication of a tendency toward popular government, if by that term is meant responsible government. The assemblies were fitted into a purely bureaucratic system, and to only a slight degree had they power to disturb the equanimity of an absolutist officialdom. How thoroughly the purposes of the oligarchy had crystallized may be best seen in the constitution and powers of the national assembly (Gi-kwai) which was set up by the organic laws of 1889.

The Constitution [1] promulgated in 1889 devoted twenty-two [2] of its seventy-six articles to the Imperial Diet. Provision was made for an annual session, lasting three months, and for extraordinary sessions when occasion required ; for the composition of the two Houses, the Peers and the Representatives, accord-

[1] *J. G. D.*, pp. 136–44.   [2] Articles XXXIII–LIV inclusive.

147

A Political History of Japan

ing to the provisions of law ; for the usual privileges
to be accorded to members, freedom of speech within
the Houses and freedom from arrest during the session,
" except in cases of flagrant delicts " ; for the attendance of Ministers of state or Government delegates
at the sittings of either House and their right to
address the members ; for holding the sessions in
public, provided that if necessary they might be conducted *in camera* ; for the quorum, which was determined at one-third of the members ; and for the
decision of all matters by majority vote, the President
deciding in case of a tie. Likewise, the Constitution
provided that every law must receive the consent of
the Diet, except that, in cases of emergency and when
the Diet was not in session, Imperial Ordinances should
have the force of law, and also, in case the Budget
was not voted upon, that the Government should put
into force the Budget of the preceding year ; that the
Diet should vote on projects of law submitted by the
Government or initiate projects of law ; that the Diet
might make representations to the Government as to
laws or upon any other matters, and that petitions from
the people might be received and considered by
the Diet.

For the present it is unnecessary to consider the
details of the organization or of the rules of procedure of the Imperial Diet, as embodied in the three
laws, " The Imperial Ordinance [1] concerning the House
of Peers," [2] " The Law of the Houses," [3] and the
" Law of Election," which were promulgated along
with the Constitution in 1889. Making allowances for
differences in circumstances, the constitutional powers
of the Diet are similar to those granted to the various
assemblies which we have already considered. As in
the case of the Fuken-kwai, the Gi-kwai was fitted
into the bureaucratic structure of the central Government and subordinated so strictly to the oligarchy that
its functions were mainly to consent to laws introduced

[1] *J. G. D.*, pp. 153–6.　　[2] *Idem*, pp. 156–70.　　[3] *Idem*, pp. 170–211.

by the Cabinet. Of necessity the setting up of a popular body in the midst of an absolutist system entailed changes the importance of which has become apparent during the parliamentary régime, but in so far as it was possible, the oligarchy anticipated those changes and provided against them. In no other way can the constitutional provision (Article LXXI) for the reapplication of a budget be explained than by the bureaucracy's fear that the representatives of the people might attempt to bring the Government to terms by refusing supply.

But the significance of the changes made in 1889 can only be estimated when the laws issued in that year are read in connection with an ordinance[1] of 1886 dealing with the organization of the departments of state. That ordinance marked the culmination of the long process of consolidating the administrative organ of the central Government. It provided for the standardizing of the various departments of state, both with respect to their official organization and their competency, and for centralizing the whole nominally in the Emperor, but actually in the Cabinet. The Constitution, by providing that Cabinet Ministers should be responsible to the Emperor (Article LV), made the bureaucracy independent of the Diet, except for the single provision that all measures introduced by the Government must receive the consent of the Diet before they could become law. The possibilities of deadlock between the representative and the bureaucratic elements, inherent in the system thus adopted, furnished what little interest there has been in the history of the Japanese Parliament, and likewise accounts for the political stagnation of the past two decades.

An interesting parallel might be drawn between the government of England during the Stuart period and that of Japan after 1890. In English history the representative device was employed early, and if sub-

[1] *J. G. D.*, pp. 109-24.

sequent facts are to be taken into account, perhaps far too early. The Model Parliament was convened in 1295, and contained representatives of the four estates of the kingdom. Parliament as thus constituted settled down during the next century and a half into practically the form in which it exists to-day, and exercised in the middle of the fifteenth century all the legislative powers it possessed in the nineteenth. But toward the close of the fifteenth century, with the accession to the throne of the Tudors, there began a period of executive despotism which did not end until the Stuart dynasty had been driven from the throne. There thus occurred a century and a half of democracy, followed by two centuries of virtual despotism, during which latter period Parliament maintained a precarious existence. The explanation of this reversal of the usual order of development is to be found mainly in the sudden creation of representative institutions upon the ruins of feudalism at the end of the thirteenth century, long before the royal power had attained anything like its full development or the popular interest in or understanding of affairs of state had reached sufficient proportions to warrant a democratic government. In 1485, on the accession of Henry VII, Parliament's control over legislation was complete, while at the very same time its control of the executive had reached the vanishing-point. The Tudor bureaucracy was vastly more efficient as an administrative instrument than anything previously known in England, and it was welcomed by the people ; the power of the throne was much greater than it had ever been, and, moreover, it was rapidly increasing, whereas the Tudor Parliaments were so subservient to the King that the people's representatives formally legalized Henry VIII's claim to devise the Crown by will to his heirs, and submitted tamely throughout Elizabeth's long reign to every kind of indignity. It was not until the seventeenth century, during the Stuart period, that a reaction set in, as a direct result of the rise of the Puritan party in Parliament. So deeply rooted was his belief in the Tudor absolutism and the Stuart theory of monarchy that the second Stuart King preferred execution to any mitigation of his executive supremacy. The tragedy of the Stuart period was the result of the creation of representative institutions before the royal power had reached its zenith, an order of development which produced a mortal struggle between a people with democratic traditions and a monarch with despotic pretensions. The principal generalization to be drawn from the constitutional history of England before the eighteenth century—the fundamental error of perfecting the control of a representative parliament over legislation without a synchronous growth of its power over the executive—finds a counterpart in Japan. For there, too, as we have seen, a representative assembly was set up, and at the same time the executive authority retained in the hands of a bureaucracy responsible to a monarch ruling by divine right. A national assembly which can legislate but cannot control the executive is, if taken seriously, the most dangerous political institution which can be created in any country.

The degree of harmony between the bureaucracy and the representatives of the people which prevailed throughout Meiji may be explained easily enough. The people had few traditions of democracy, the theory of divine right was firmly believed, the reign of the Meiji Tenno was one of brilliant achievement, the bureaucracy was efficient, and the representatives venal or complaisant. In some respects the period may be contrasted with the era of Elizabeth, in others with that of James I. It is true that political progress was retarded, and came to a standstill after 1896, but so long as the oligarchs remained united—and that the Meiji Tenno was able to secure—the people were unwilling to insist upon their claims as against the Government.

But that the system of government established in

A Political History of Japan

1889 has in it the elements of danger which characterized the Stuart system there cannot be the slightest
doubt, nor can it be denied that Japan is preparing
for political and constitutional changes as great as
those which England witnessed in the eighteenth
century. That the advent of responsible government
will be marked by revolutionary excesses is not
probable, for the monarchy has no firm convictions on
the subject of divine right, and the oligarchy, which
has mainly profited by the sedulous cultivation of that
myth, has already been internally disrupted into
opposing Choshu and Satsuma factions, and for the
time being the government is in the hands of
outsiders.[1]

[1] Okuma, Kato, and Ozaki are all outsiders from the point of view of the
clan oligarchs.

CHAPTER VII

POLITICAL ISSUES AND MORALITY

In 1873 the Restoration Government definitively committed itself to a policy of domestic reform and reconstruction, and turned its back upon the chauvinistic pre-Meiji programme of military expansion in Asia. It happened, however, that the influential class of samurai was opposed to the Government's decision, since the development of agriculture, commerce, manufactures, and transportation was an essentially non-military undertaking ; the adoption of such a policy was not only a repudiation of the teachings of the " patriotic schools " of 1840-67, but a blow to the pretensions of the old feudal aristocracy. Until 1877 the dispute between the Government and the samurai was of such seriousness that it occupied public attention to the exclusion of nearly every other issue.

One most important exception, however, was the question of popular rights. As we have seen, a number of ex-Councillors of State, the best known of whom were Itagaki, Soyejima, and Goto, memorialized the Daijokwan in 1874, praying for the immediate establishment of an elective assembly. They based their claim for representative institutions not only upon the first article of the Imperial oath, but upon the natural rights of the people to a share in the government. This issue between absolutism, whether of a monarchy or an oligarchy, and democracy was the storm centre of Japanese politics after 1877 until 1889. A minor exception is also to be found in the affairs of the Hokkaido Colonization Board (Kaitakushi). The popular interest in the development of the northern island never was keen until 1880, but during that year and the first half of 1881 public attention was focused upon the project with an intensity new in Japan, and interesting not only for its direct results but as an illustration of the power which a Tokyo mob may exercise over the Administration.

Apart from these purely domestic questions, the revision of the treaties with the Western Powers entered most largely into political discussions. The interest in this project, which had been aroused first in 1871, grew in strength as time went on, and reached its climax in 1887-9. The Government, under the pressure of popular criticism, made numerous attempts at revision, each one of which ended in failure, chiefly owing to the people's unwillingness to accept the terms demanded by the Treaty Powers.

As described above, the Government fought out the issue with the samurai in 1877, and emerged completely victorious at the conclusion of the hostilities in Satsuma. It had destroyed the last vestiges of the feudal régime, which had persisted for more than a thousand years, and from that time until the end of the reconstruction period militarism was crushed. Modern Japanese militarism, which made its appearance in 1894, had a different origin and to a certain extent a different object from that of the feudal aristocratic warrior caste of the early days of Meiji.

The issue between the central Government and Satsuma having been decided, the Government turned to face its more peaceful but even more dangerous opponents, the agitators for representative government. As we have seen, various concessions had already been made to the Opposition in 1874 and 1875. The reorganization of the institutions of state undertaken as the outcome of the Osaka Conference was the result of an effort to reunite the oligarchy's divided ranks and to arrest the progress of the agitation for a national assembly by placating its leaders. Similarly, the creation of the Chihokwan-kwaigi was an attempt to satisfy the rank and file of the agitators by giving them not what they demanded, but a substitute which was represented as capable of serving their purpose.

By 1876 the futility of the concessions of 1875 was generally admitted. The Genro-in was so organized as to rob it of any real power over the decisions of the oligarchy, and the Chihokwan-kwaigi, composed of the leading members of the local bureaucracy, could not have acted as an assembly of representatives of the people, even if it had not been emasculated by the regulations governing its conduct of business.

Thus far the oligarchy had been successful in preserving its absolute powers intact, but at the same time it had embittered the Opposition and driven it to devices far more formidable than the dispatch of memorials to the Government or newspaper controversies upon the rights of the people. It is true that during the Satsuma Rebellion the agitation for a popular assembly had subsided : even though its champions objected to the tyranny of the central Government over the people, the design of Satsuma to throw the whole country back into feudalism was still more abhorrent. As the cause of popular government would have been completely extinguished by the triumph of the Western rebels, for the brief period of hostilities the Government had the support of its quondam opponents. Loyalty on that occasion was a tribute to the real patriotism of Itagaki and his followers.

But with the suppression of the rebellion the agitation was straightway revived. A memorial, not from Itagaki in person, but from the members of a political society (Risshisha), which he had established in his native province of Tosa, was sent to the Emperor. This long document [1] reiterated the demands of the people for an assembly, and attacked the Government as an oligarchy which had thwarted the Emperor's express designs and driven the people to the verge

[1] *J. G. D.*, pp. 457-80.

of revolt by its despotic measures. Not so much because of its contents but because of its origin does this memorial mark a new stage in the campaign for popular government. The political society fathered by Itagaki in Tosa was duplicated by others in different parts of the country, the parent societies establishing branches here and there, thus welding into one body the scattered elements of the opposition to the Government. They set up newspapers as their organs, or enlisted the services of already existing papers for the spread of their propaganda. It was this organized pressure that caused the Government in 1878 to grant representative assemblies to the Fu and Ken, and in 1880 to the cities, towns, and villages.

At the same time that these concessions were made the Government took steps to protect itself against the attacks of its opponents. The Press Law [1] of 1875 was strictly enforced and political meetings [2] were forbidden, except with the consent of the police and under their supervision. Various classes of the people, officers of the army and navy, officials of the Government, and teachers and students, were forbidden to attend or speak at political meetings. A provision which forbade a political society to have affiliations of any sort with a similar society, either in the same place or in another part of the country, practically destroyed the organizations which had been built up in opposition to the Government.

This policy of suppression, ruthlessly carried out, had the effect of driving the agitators into secret societies, or in some parts of the country, especially in the north, into open defiance of the regulations.

In 1881 the interest in the general agitation, which had become all the more dangerous because it was hidden, was eclipsed for a short time by the action of Okuma, the present Prime Minister, at that time the Minister of Finance. Okuma had held office in the Finance Department continuously since 1872,

[1] *J. G. D.*, pp. 539-43. [2] *Idem*, pp. 495-9.

Political Issues and Morality

and after the death of Okubo had become one of the foremost members of the Government. He had grown rich, it is currently believed, as a result of his measures in financing the campaign for the suppression of the Satsuma Rebellion, and being of a restless, daring disposition and a demagogue as well, he undertook an enterprise in 1881 which he hoped would carry him to the position of Prime Minister. It was in this connection that the affairs of the Kaitakushi were brought prominently before the public. The Hokkaido Colonization Commission, established in 1872, had received a yearly grant of 1,000,000 yen for a period of ten years. Kuroda Kiyotaka, a member of one of the historic families of Satsuma, was appointed chief of the Commission at the time of its creation. Its business was to develop the resources of the northern island by encouraging immigration and providing the necessary public works, " roads, bridges, harbours," etc., for the new community. As early as 1874 the projects undertaken in the Hokkaido had been subjected to trenchant criticism. In a summary of the events of 1873 the editor of the *Japan Weekly Mail* [1] expressed himself on the subject of the Kaitakushi in the following terms : " We shall hardly be wrong in saying that there has been an enormous, if not an iniquitous, waste of money in this department. Roads leading nowhere ; piers with no possible water approach to them ; a new capital created by no trade and with no trade to support it : these are some of the more expensive features of the new department. We have little doubt that the department would be found a

[1] January 24, 1874, p. 60. The *Japan Weekly Mail* was edited in 1874 by G. W. Howell, a journalist of remarkable powers, and after 1880 by the late Captain Frank Brinkley, R.A., Yokohama correspondent of the London *Times*, contributor of the article "Japan" to the *Encyclopedia Britannica*, 11th edition, and author of a monumental work on China and Japan. The files of the *Japan Weekly Mail* are an almost indispensable source book for the history of the Meiji Era. After 1900 their value rapidly diminished, however, for the editor about that time was offered and accepted a subsidy from the Japanese Government, and thereafter became a thick and thin supporter of the Administration and its measures.

perfect sieve for the manner in which money has flowed through it, and that a vast percentage of that money has found its way into the pockets of those who were appointed to see it properly spent."

Whether all the accusations brought against the Commission were true or false is neither here nor there, for the Government continued to support it. As the term of the subsidy drew to its conclusion, in 1881, Kuroda, the chief of the Kaitakushi, presented to the Daijokwan a scheme for winding up the affairs of the Kaitakushi, which was considered and accepted, though it was destined never to be carried out, for it was at this point that Okuma saw fit to attempt his *coup*. The nature of Kuroda's scheme was so flagrantly dishonest that when once its terms were divulged the Government itself felt obliged to reconsider its decision and withdraw its consent.

According to the terms of the proposed arrangement the existing members of the Commission, having formed a private company, were to purchase all the establishments in the nature of productive enterprises which the Government owned in the Hokkaido : in effect, it provided for the reversion to private ownership of what had hitherto been public. Thus far the measure was undoubtedly a wise one, neither was there any serious objection to the former members of the Commission organizing a company to take over the property in question ; it was the price to be paid for that property which furnished the main element of scandal. The Government had contributed 10,000,000 yen of public money, and Kuroda proposed to sell out for a fraction of a million. The only conclusion to be arrived at in the circumstances was either that the money had been squandered by the members of the Commission or that they were now attempting to get possession of a valuable property on terms so ludicrously inadequate as to amount to theft.

Okuma, as Finance Minister, was the natural channel through which such a scandal should have been brought to the notice of the public. He called a meeting of the citizens of Tokyo and divulged the nature of the plot, not only raising thereby a storm of protest against the Government, but making himself the idol of the people. While carried along on the crest of this wave of popularity he addressed a memorial to the Emperor praying for the establishment in *1883* of a National Parliament.

The Government's action was instantaneous. The memorial was received on the eve of the Emperor's departure upon a tour of the north, and before twenty-four hours had elapsed the Parliamentary Rescript [1] was issued. " We therefore hereby declare," it read, in part, " that We shall, in the 23rd year of Meiji (1890), establish a Parliament, in order to carry into full effect the determination We have announced, and We charge our faithful subjects bearing Our commissions to make, . . . in the meantime, all necessary preparation to that end.

" We perceive that the tendency of Our people is to advance too rapidly, and without that thought and consideration which alone can make progress enduring, and We warn Our subjects, high and low, to be mindful of Our will, and that those who may advocate sudden and violent changes, thus disturbing the peace of Our realm, will fall under Our displeasure."

This was Okuma's answer, as well as that to all the other agitators for the immediate establishment of an elective National Assembly. The Minister of Finance resigned his office, and for the time being the issue was dropped. The Emperor had voiced the Government's decision, and had even threatened the Radicals with his displeasure. The results of this abortive *coup d'état*, if disastrous to the pretensions of Okuma, were satisfactory in many respects. In the matter of the already accepted Kuroda scheme for the disposal of the property of the Kaitakushi, the Government reversed its decision. A notification

[1] *J. G. D.*, pp. 86-7.

of the Privy Council, addressed to the chief of the Colonial Commission, was issued in the following terms : " You are hereby notified that the permission lately accorded, in reply to your application, for the sale of the industrial undertakings connected with your department, is, upon further examination, withdrawn." The definitive choice of a date for the opening of the Parliament was also a matter for congratulation, for thereby was granted in principle the main contention of the agitators.

In this series of events some characteristic features of Japanese political morality stand out clearly. Kuroda and his subordinates in the Kaitakushi were not the only grafters of their day, for there was little, if any, public sentiment against dishonesty in public life, venality in the rulers being taken as a matter of course, as it was and is in China. Salaries were inadequate, ostensibly to reduce the great disparity in the social status of rulers and the ruled, but really to justify peculation of public money. It seems incredible, yet such was the Chinese argument in defence of this system of universal official corruption. Likewise, the general public in Japan regarded a public man as abnormal if, during his term of office, he did not acquire for himself an ample competence. Nor was malfeasance of public funds a sufficient offence to drive a public man from office under ordinary circumstances. With remarkably few exceptions, Kido, Ito, Okubo, Itagaki, and Goto Shojiro conspicuous among them, the promoters of the Restoration have died millionaires or are still living as rich men. The late Prince Katsura was reported to have amassed a fortune of 15,000,000 yen, though he had served the Government as a soldier for most of his life, with no independent income. One of the recent Prime Ministers, Yamamoto Gombei, refused to permit an inspection of the value of his property even after he had been accused in the Diet of diverting large sums of public money into his own pocket. In the case of Kuroda, in 1881, his offence

was noised abroad not so much for its own sake as
to serve the purposes of Finance Minister Okuma in
discrediting the Government which he was planning
to overthrow. That Kuroda's dishonesty was not taken
seriously was made manifest by the manner in which
his colleagues disposed of him. Instead of being dismissed, he was removed to an even more influential
office, that of Cabinet Councillor.

One of the results of Okuma's plot against the
Government—for it is a question whether Okuma was
moved to action by any genuine reprobation of
Kuroda's dishonesty—was the rising of a great Tokyo
mob, which threatened violence against the members
of the oligarchy, the terrorized Government repudiating
its decision as to the disposal of its property in the
Hokkaido and promising what it had persistently refused to grant while the populace was peaceable, the
convoking of a National Assembly. Threats of violence
have been since that day the most potent solvent of
disputes between the Administration and the people.
Cabinets have fallen in answer to the mob's demands,
and even foreign policy has been shaped by the same
means. A despotic Government can, perhaps, only
be brought to terms by violence ; at any rate, the
events of 1881 constitute an early example of the
kind of pressure which was to be frequently exerted
in subsequent years.

In meeting the onslaught of its opponents in 1881
the oligarchy set the Emperor between itself and the
people, nor was this the first occasion upon which it
had taken shelter behind the throne. In the light
of documents issued in 1885, when the Daijokwan
was replaced by the Naikaku, it cannot be asserted
that even a nominal personal government by the
Emperor was in existence in 1881. The Daijokwan
was still the " supreme authority," and it is natural
to suppose that it would have borne the consequence
of its policy. It was impossible, however, for the
whole body of oligarchs to resign when public opinion

turned against them, since such an action would be contrary to the very existence of an oligarchic régime. In such a dilemma the practice of reversing the shield and turning the Emperor toward the people, which involved no serious consequences as far as the throne was concerned, was invariably resorted to. This baffling game of Emperor and oligarchs, strange as it may seem, because it was perfectly well understood by all parties concerned was played successfully throughout the whole era. The adroitness with which the Government discomfited Okuma and his mob of excited Tokyoites by publishing an Imperial rescript, partly acceding to and partly refusing their demands, commands our admiration as an example of political prestidigitation. But the continued repetition of such a feat, however clever, will ultimately make any nation impatient, and therein lies the danger for the Japanese Imperial house.

The Kaitakushi affair had the result of immensely stimulating the already highly interesting agitation against the oligarchy and the absolutist ideas of government. The mob, having discovered its power, was the more inclined to exercise it, while the Government, realizing that punitive measures were necessary, began to bring to bear all the pressure it could against every kind of political propaganda, beginning with a wholesale muzzling of the Press by the suspension of newspapers and imprisonment of editors and owners. The tension visibly increased during 1883, and in 1884 a crisis was reached. Riots broke out in the provinces ; in Fukushima, Saitama, and Ibaraki they were especially violent, though in nearly every other Ken there were disturbances of a more or less serious nature. The causes of this crisis were partly political, partly economic. Beginning with 1880 a period of industrial depression had set in, a reaction which followed undue stimulation of business and the rise of prices caused by the inflation of the currency in 1877. Paper was inconvertible, and as the inevitable result

Political Issues and Morality

of its over-issue depreciation of its value occurred, the notes falling to a discount of more than 50 per cent. Naturally for this monetary disturbance the Government was blamed. The political societies which had arisen in 1877 and 1878 gave place in 1881 and 1882 to so-called political parties,[1] the Liberal party (*Jiyuto*), which was established by Itagaki and Goto in 1881, the Liberal Conservatives (*Kaishinto*), by Okuma, Ono, Mudaguchi, Aoki, etc., in 1882, and the Conservatives (*Teiseito*), by Fukuchi, in the same year. The Jiyuto and Kaishinto were more or less directly connected with the exhibitions of violence in the provinces, though it is not likely that the leaders of either countenanced the measures adopted. To clear itself of the stigma of inciting to rebellion, the Jiyuto, at a general meeting held on October 29, 1884, in Osaka, resolved to disband " and wait for an opportunity when society will be prepared for its reconstitution." The Kaishinto refused to disband, and some of its leaders—Okuma, Kano, and Mayeshima—severed their connection with the party on December 21, 1884. The Teiseito, never a popular party, had already dissolved for lack of support in 1883.

In Ibaraki and Saitama the rioters were composed of the debtor class, mainly the ex-samurai and their descendants, their object being to destroy the evidences of their indebtedness. On September 31, 1884, at the village of Fubu, in Saitama, a mob of over two thousand persons destroyed property and killed policemen, burning all the papers recording their debts to the usurers. Connection between the political parties and the rioters being assumed, the *Nichi Nichi* and other Government papers asserted that there was an organized attempt by the Liberal party to overthrow the Government. The dissolution of the party before the close of the year might, perhaps, be cited as substantiation of the charge.

[1] For the manifestoes of the various parties see Lay, A. H., *History of the Rise of Political Parties in Japan. Trans. A.S.J.*, vol. xxx., Part III, Yokohama, 1902.

A Political History of Japan

During the years between 1881 and 1884, especially in the latter year, the newspaper Press suffered great, though probably merited, punishment at the Government's hands. To a considerable extent the basis of this persecution was to be found in prohibitions imposed by the Press Law and Criminal Code upon publication, without permission, of reports of preliminary trials and the texts of state documents. For offences of this kind a number of papers, among them even the most respected in Tokyo, the *Jiji Shimpo*, were punished. Other offences in the eyes of the Government were attacks upon the officials and the policy of the Administration. During the riots of 1884 the local Governors and police, especially in Fukushima, Saitama, and Ibaraki, were soundly abused, the former for incompetency, the latter for cruelty in connection with the prosecution of the ringleaders among the rioters. The official statistics enumerate a list of forty-nine suspensions of newspapers in 1883, and in 1884 the majority of the Opposition papers employed upon their staffs " jail-editors," whose sole function was to serve terms in prison.

The disorders occurring in 1884 gradually subsided under the Government's firm hand, and with 1885 a new trend became visible in politics. The oligarchy, by the abolition of the Daijokwan and the establishment of the Naikaku, made it somewhat more dangerous for political agitators to carry on their work. Though the Naikaku was made up, with the exception of Sanjo Saneyoshi, of the men who had been associated with the Daijokwan, and the little ring of oligarchs remained unbroken, yet the Government outwardly had ceased to be oligarchical, and had become a personal despotism of the Emperor. Reverence for the latter was so profound among the people that only the most radical were willing to adopt an attitude of hostility to the Administration, for it was now almost impossible to dissociate the Government from the monarch, and any opposition became treasonable. Partly for this reason,

Political Issues and Morality

the agitation carried on during the past four years by the political parties subsided, and interest shifted from domestic to foreign policy, centring upon the revision of the treaties.

As we have seen, treaty revision had agitated the people at intervals ever since 1871, but it was not until 1887 that the subject became all-absorbing. In that year Inouye, who occupied the Foreign Office, took up the question, and secured the Government's consent to a programme of treaty revision which he had determined to put into execution. Preparations for the event were made on an elaborate scale and by devices which, to say the least, were as amusing as they were abortive. A great hall was built in Tokyo, and the Government began to encourage social relations between the people and the resident foreigners. Balls and musical performances, participated in by both natives and foreigners, followed upon each other in a round of gaiety such as Tokyo society had never before witnessed. Dancing academies sprang up overnight, and little circles of men and women worked diligently to master foreign languages, etiquette, and amusements. The winter months of 1886-7 were for Tokyo a season never to be forgotten. Among the lower orders the wearing of foreign articles of dress was advocated, and in every direction it was evident that " foreign ways " were to be adopted with all possible speed. The meaning of this official encouragement of the imitation of foreign manners was not evident to the people, either high or low, until well on in the year, when it was noised about that negotiations to abolish extra-territoriality had been going on with the representatives of the Western Powers and had reached the point where it only remained to append the signatures of the contracting parties. The main purpose of these negotiations was to restore to Japan its judicial autonomy, which had been granted away by the extra-territorial provisions of the original treaties. In order to abolish the jurisdiction of the

A Political History of Japan

Consular Courts, Inouye was willing to permit the establishment of mixed tribunals, collegiate courts, composed of both Japanese and foreigners, for the trial of cases involving the nationals of Western countries. When this fact became known the whole attitude of the public changed. The adoption of foreign customs and the erection of mixed tribunals were denounced with a vehemence which even the Government could not refuse to notice, and the Naikuku was compelled, not unwillingly, to repudiate the negotiations and accept Inouye's resignation.

This incident was a startling illustration of the temper of the people, all classes desiring the revision of the treaties, which in their existing form were felt to be derogatory to the national pride, both as an infringement of the sovereign rights of the Empire and as a slur upon Japan's civilization. As we have seen, the treaties did limit the fiscal independence of the Government in the matter of imposing a tariff of Customs duties upon imports ; and, what was even a more serious cause of offence, by stipulating that the Consular Courts should have jurisdiction in all civil and criminal cases in which foreigners were concerned, they offered silent but eloquent testimony to the contempt with which Westerners regarded the administration of justice by the Japanese courts. Nevertheless, while the Japanese were extremely impatient at the Government's delay in effecting the revision of the treaties, they were highly sensitive on certain points, and were unwilling to accomplish their purpose by a sacrifice of their national pride, for the mixed tribunals with prosecuting attorneys of foreign birth, as well as the wholesale adoption of Western manners, were a virtual confession of inferiority. Especially among the upper classes was there a genuine dislike of foreigners, who were often offensive to the more punctilious Japanese both in manners and appearance, and this aversion was no doubt heightened by the feeling, naturally unconfessed, that the foreigners

Political Issues and Morality

were superior in many respects, especially in their mechanical and scientific achievements in the fields of war and peace. The resident foreigners, confident of their own superiority, probably did little to decrease the innate dislike of the upper and more conservative classes in Japan. The activity of the foreign missionary, too, was an implied slur upon the native religions, Buddhism and Shinto, the necessity of employing foreigners as teachers and advisers was a humiliating confession of backwardness, and the monopolizing by the foreign merchant of the import and export trade seemed a usurpation of the business opportunities which should be enjoyed by Japanese. Misunderstandings were as frequent as they were lamentable. Even among the rank and file of the nation conservatism was intense and the dislike of foreigners universal. The radical elements, which proved so troublesome to the Government, were by no means admirers of the Western nations. The national traditions cultivated from time out of mind had been of such a nature as to cause the Japanese to think of themselves as a peculiar people, especially favoured by the gods, and of their civilization as a culture compared with which that of every other people was new and barbarous, though it is true that foreign intercourse had done something to diminish this extravagant self-esteem.

In addition to this psychological process, it is probable that the Opposition, for reasons of their own, attacked Inouye's treaty-revision programme by appealing to the pride of the nation. To permit the Government's successful revision of the treaties would have been to allow the removal from the sphere of politics of an issue of great possibilities. The prestige of the Government would have been thereby increased, and the strength of the Opposition correspondingly diminished. However the emphasis is to be distributed among the contributory causes, the fact remains that the storm of protest against Inouye's project, which was represented as "treasonable and disloyal," a surrender of the nation's customs and traditions and an adoption of those of foreigners, drove him from office.

The failure of treaty revision in July 1887 had the effect of redoubling the agitation in its favour. Toward the close of the year, Tani, who was a member of the Cabinet as Minister of Agriculture and Commerce, forwarded a memorial [1] on the subject to the Prime Minister, advocating the denunciation of the treaties and the publication of the terms upon which Japan would continue to act with relation to the resident foreigners. The result of such action, he predicted, would be the calm acquiescence of the Powers in the Japanese dictum. This alarmingly indiscreet proposal was suppressed by the Government, but, nevertheless, it was secretly circulated, and served as the nucleus for a dangerous propaganda. The enforced resignation of his office by Tani only served to add strength to the movement, which was suppressed by a reign of terror initiated toward the close of the year with the promulgation of the Peace Preservation [2] Ordinance on December 25th. This draconian law forbade all assemblies of a political character, whether secret or open, imposed severe penalties upon persons who persisted in agitating, and provided for the declaration of a state of siege in any district where peace and good order were threatened. It had the effect of driving out of Tokyo some three hundred suspects, the best known of whom were Ozaki Yukio, editor of the *Choya Shimbun*, at present Minister of Justice, Hoshi Toru, editor of the *Koron Shimpo*, Shimamoto Chudo, Nakashima Nobuyuki, and Hayashi Yuzo. The *Nichi Nichi*, commenting editorially upon the ordinance, remarked that it had been made necessary by the foolish policy of the Government in suppressing public discussion, thereby driving into dangerous and

[1] *J. G. D.*, pp. 596–604. [2] *Idem*, pp. 502–4.

Political Issues and Morality

secret channels feelings and ideas which, if publicly uttered, would have been comparatively harmless. The *Jiji Shimpo* and many other Tokyo papers openly approved of the measure, while those which objected to it were perforce silent. The *Japan Weekly Mail*, at that time edited by the late Captain Brinkley, regarded the law as an unfortunate incident not to be taken as an expression of the Cabinet's general policy. It generally approved of the Government's action, so far as it would operate to repress " everything savouring of secret conspiracy and covert combination to disturb good order."

Under the enforced quiet of the Peace Preservation Ordinance, which was not repealed until 1898, events moved on toward the consummation of the reconstruction programme. The even tenor of the year 1888 was not, however, unbroken by untoward incidents. In February the Government essayed once more to revise the treaties, only again to meet with failure, owing to the opposition of the people to an essential part of the policy of the Foreign Office. After Inouye's resignation in July 1887, Ito had resumed the portfolio of Foreign Affairs in addition to his office as Minister President of State, but in February 1888 Okuma was taken into the Cabinet, largely to placate his large political following and to make a final effort before the new régime began to solve the problem of treaty relations with the Western Powers. The plan adopted by Okuma was to set up mixed tribunals for the trial of cases involving foreigners. This device the Powers were ready to accept, but when the proposal was made public it was denounced as derogatory to Japan's integrity and independence and contrary to the spirit of the Constitution. The vehemence of the popular objection found its culmination in a murderous attack on the Foreign Minister, whose carriage was blown to pieces by a bomb. Though seriously injured, Okuma escaped with his life. Thus ended the last of the pre-Constitution attempts to revise the treaties.

The Cabinet stopped the negotiations and in due time Okuma resigned.

A further cause of contention between the Government and its political opponents calls for consideration, and this is the system of so-called clan government (Hambatsu Seifu). Popular opposition to the oligarchy was based not only upon its despotic rule and its usurpation of powers which belonged by right to the Emperor, but upon the monopolizing of all offices by Satsuma and Choshu men. This particular agitation cropped up periodically throughout the Meiji Era, and because it was more violent before 1888 than at any other time except during the closing years of the reign, it is advisable to make at this point a somewhat extended statement of what is meant by clan government.

Generally speaking, the origin of clan government is to be found in the survival of the spirit of feudalism. That spirit was essentially sectional, not national, and it bound the samurai of a clan in a common loyalty to their lord, and to the interests of their fellow-clansmen : to exalt the clan was the samurai's highest duty. National interests did not enter his field of vision except in so far as the defence of the Empire against foreign encroachment was a part of the clan's duty. A national outlook upon life had been lost during the two centuries of seclusion which followed upon the closing of the country in 1636, and it had hardly been reacquired when the Restoration occurred. It is not too much to say, therefore, that in 1867 the samurai were capable of comprehending their duty and willing to give their services to preserve the independence of their country, but that they did not set distinctly national interests, as such above those of their immediate clans. Japan entered upon the modern era hampered by a feudal sectionalism among the whole privileged class.

By force of circumstances which we have already detailed, a few of the clans residing in the south-

Political Issues and Morality

western parts of the Empire became the protagonists of the movement which culminated in the Restoration. When the task of carrying on the restored government came to be undertaken, it was natural that the men who had been active in overthrowing the Shogun's power should be appointed to office; once in office it was equally natural that they should remain there, and the longer they remained the more indispensable some of them became. Thus far the process is perfectly intelligible, and instances of it are to be found in every country. When a Prime Minister is appointed in England, for example, and he undertakes the formation of his Cabinet, all the men who have sat in the previous Cabinets of the party, who are still eligible and desirous of office, have the first claim upon his consideration.

But in Japan the spirit of feudalism, as manifested in loyalty to fellow-clansmen to the exclusion of outsiders, resulted in filling the various minor offices with friends and relations of the higher officials, without any regard for efficiency. That natural tendency was strengthened after 1873, at which time the Government had determined to disinherit the military class by commuting the pensions on which they lived. There was a rush of needy samurai for all sorts of offices in the pay of the State. Every member of a clan to which a highly placed official belonged claimed his patronage, and refusal of an appointment was nearly impossible. Not only did the percentage of officials drawn from the Western clans reach very high figures, but what was an even greater menace, the actual number of officials soon grew so large as to be out of all proportion to the work to be done. Though thousands of the minor officials were dismissed periodically, the process of inflation straightway began again. So persistent has this tendency been throughout the Meiji Era, and so disastrous its results, especially to the Treasury, that hardly a year has passed since the Parliament began to meet without some protest being made or committee appointed to examine into the matter of administrative reform, in the sense of reduction of the number of officials in the employ of the State.

But if clan government had meant merely bestowing office upon the leading men of the Western clans and filling minor Government positions with their fellow-clansmen, no serious objection would have followed, for the development was a natural outcome of the situation. As a matter of fact, after 1885, civil service regulations [1] were promulgated, and it became more and more difficult to get into the Government's employ merely through nepotism, or for a Minister of a Department to flood his office with unnecessary officials. Furthermore, when once the system of competitive examinations for entrance to the civil service was established, the way was opened to men of talent, no matter what their clan affiliations might be. No one need accuse the Government of the present day of excluding from the public service, upon the score of birth in Northern or Eastern Japan, any candidate of unusual ability. In that sense the monopoly of the Western clansmen has disappeared, and even in another and more important respect a distinct change has taken place since 1890 in the meaning of the shibboleth *Hambatsu Seifu*. With the erection of a Parliament and the beginning of public discussion of affairs, it has been necessary for the Government to include in the Cabinet representative men from different parts of the country. Examine the modern lists of Cabinet Ministers and you will find the names of many men who have had no affiliations, in their own persons or through their ancestors, with either Satsuma or Choshu. The apportionment of offices, high and low, among the whole people is one of the most conspicuous changes of the second half of Meiji, and yet there probably never was so much animus displayed against clan government during the early years of the era as there was in the spring of 1913.

[1] *J. G. D.*, pp. 99–108 and pp. 109–27.

Political Issues and Morality

It is obvious, therefore, that the domination of the Western clans has gone through a process of evolution, and that its power does not reside now where it once did, in the monopoly of the administrative offices. To get at the root of the matter it is necessary to go back to the early years of the period, when the Department of War was subdivided into the two offices of the Army and Navy, and these two branches of the military service became the special preserves of Satsuma and Choshu.

It was natural that the desires of the two greatest military clans in the country should turn toward these services, and that Satsuma should choose the Navy and Choshu the Army was the outcome of previous training and contemporary circumstances. Satsuma had long been an *imperium in imperio*, and its military policy for generations had been that of an independent kingdom. At the Restoration the greatest military genius in Japan was Saigo Takamori, the leader of the Satsuma samurai. Yet in spite of the fact that Satsuma was pre-eminent among the clans both on land and sea, it was policy that dictated handing over control of the Army to Choshu. Okubo, though a Satsuma samurai, was wise enough to see that Saigo was unsuitable for the Government's purpose, and that no other man in Satsuma could be chosen over his head to fill the post of Minister of the Army.

Too much importance, however, should not be attached to the specific acts of the Restoration Government during these early years, and it would be erroneous to suppose that military designs occupied the first place in the minds of the leading members of the Government. In 1873 the civil party gained the ascendancy over the military, and held it for twenty years. During those two decades military progress was by no means suspended, neither could it be said that the alliance between Satsuma and Choshu was broken. As long as Okubo lived he remained the leading figure in the Government, and after his assassination Ito, a member of the Choshu clan, stepped forward to occupy his place. But during these changes two men, Kawamura and Yamagata, the former from Satsuma, the latter from Choshu, occupied almost continuously the ministerial posts of the Navy and Army respectively. They seemed to have been devoted to the technical interests of their services, although Yamagata did achieve the distinction of becoming Prime Minister even before the constitutional régime was inaugurated. However much he dabbled in general politics, his chief interests remained the Army and its development.

The policy of these two men, Kawamura and Yamagata, was doubtless to favour their clansmen, but as the training of a military officer continues through life and involves promotion to the highest ranks of the service more or less according to seniority, there were no such opportunities in the Army or Navy as there were in the civil departments of getting rid of men who received appointments on the ground of clan ties. It would be quite erroneous to say that *all* the high officers of either the Army or Navy were at any time in Japan's modern history Choshu or Satsuma men, nor is it necessary to an understanding of clan government to presuppose such a fact. There is a solidarity about a military service, with its strict discipline and jealously guarded secrets, an *esprit de corps,* which binds inferiors to superiors, especially when the ultimate control of the organization is entirely in the hands of military men. A man of Yamagata's type, who had fought in the wars of the Restoration and had held the highest military post in the Government for a number of years, finally arrived at a position where nearly all the officers in the Army owed their promotion to him and thus might almost be counted as his personal henchmen. Such was the nature of the evolution which took place in the military departments, Choshu being represented by Yamagata and a small group of his personal friends and favourites, Satsuma by Kawamura and his friends.

Political Issues and Morality

However widely these services were opened in later years to men of other clans, and whatever the influx of Satsuma men into the Army or of Choshu men into the Navy, pre-eminence was jealously guarded by the representatives of the two great clans. Outsiders were made to feel their domination, and only those who proved pliant were advanced to the rank of Lieutenant-General or Vice-Admiral. In the Russian war Togo, a Satsuma man, was the Admiral in command of the fleet, while Oyama, another Satsuma man, was Field-Marshal of the land forces, but Katsura and Kodama, two faithful henchmen of Yamagata, were Minister of War and Chief of Staff respectively.

The two clans hung together until after the Meiji Era had closed. During Ito's long régime he was associated with Kuroda, Terashima, Matsukata, and other representatives of Satsuma, and it would be difficult to point to any single instance, except the Okuma-Itagaki Ministry in 1898, when the office of Minister President of State was not held by a member of one or other of the two clans, at least until after the Russo-Japanese War. Even then the only outsider who was admitted to the post during Meiji was Saionji. As we shall see in another connection, the change to a constitutional monarchy in 1889 was so contrived that the political power of the Sat-cho combination was not seriously affected, and such effects as were noticeable were dealt with in 1894 by the first purely military Government which the modern nation had had. In that year, under the presidency of Yamagata, an ordinance was passed by the Privy Council which stipulated that the Cabinet offices of the Army and Navy should not be held by any but officers in active service of at least the rank of Lieutenant-General or Vice-Admiral. This ordinance remained in force until 1913, when it was modified, not in order to admit civilians, but either active or retired military officers of the ranks stipulated.

The influences of this ordinance in strengthening the

Sat-cho combination will be pointed out elsewhere ; at present it is sufficient to say that it enabled the Army and Navy, or the parties in control of those services, to unmake any Ministry whenever they saw fit.

One other institution must be mentioned in this connection if a complete understanding of clan government is to be obtained, and that is the Genro, or Council of Elder Statesmen. This body, more or less informally constituted toward the end of Meiji, was not provided for in the Constitution ; nevertheless, men have been specifically called to it by Imperial order since the era closed ; during the reign of the Meiji Tenno, however, the Elder Statesmen were what the name signified, the surviving members of the original group of samurai who had promoted the Restoration and been active in the Government through the first thirty years of the reign. The Emperor consulted them semi-privately on matters of importance, such as the beginning and termination of hostilities in the Russo-Japanese War. The Cabinets of the day also consulted with, or rather submitted to the direction of, the Elder Statesmen. Their position in national affairs, in short, was the more or less exact counterpart of that of the elders in any ordinary Japanese family council ; they are old and therefore wise in experience, and their advice should be followed. So far the Elder Statesmen as an informal body of advisers to the Emperor and the Cabinet seems a natural product of Japanese tradition, but the rôle played by these advisers was open to misunderstanding in political circles, and their extraordinary power liable to grave abuse if arbitrarily exercised. For example, when in 1908, after being returned by the people at a general election, the Saionji Cabinet resigned before meeting the Diet, it was impossible to account for the event except by suspecting the machinations of the Elder Statesmen. The intrigue against the non-clan Saionji Cabinet was set on foot by Katsura, who, desirous of taking up office again, prevailed upon Yamagata to oust Saionji. Yamagata,

Political Issues and Morality

Inouye, and Ito became the principals in the action, making three Choshu men against Oyama and Matsukata, the two Satsuma representatives in the Genro. It was not a case of strife within the Elder Statesmen's Council between representatives of the two clans, since Saionji was not a Satsuma adherent but a Kuge who had succeeded Ito as leader of the Seiyukai (Constitutional party). Whatever the details of this intrigue or the means by which the Choshu faction attained their object, here was a case in which the Elder Statesmen may be said to have arbitrarily used their immense influence in the field of domestic party politics. It would be a grave error, however, to imagine that the Genro were wholly employed in intriguing against the party politicians. In 1905 it was their wisdom which suggested the termination of hostilities against Russia, even though the nation objected vehemently to the terms of peace which the Elder Statesmen were willing to accept. Nevertheless, the Genro have been so often brought prominently into public notice in connection with Cabinet changes that their reputation in Japan is mainly based upon their connection with party, as distinguished from national or international, politics.

In summing up, it may be pointed out that clan government, while it grew naturally out of feudalism and the perpetuation of the clan spirit in the modern period, would have disappeared long ago if other elements and aims had not been introduced. In the evolution of Japanese politics all administrative offices have been opened to ability, wheresoever found, except in the military services, and these have been closely and jealously restricted to members of the new military class. In the process of time, by various disingenuous devices, this class has succeeded in securing and retaining control of the administration, and hence clan government has come to mean primarily a government by the military party.

CHAPTER VIII

END OF THE RECONSTRUCTION PERIOD

THE period of political reconstruction may be said to have terminated with the promulgation of the Constitution and its accompanying laws in 1889. Beginning with the confusion characteristic of every transition stage, manifested in this case by the conflicting jurisdictions of the Imperial and feudal governments, it ended with a highly centralized organization, founded upon a divine-right theory of monarchy and operating through a bureaucracy. At the apex of the system was the absolute monarch, whose prerogatives were exercised by and with the advice of the Privy Council and Cabinet and the consent of the Imperial Diet, and in accordance with the terms of the Constitution. Similarly, in the sphere of local government the prerogatives of the monarch were exercised to the remotest corners of the Empire through the local bureaucracy with the consent of the various local assemblies.

The overthrow of the Shogunate in 1867 transferred the exercise of despotic powers from the adherents of one great family, the Tokugawa, to the henchmen of a league composed of the feudal houses of South-western Japan. Nominally, the Restoration League governed the people in the Emperor's name and with his consent, but actually a small group of the most active samurai of the Western clans constituted themselves an oligarchy and in accordance with their own purposes and ideas exercised the despotic powers of the throne. In 1885 the virtual regency of the oligarchs ended and a personal rule by an absolute

End of the Reconstruction Period

monarch began. But only the semblance of oligarchy perished in that year ; in the hands of his Cabinet the Emperor was controlled as completely as he had ever been by the Daijokwan.

The devious devices by which the oligarchy had managed to neutralize opposition to its course by suppressing sternly all attempts to subvert the Government, or yielding partially to the demand for a popular government, have been described in the foregoing chapters. It remains only to analyse the institutions created in the culminating stage of the reconstruction and to determine the nature of the government with which Japan set out upon its constitutional régime.

It would be in contravention of the principle of continuity, as exemplified in the history of nations, to expect that any radical changes could be introduced into the Japanese political system by the mere promulgation of a Constitution. It would be more in accord with history to conjecture that the Constitution merely crystallized political ideas and forms already familiar to the ruling class. Institutions seldom thrive in an unprepared soil. Too liberal a form of government for the times is as impracticable as the reverse ; thus the Chinese republican institutions of 1912 have perished except in name, whereas the reactionary institutions established in Japan in 1889, with a definitiveness that almost paralleled the immutability of the laws of the Medes and Persians, immediately began to hamper and restrict the nation's political progress. Rapidly changing political conditions demand a high degree of elasticity in the institutions of government. To attempt to check an active progressive nation in its career is a type of folly bred by caste or ignorance. A stable equilibrium is unthinkable in the political development of a nation, and its appearance is merely a sign of complete retardation of progress. An individual, if born within a caste, is likely to be held fast by its bonds, but if in a free society the limits of his progress are determined only by his ability. A nation, it is true, may be bound down by a system such as the Japanese endured for more than two centuries during the Tokugawa régime, but in a nation's life a thousand years are indeed but a day, and the time must come when the " cake of custom " is at last broken. Thus the year 1867 witnessed in Japan the bursting of the bonds imposed in 1603 by Tokugawa Iyeyasu, whereas the Constitution, by its claim to immutability, marked the beginning of a new period of political stagnation, after a few brief years of readjustment and change.

The struggles of the people within the bonds of the Constitution, the efforts of the governing clique to distract them and prevent their realizing the existence of the web of despotism in which they were being enmeshed, are matters which will occupy our attention in the succeeding chapters. The devices adopted by the constitutional oligarchy—the diligent cultivation of a popular belief in the peculiarity and inherent superiority of the Japanese monarchy,[1] with its heavenly origin and unbroken lineage, the diverting of the nation's energy from domestic to foreign policies, the securing of a place in the comity of world Powers— are as old as history and as modern as the twentieth century. But despite the wonderful record of progress achieved by the people in the second half of Meiji, the era closed in a storm of protest against the institutions established in 1889—a storm which will continue to rage until the insurmountable barriers against political progress erected by the Constitution have been removed by the revision of that instrument.

When in 1881 there was extracted by force from the Daijokwan the promise to establish a constitutional monarchy, the members and supporters of the political societies hailed the rescript as assuring the fulfilment of their aim, the establishment of responsible government. That document stated that the limitations upon

[1] See Chamberlain, B. H., " The Invention of a New Religion," *Literary Guide*, London, 1911.

End of the Reconstruction Period

the Imperial prerogative and the constitution of Parliament would be announced in due course, and the statement was accepted as additional proof of the coming abolition of despotic oligarchy or monarchy and the approach of popular control of the executive. Had the agitators been more deeply read in their own history or that of other nations, or less carried away by enthusiasm for democracy, they would have been able to gauge the real value of the promise. Three years before, elective assemblies had been established in connection with the Fu and Ken, but no substantive powers either in legislation or administration had been bestowed on them, nor on the similar assemblies which had been created in the various municipalities in 1880. It would seem that no great perspicacity was necessary to judge correctly the nature of the powers likely to be bestowed upon the National Assembly.

Moreover, it was not in reason to expect that the members of the Daijokwan, who had tasted the delights of office for nearly fifteen years and were knit together by a common belief in the principles of absolutism and by ties of clan as well, intended to divest themselves suddenly of place and power. No matter what new institutions were created or constitution promulgated, mere common sense would lead the politicians to expect the perpetuation of despotic government and control by the oligarchs. Only by revolution can power be wrested by one class from another. The ordinary processes of nature, evolution and decay, are too slow to accomplish any sudden changes. The span of man's life covers not one, but two or three generations, and thus traditions of one age are necessarily handed down to the next. At the end of Meiji some of the promoters of the Restoration were still alive ; one of them, Okuma Shigenobu, is at present the Minister President of State, and at least two others are influential Genro. The oligarchs of 1881 not only drained their cup of power, but they had time likewise to bring up in their own political philosophy a new generation to carry on into the future the traditions of the past.

The steps by which the *dénouement* of 1889 was approached have been to some extent anticipated. In 1883 Ito was transferred from the Home Office to the Household Department. His appointment was significant, both because of the man and the office. In 1878 he had assumed Okubo's place as head of the Department of Home Affairs and likewise his dominating position in the Daijokwan, and it was during his régime in the Home Office that the local elective assemblies were created and emasculated by being subjected to the bureaucracy. Ito's appointment as the responsible head of the department which was to draft the Constitution could hardly be interpreted otherwise than as foreshadowing the nature of the changes impending. Moreover, the office of the Household Department had never before been filled by a commoner, but always by men of Kuge origin, and no greater tribute to the importance of Ito in the counsels of the Government could have been given than his selection for the post.

Shortly before assuming office he had headed a mission to America and Europe for the study of constitutional forms and practices, and had come under the spell of the most imposing political figure in Europe, Prince Otto von Bismarck. His study of the Prussian system, which undoubtedly captivated him completely, determined in his mind the form and content of the Constitution which by his instrumentality was subsequently imposed upon Japan. Upon his return in 1883 there followed in quick succession three events, all of which are to be at least partially attributed to Prussian influence. In 1884 a bureau for the study of constitutional and administrative reforms (Seido Torishirabe Kyoku) was established in connection with the Household Department, so that the drafting of the Constitution might proceed under Ito's supervision, not only in absolute secrecy, but, as it were, under

End of the Reconstruction Period

the personal direction of the sovereign. During the same year the nobility was rehabilitated, and five orders created in the Prussian manner. It will be remembered that among the early acts of the Restoration Government was the abolition of the old system of honours by which the Court and territorial nobles were sharply distinguished, and in its place a single order, *Kwazoku*, was established. In 1884, five hundred patents of nobility were issued. In the order of Princes were included the five families of the Kuge of the First Class (Sekke); the Tokugawa in the direct line from Iyeyasu; Satsuma, Choshu, and their Excellencies Sanjo and Iwakura. Among the Marquises were three houses of new creation, those of Okubo, Kido, and Nakayama Tadayoshi, the grandfather of the present Emperor. The names of the foremost members of the oligarchy were found in the order of Counts, Hirosawa, Higashikuze, Oki, Yamagata, Ito, Saigo, Kuroda, Inouye, Yamada, Matsukata, Oyama, Kawamura, Sasaki, and Terashima. In that of Viscounts was a number of the leading military and naval commanders of the time, nearly all of them Choshu or Satsuma men. The order of Barons was composed entirely of the former territorial nobility or their descendants. The establishment of these various orders of nobility has often been interpreted as necessary for the composition of the projected House of Peers, but a much more direct explanation lies in the connection which exists between a despotic monarchy and the bureaucracy through which it expresses its will. "Honour," said Montesquieu, "is the principle of monarchy." If the service of the monarch is to appeal universally to the people, then high honours in the form of ranks of nobility must be attainable by those who rise to the highest posts in the bureaucracy.

In 1885 the change was accomplished which most clearly shows the desertion of Chinese or ancient Japanese tradition in favour of that of modern Prussia. The Council of State system was abandoned and the Cabinet form of Government adopted. At the head of the Cabinet, which was composed of the Ministers of the various administrative departments, stood the Minister President of State, with powers of supervision and control which made him a Japanese counterpart of the German Chancellor. Ito secured his own appointment to this latter office, and for the time being the main outlines of the Prussian system were adopted in Japan. The Emperor appeared as a personal despot, exercising absolute powers, in accordance with the advice of the Minister President of State, through the members of a bureaucracy who were entrusted with the details of administration. This was the system which was embodied in the Constitution, and if the Imperial Diet is appended to the monarch, Minister President, and bureaucracy, the nature of the constitutional régime in Japan is not difficult to understand.

Meanwhile the work of the bureau for the study of constitutional reforms continued under Ito's direction. Associated with him as his principal colleagues were Inouye Ki and two of Ito's personal followers, Ito Miyoji and Kaneko Kentaro. These four men may be considered the principal authors of the Constitution, but surrounding them in all their work was the atmosphere of the Household Department. Nothing was done to appease the curiosity of the people as to the nature of the instrument while it was in the making; on the contrary, its secrets were kept inviolate, and all public expression of opinion, at least of a critical nature, upon the subject was forbidden. Thus in November 1888 the publication of Count Shojiro Goto's organ, the *Seiron Zasshi*,[1] was suspended for printing an article entitled "Cabinets responsible to Parliament," in which it was said plainly that as the present clan government was not likely to endanger its tenure of office, the people should make prepara-

[1] The editors of this paper were Messrs. Suge and Nakaye, the latter a well-known French scholar, among those proscribed in 1887. Suge had studied in England.

End of the Reconstruction Period

tions for the emergency which would arise when Parliament assembled. In the course of fourteen months the *Seiron Zasshi* was compelled to suspend publication three times for periods of considerable duration, nor was the fate of other Opposition papers different.

How totally unaffected by the agitations of the Radicals were the deliberations of the framers of the Constitution may be seen by contrasting the instrument as it finally was promulgated with a document [1] which was widely circulated among the political societies in 1881, at the time the Parliamentary Rescript was issued. That so-called " Draft of a Constitution " outlined a form of parliamentary government in which the Cabinet should be responsible to the elected representatives of the people, while legislation passed by the two Houses in due form should receive the Imperial sign-manual and become law. These principles had become an essential part of the stock-in-trade of the Liberal party, and their wisdom had been gradually confirmed by the growing familiarity of the politicians with English books on parliamentary government.

As the time for the promulgation of the Constitution approached, the Government established the Privy Council (Sumitsu-in), for the purpose of shaping its final form and ratifying it before promulgation. Ito resigned his office as Minister President and assumed the Presidency of the Council. Count Terashima was Vice-President, and the other members were Counts Kawamura, Yoshii, Sasaki, Oki, Higashikuze, Soyejima, Katsu Awa, Viscounts Fukuoka, Shinagawa, Sano, and Mr. T. Kono. The Secretary General was Inouye Ki. In an account which Ito has left of what took place at the meetings of the Privy Council while the draft of the Constitution was being considered, the Emperor is represented as taking a lively interest in the proceedings, entering the meetings informally and listening to the expression of the views of the members. Whether or not this is true, and it may be, the statement

[1] *J. G. D.*, pp. 484–95.

which Ito makes in this connection that the Meiji Tenno gave "reasonable consideration to all the conflicting views of Liberalism and Conservatism," is obviously misleading, and was designed to impress the Japanese people with the fact that the Emperor himself was responsible for the provisions of the Constitution. Few monarchs, and certainly the Tenno was not one of them, would be able to draft the outlines of a national Constitution. We may therefore be pardoned for believing that the Constitution was formulated by the reactionary members of a small bureau, ratified by the Privy Council, and sanctioned by the Emperor in fulfilment of a promise given some years before to the nation by the Daijokwan.

The day set for the ceremony of promulgation was the 11th of February 1889, a date since observed as a national holiday, *Kigensetsu*, in honour of the event. Among other preparations made for the occasion was the suppression of practically all the Radical newspapers in Tokyo, and the issuance of strict injunctions to the rest of the Press that no unfavourable comments were to be made, for the time being, upon the Constitution. Apart from two incidents, the events of the celebration occurred without a hitch. The ceremonies were performed at the Palace in the presence of high officials, the diplomatic corps, and other invited guests. The streets were gay with flags and bunting, and filled with a holiday crowd who watched, silent, but full of curiosity, as was their habit, the steady stream of carriages and jinrikishas bearing officialdom, in gold lace and cocked hats, to and from the Palace. There was no attempt at mirth or frolic : the occasion was a solemn one, and the people behaved accordingly. Neither was there any effort made to include the populace; the Constitution was not read in public to the citizens of the capital. The instrument had been framed in secret, ratified by the aristocracy, and promulgated before an audience of officials. It was the Government's affair from beginning to end.

End of the Reconstruction Period

The day had begun most inauspiciously, however, with the regrettable assassination of Mori Arinori, the Minister of Education, as he was about to start for the Palace to participate in the ceremonies. The assassin had no grudge against the Government on the score of the Constitution, but with a curious sense for effect chose that occasion to wreak vengeance upon an individual whom he regarded as deserving of death. In his eyes, Mori's offence had been the violation of the sacred shrine at Ise, by raising a curtain in order to look into a shrine forbidden to all save the Emperor. That Mori may have been unthinking in his behaviour at Ise is admitted, but he had certainly intended no sacrilege, and the priests of the temple afterwards deposed that he had made ample apology to them, and that both he and they had considered the incident closed. Mori was a samurai of the Satsuma clan who had been ennobled as Viscount in 1887 ; he had lived and studied abroad, especially in England, and was held in the highest esteem in his own country as a scholar and patron of learning.

The other incident of the day was of an entirely different nature. Despite the fact that all the documents which the Emperor was to read had been read and re-read by the officials entrusted with their preparation, an error in the text of the Preamble of the Constitution as to the date of the promulgation of the Parliamentary Rescript escaped their notice. The rescript had been issued on October 12, 1881, whereas in the Preamble the date was given as the 14th. As soon as the Emperor uttered the words, there were a dozen men in the audience who recognized the blunder and trembled. Ito that very day handed in his resignation, but the Emperor regarded the matter lightly, and good-naturedly bade him think less of such trifles and continue in the performance of the duties of his high office.

As the contents of the laws proclaimed in the Palace on February 11 were published, the loyal Government papers acclaimed them as the dawn of a constitutional régime. The Constitution itself was described as something new in Japan, and in a sense it was. Never before, at least not since 1868, had a Constitution been issued, and certainly never before had the Emperor been so closely connected with a similar instrument. The Constitution of 1868, based on the terms of the Imperial oath, had been the creation of the Daijokwan, and was issued in its name. In many respects, however, it deserves the title of the Japanese Magna Charta, but, like the English original, it was too highly coloured by the then existent conditions of feudalism to long survive the collapse of that institution. It contained, however, the promise of representative institutions; it guaranteed freedom of speech, and set up a feudal council. Contrasted with the spirit of the Constitution of 1868, that of 1889 was distinctly reactionary, especially in the theory of monarchy it announced and the provision made for popular government. But the Press, in so far as there was comment at all, sought to direct the attention of the people to the significance of the event, independent of the nature of the contents of the Constitution. It was pointed out that the Emperor, to whom both land and people belonged, whose absolute control of the property and lives of his subjects was inherent in the commission received by the Imperial Ancestor from the Sun Goddess Amaterasu, had out of his wisdom and beneficence voluntarily limited his powers, or at least had consented to exercise them in accordance with the laws, and had bestowed upon the people rights and liberties and a share in the determination of national affairs.

In this presentation of the matter the editors had taken their cue from the various Introductions to the Constitution, not from the provisions of the instrument itself. They likewise had read their history in the way which was officially prescribed. In any critical view of that history it is impossible to support the official thesis that the thousand years of feudalism and

the eight centuries of almost unbroken usurpation of
the administrative powers of the throne by the Shoguns
are compatible with the rule of an absolute monarch,
and are to be explained away by saying that the
usurpers were the Emperor's Lord High Constables,
exercising legitimate functions in the Imperial name,
or that the territorial nobility were the vassals of the
Court. In the ceremony which was performed early
in the morning of the promulgation day at the
Sanctuary of the Imperial Ancestors, great emphasis
was laid upon the continuity of the Imperial polity.
The Constitution, it was maintained, broke with no
traditions of the past. It merely served to enunciate
in the progressive nineteenth century and amid new
surroundings, by means of express provisions of law,
the unwritten principles which had always underlain
the ancient form of government. " These laws," the
Emperor read, " amount to only an exposition of grand
precepts for the conduct of government, bequeathed
by the Imperial Founder of Our House and by Our
other Imperial Ancestors." [1] This claim of continuity
is absurd, and the editors very correctly made little
of it, except in so far as they used it to prove that
from the beginning of Meiji there was a line of continuity stretching from the Imperial oath in 1867 to
the Constitution, a gradual development of representative institutions. They preferred to lay stress upon
the changes which had been brought about and were
embodied in the Constitution. " In consideration [2] of
the progressive tendency of the course of human
affairs, and in parallel with the advance of civilization,
We deem it expedient, in order to give clearness and
distinctness to the instructions bequeathed by the
Imperial Founder of Our House and Our other Imperial
Ancestors, to establish fundamental laws formulated
into express provisions of law, so that, on the one
hand, Our Imperial posterity will possess an express
guide for the course they are to follow, and that, on

[1] *J. G. D.*, p. 145.   [2] *Ibid.*, p. 144.

the other, Our subjects shall thereby be enabled to enjoy a wider range of action in giving Us their support, and that the observance of Our laws shall continue to the remotest ages of time." So likewise in the Preamble to the Constitution the sentiments which were taken up and commented upon most freely by the Press were embodied in the following paragraphs :—

" We hereby promulgate . . . a fundamental law of state, to exhibit the principles by which We are to be guided in Our conduct, and to point out to what Our descendants and Our subjects and their descendants are for ever to conform.

" We now declare to respect and protect the security of the rights and property of Our people, and to secure to them the complete enjoyment of the same, within the extent of the provisions of the present Constitution and of the law."

In the light of the facts in our possession there is much in these Imperial statements, prefatory to the Constitution, which traverses both the truth and the laudatory views of the Press. To set up the divine-right dogma, based upon the myth of the Emperor's heavenly lineage, for the purpose of giving sanctity to a Constitution which was not Japanese but Prussian in its origin and in many of its chief characteristics —and that is what the Government deliberately did— was, to put it mildly, to ignore the facts of Japanese history and proclaim belief in what was scientifically impossible. Likewise, to declare that the Constitution was merely a revision of " the ancient form of government " leads the reader to ask, " What ancient form of government? " If that of *Tai-ho* (701-4), then the elaborate statement of Sanjo Saneyoshi, made in 1885 upon the occasion of the abandonment of the " Council of State " system and the adoption of Ito's adaptation of the Prussian system, must be completely ignored ; if that of Jimmu Tenno, the mythical founder of the Imperial house, the reader is entitled to point out that no one can possibly know anything about the form of government in vogue during a supposititious period which antedates all Japanese historical records by a thousand years. Furthermore, to establish the Constitution as a law which was to continue " to the remotest ages of time " was to deny all presumption of change in an effort to enforce obedience to the provisions of the instrument.

As time passed by, the newspapers which had been suppressed as a precautionary measure were permitted to resume publication, while those which had been cautioned to be careful in their comments grew bolder, · and the discussion of the Constitution was taken up. Fukuzawa Yukichi,[1] the owner and editor of the *Jiji Shimpo*, who had at the beginning of 1889 decided against responsible government on the ground that it would be mean-spirited for men to give up office merely because their opponents wished them to do so, but at the same time counselled against the Cabinet's tenacious holding to office after the Parliament had declared a want of confidence in the Administration, voiced the opinions of the educated classes of the community in March of that year in a series of articles [2] on " The History of the Japanese Parliament." He welcomed the Constitution as ushering in " a stupendous change," and pointed with pride to the method of its attainment as different from the experience of other nations in similar crises. He said : " Our Constitution has been promulgated and a Parliament provided under the most auspicious circumstances of a tranquil and prosperous reign." He further recorded the fact that various comments had been made by the politicians, some of whom regarded the Constitution as " too liberal," others as " too severe," but he declined to enter into any criticism of its provisions until some experience of their operation had been obtained. Such

---

[1] Fukuzawa was a voluminous writer, and the pioneer of modern education in Japan. The school which he founded during the era of Keio has grown into a great educational institution, the Keiogijuku.

[2] *J. G. D.*, pp. 577–93.

was the attitude of many true Liberals who stood more
or less aside from active political life. The more
Radical editors seized at once upon the 55th Article
of the Constitution, upon the interpretation of which
hung the fate of responsible government. That article
read ambiguously as follows : " The respective
Ministers of State shall give their advice to the
Emperor, and be responsible for it." Responsible to
whom? was the question, to the people as represented
in Parliament or to the Emperor? Even the *Nichi
Nichi* professed itself as believing that the former
interpretation was correct, and the question was not
decided in the contrary sense until Ito's " Commentary
upon the Constitution " appeared.[1] Other ambiguous
provisions were discussed, but, generally speaking, only
a few of the newspapers undertook to condemn the
Emperor's gift as not what the nation desired or
expected.

Thus were the Constitution and its accompanying
laws providing for the Imperial Diet launched, and
accepted quietly by the nation. The lower orders of
the people were only vaguely aware of the event, and
troubled themselves little about the contents of the
laws ; the more conservative Liberals were content
to await the progress of events and the establishment
of the Parliament ; the advocates of responsible
government alone were disappointed, and the great
majority of them were afraid to speak openly what
was in their minds.

At this distance from the event there is little difficulty in estimating the quality of the institutions
provided for. The " immutable law," it is true, has
not been set aside, nor has its amendment been publicly
advocated by any responsible politicians. But the dissatisfaction with the Government has from time to
time become intense, and on many occasions a Cabinet
has been compelled to resign by the force of hostile
public opinion. Nevertheless, the Opposition through-

[1] P. 90.

out the second half of Meiji never saw the necessity of demanding, or perhaps never had the temerity to demand, a constitutional amendment for the purpose of making the Cabinet responsible to the people. The outcry has always been against clan government or the Genro, never against the Constitution itself.

The first chapter of the Constitution is entitled " The Emperor," and contains seventeen articles. Except for the first of these, which declares that " The Empire of Japan shall be reigned over and governed by a line of Emperors unbroken for ages eternal," there is nothing in the chapter which would be unfamiliar to a student of the Constitution of the German Empire. The prerogative is described in general terms in the fourth article, which runs thus : " The Emperor is the head of the Empire, combining in himself the rights of sovereignty," and more specifically in the provisions that immediately follow. His powers may be summarized as : exercise of legislative and executive authority by sanctioning and promulgating laws and ordinances, by convoking and dissolving the Imperial Diet, by determining the organization of the different branches of the Administration and the salaries of civil and military officers, and by the appointment and dismissal of the same ; supreme command of the Army and Navy ; the right to declare war and conclude treaties of peace, and to confer titles of nobility and other marks of honour ; the ordering of amnesty, pardons, commutation of punishments, and rehabilitation. Provision is likewise made for a Regency to exercise all the Imperial prerogatives in the name of the Emperor.

The second chapter contains fifteen articles relating to the rights and duties of subjects. But in order to understand the provisions of this chapter it is necessary to notice, first, that a strict line of demarcation is drawn between the civil and military classes, and second, that times of war or other national emergency are sharply differentiated from those of peace. The rights and duties of subjects, as mentioned in these provisions, do not apply in their entirety to the military class, nor to any class of the people under the special circumstances mentioned above. Moreover, no absolute rights are granted to any class of subjects under all circumstances ; all rights, privileges, and duties are limited by the provisions of law. When it is remembered that the Peace Preservation Law remained in force for a decade, there is little significance in Article XXIX, which reads : " Japanese subjects shall within the limits of the law enjoy liberty of speech, writing, publication, public meetings, and associations." Nor, in view of the nature of the Code of Criminal Procedure and the ordinary practices in preliminary trials, can much protection be claimed under the terms of the following article : " No Japanese subject shall be arrested, detained, tried, or punished, unless according to law." Generally speaking, all the provisions of this chapter are so stated as to avoid a categorical announcement of positive rights which appertain to the status of citizenship. The provisions of law determine and limit in every case the rights of the subjects. But the Japanese people had no traditions on the subject of natural rights, and during the long régime of feudalism they had been accustomed to only those rights and liberties which were determined by custom or the arbitrary will of their lords. Hence it is probable that the adoption in the Constitution of the Continental rather than the Anglo-Saxon theory of rights seemed a matter of small consequence.

The Imperial Diet is the subject of Chapter III, and its provisions, if taken in conjunction with those of the chapter immediately following, entitled " The Ministers of State and the Privy Council," contain what the Constitution determined with regard to the exercise of legislative and executive functions. In a preceding chapter [1] we have already summarized the contents of the twenty-two articles on the Imperial Diet. It is sufficient to say in this connection that the legislative powers of the Diet are limited to giving consent to laws or voting on projects of law submitted by the Government, for the provision enabling the Diet to " initiate projects of law " is completely offset by the Emperor's right of sanction and promulgation as well as by his power to order or refrain from ordering the execution of any law.

But inadequate as the provisions of Chapter III are for the creation of a Diet authorized to exercise substantive powers in legislation, the two provisions of Chapter IV do not even mention the Diet in connection with the executive power. The Ministry and the Privy Council alone have access to the executive head of the State, except for the Diet's privilege of presenting " Addresses " to the Emperor. On all ordinary matters the Ministers give advice to the Emperor, but whenever he so desires he may consult the Privy Council and be advised by them on " important matters of state." As Ministers and Privy Councillors are alike appointed by the Emperor and can be dismissed by him alone, their naturally acknowledged responsibility is to the sovereign, not to the people. Quite as significant as this subordination of the Diet to the Cabinet and Privy Council is the provision against unity of action by the Cabinet. The " respective Ministers of State " are to act as individuals in advising the Emperor, just as by the second article of an Imperial ordinance [1] of February 26, 1886, they were " held responsible for all matters falling within their competency." This provision, when taken in connection with the pre-eminence of the Minister President of State, reveals distinctly Ito's intention of instituting a German chancellorship, combined with a Cabinet composed of a number of Secretaries of State occupying subordinate and mainly administrative posts. The power of the Privy Council, too, was carefully limited to giving advice, when consulted, to the Emperor and

J. G. D., p. 110.

195

his Minister President. How this system was subsequently transformed by Yamagata in the interests of the militarist faction we shall see in due time, and also how the Cabinet, except for the Ministers of the Army and Navy, has succeeded in unifying itself, in spite of the express provision of the Constitution to the contrary. Whether it was that there appeared no Bismarck among the Japanese oligarchs or that conditions were different in the two countries, the system of government so carefully adapted from the Prussian model has proved unworkable in Japan almost from the beginning.

The five articles of Chapter V on " The Judicature " provided for a system of law courts, organized according to law [1] ; for judges to be appointed from among those possessing proper qualifications, to hold office for life during good conduct ; for public and secret trials ; and for administrative courts established by law. Three kinds of courts of law were thus established—ordinary civil and criminal courts, courts of administrative litigation, and special tribunals sitting *in camera* if the nature of the case warranted. The system, to be understood, must be studied in connection with the Codes of Law and Procedure and the actual practice of the courts in administering justice. But from the constitutional provisions it is evident that the Anglo-Saxon system was rejected in favour of that of France and continental Europe, especially in the matter of providing administrative courts for the protection of the bureaucracy.

The Budget is the subject of the eleven articles of Chapter VI. Therein it is provided that the Budget shall be presented first to the Lower House of the Diet, and subsequently to the Peers. If the circumstances are such that the Diet cannot be convoked, the Government is authorized to take all necessary financial measures by Imperial ordinance, or if the Budget does not pass the Diet, the Government shall carry out the

[1] *J. G. D.*, pp. 625-59.

provisions made for the previous year. A Board of Audit is also provided for. Except for certain charges upon the national treasury, such as the civil list and " fixed expenditures," all appropriations require the consent of the Diet. Among the so-called " fixed expenditures " are the salaries of military, civil, and police officials and departmental expenses, the cost of the maintenance of the Army and Navy, as well as the interest on the national debt and all expenditures arising out of treaties with foreign countries. As to the items contained in this long list,[1] the Constitution provided that they might not be rejected nor reduced by the Diet without the consent of the Cabinet. As to the methods of raising a revenue, taxes are to be determined by law, and all public loans require the consent of the Diet. These articles furnish the Government with the powers necessary to carry on the administration independent of the Diet, in case the latter should refuse to vote supplies. The appropriations necessary for the essential services are fixed charges upon the treasury, and in respect of other outlays, though it may be inconvenient to continue indefinitely to reapply the Budget of the previous year, it is infinitely less embarrassing than a complete stoppage of income. In respect to finance, the Japanese Constitution departs as radically from the English practice as it does in respect to the administration of justice or the relations of the Diet to the Government.

The four Supplementary Rules which make up the concluding chapter apply mainly to the revision of the Constitution. Although the instrument is described in its Preamble as a " fundamental law of state, to exhibit the principles by which We are to be guided in Our conduct, and to point out to what Our descendants and Our subjects and their descendants are for ever to conform," nevertheless, with an astonishing inconsistency, the same Preamble recites the terms according to which the provisions of the Constitution are to be

[1] *J. G. D.*, pp. 233–6

amended. The Preamble begins by describing the Constitution as an "immutable law" and ends with the presumption that revision of its provisions will become necessary in time. "When in the future it may become necessary to amend any of the provisions of the present Constitution, We or Our successors shall assume the initiative right, and submit a project for the same to the Imperial Diet." In such a case, the Supplementary Rules provide that the Diet shall not consider the amendment unless two-thirds of the whole number of members are present, and no amendment shall be passed by either House except by a two-thirds majority of those present. If we assume the minimum requirement as thus described, it would be possible for a strong Government to initiate and carry through the Diet an amending project by controlling 171 votes in the Lower House and about the same number in the Peers. But the difficulties are not adequately represented by these figures. If the present Government, which controls a majority of the Lower House, should introduce the amendments necessary to secure responsible government, and that is the policy which the Prime Minister and various members of his Cabinet have advocated for years, even if the Bill were passed by the Lower House it would certainly be rejected by the Upper, for the majority of the Peers have always been, and are still, opposed to party government. It is probable, too, that the Genro would insist upon the immediate resignation of a Ministry which sought to secure the Emperor's consent for a measure the purpose of which was to change any of the provisions of the Constitution. There are difficulties, therefore, attendant upon such a project which are not taken into account in the Supplementary Rules of the Constitution.

The constitutional monarchy established in 1889 in Japan is not to be understood as the equivalent of parliamentary government under a limited monarchy. It is true that a change from absolute to limited monarchy took place, but the significance of that change may easily be overestimated. Any one familiar with Japanese history, either during the feudal régime or the first eighteen years of Meiji, would not be likely to maintain that the Emperor was *de facto* an absolute monarch. For centuries the traditions of divine right and absolutism had been maintained, even though the usurping military dictators were the actual rulers in the land, and after the Restoration these traditions were perpetuated by the Daijokwan or oligarchy. At the end of 1885 the outward organization of the Government was made to conform, arbitrarily and by direct imitation, to the system established in the German Empire, except for the Constitution and Parliament, which institutions were added four or five years later. Under her great Chancellor and by his shrewd calculation the organization for government in Germany had been so devised that it served the purposes both of a divinely anointed monarch and an aspiring democracy. The situation in Japan in 1881 was essentially similar to that of Germany after 1866, and Ito became convinced that Bismarck's scheme for Germany could be applied bodily in Japan. The traditional claims of the throne could be satisfied, the petitions of the people for a Parliament granted, and the powers of the oligarchy over both Emperor and Diet preserved. When in 1889 the Constitution was promulgated and the Imperial Diet provided for, practically every institution and principle which had been used by Bismarck in constructing the constitutional monarchy of Germany made its appearance in Japan.

Under a constitutional monarchy, in this German-Japanese sense, the force of public opinion must eventually determine the policy of the State, and therefore this form of monarchy is in this sense a government by the people. To what degree of intensity the conflict between the absolute monarch and his subjects may increase depends upon the success of the Government in creating a public sentiment in favour of its policies. To persist long in any course which is objectionable to public opinion is to court disaster, but the danger of popular revolution on a scale sufficiently great to imperil the throne is so remote, and the possibilities of swaying public sentiment by means of the Press and the schools so great, that the will of the Government is to all intents and purposes the law of the land. To what extent parliamentary government in a democracy differs from that in a constitutional monarchy in this fundamental respect it is most difficult to determine. The will of the Government in a democracy is that of the party which controls a majority of the representatives of the people, and the only safeguard of minority opinion lies in the possibility of turning it into the majority opinion. In a parliamentary government, the transformation by a general election of a minority into a majority results immediately in a change of policy, or at least the possibility of a change. In a constitutional monarchy of the Japanese type the swinging of the majority from one party to another does not necessarily nor often result in any change in the personnel of the Government or the character of its policy.

PART II

THE PARLIAMENTARY RÉGIME

CHAPTER IX

THE FIRST FOUR YEARS

IF the Constitution had been promulgated in a period of sabbath calm, induced by the wholesale suspension of the Opposition Press as well as by an appreciation upon the part of the educated classes of the event's significance, the spell was soon broken. In a few months editors and politicians regained their accustomed volubility, and long before the Diet was elected the political arena was again the scene of turmoil. Itagaki and Okuma, the two foremost party leaders, quickly decided upon the action which the situation demanded. Itagaki had stood outside the oligarchy, a voice crying in the wilderness, practically throughout his whole career, and he knew only too well after a single perusal of the provisions of the Constitution that his demands for an Executive responsible to the Diet had not been heeded. Article LV alone would have been enough to have driven him into Opposition once more. Okuma, on the other hand, having been a member of the oligarchy which drafted and issued the instrument, may be regarded as having consented to its terms : his quarrel, therefore, was not primarily with the terms of the new Constitution, but with the two leading Choshu members of the Government, Ito and Inouye. In 1881 they had ruined his political career by defeating his scheme for a Parliament in 1883, and six years later they had again triumphed over him. Toward the close of 1889 these two men headed the opposition within the Cabinet to his treaty-revision negotiations, and forced him out of the circle of the oligarchs. Okuma's revenge is written large upon the parliamentary records of the period which followed, from 1890 to 1894.

But in order to understand the events of these four years, the previous history of the political parties must be recounted in some detail. It has already been related how Itagaki's party, the Jiyuto (Radicals), was dissolved in 1884 because of the participation of some of its members in the Fukushima plot and the Ibaraki and Saitama riots, not to mention the Korean embroglio of 1882-4. Okuma's party, the Kaishinto (Progressionists), was disrupted in the same year for similar reasons. But whereas the Jiyuto dissolved its organization, the Kaishinto was kept alive by a section of the party which rebelled against its leaders' action. The next year, 1885, in its first few months witnessed the conclusion of treaties with Korea and China, both of which were denounced by the public as proving the weakness of the Government's foreign policy. The Korean treaty provided for the opening of that country to Japanese trade, but as it was followed almost immediately by similar treaties between Korea and Western nations, the Japanese saw Korea slipping out of their grasp. The terms of the treaty with China, signed at Tientsin by Ito in April 1885, seemed even more unfavourable—in fact, a surrender of Japanese rights in Korea. By the articles of this treaty Korea's independence was acknowledged by both China and Japan, and both countries agreed to withdraw their troops from the peninsula, and further, if at any time in the future it was necessary to intervene in Korean affairs, neither of the contracting parties was to dispatch troops without previously notifying the other of its intention. How the terms of this convention were used a decade later to justify Japan's attack upon China we shall see in the next chapter; here it is only necessary to point out that the recognition of the independence of Korea and the withdrawal of Japanese troops from the country was popularly denounced as a betrayal of Japan's legitimate interests in Asia.

The First Four Years

A few months later, Ito launched the first of his Prussian innovations by abolishing the Daijokwan and setting up in its place the Naikaku. The real significance of this change was not apparent at the time, nevertheless it served to raise the question of the responsibility of the Cabinet and caused a fresh outbreak of the old controversy over independent *versus* responsible executives. With these two burning political questions, the one concerning foreign and the other domestic policy, thus brought into prominence, the voracious appetite of the public for discussion could be easily fed with sensations, and to say that men like Ozaki, Hoshi, Nakaye, etc., were the editors of the leading Opposition papers is assurance enough that nothing was left undone to sharpen the Radicals' animosity against the oligarchy.

Towards the end of 1887 the *Yoron Shinshi* defined the objects of the political agitation of the past two years as "thoroughness in foreign policy"—which meant the revision of the treaties in such a manner as to restore the nation's judicial and fiscal autonomy, and the extension of Japanese control over Korea; "reform of the domestic policy" by abrogating the oppressive regulations governing the Press and public meetings and by establishing a Parliament to which the Naikaku would acknowledge responsibility; "increase of national power," and "the immediate publication of the outlines of the Constitution."

The results of this campaign of the Radicals were, on the one hand, the formation of all sorts of secret societies, for the law of public meetings was enforced so strictly that no public political associations could be organized, and on the other the creation of a dangerous class of political rowdies called *Soshi* (Enterprising Persons). These *Soshi* were not merely ruffians whose services could be obtained for a price to perform any kind of political crime, even assassination, but they represented an unusual but quite conceivable line of cleavage in the educated classes

o

of the day. Over against the *Soshi* were the *Koshin* (Distinguished Persons), who were the men in office, the oligarchs and bureaucrats. The vast majority of the citizens, even those of the capital, had little interest in politics, and consequently stood outside of these two groups. The struggle between the ins and the outs, the *Koshin* and the *Soshi*, was the more severe because the position of the former was impregnable. From open denunciation of the oligarchy the *Soshi* were driven by the Government to secret plotting and violence. The *Koshin* were waylaid and beaten, their houses broken into and looted, and their families terrified by threats. At last the Government determined to put an end to these disturbances, and issued on December 25, 1887, the Peace Preservation Ordinance, which practically declared a state of siege in Tokyo and for seven miles in every direction from the Imperial Palace. Five hundred suspects were driven out of Tokyo, of whom many were *Soshi*, but among the number were men of position and ability like Ozaki, Hoshi, Nakajima, and Hayashi Yuzo, whose inveterate hatred of the clan system was intensified a thousand-fold by their proscription, and who during the early years of the Diet's history ably seconded the efforts of Itagaki and Okuma to overthrow the oligarchs.

In February 1888, Okuma was taken into the Cabinet as Minister of Foreign Affairs, so that the popular demand for a forward foreign policy might be satis-fied. As the year wore on and nothing was done toward revising the treaties, the politicians who had been suffered to remain in Tokyo in December 1887, with others who were exiled to the provinces, began to concert measures for bringing pressure upon the Cabinet. The agitation took two very different forms, one represented by a society called the Minken-to (Popular Power Party), the other by Goto's Daido Danketsu (Union-in-Large Party). These organizations had few of the characteristics of a political party; the former was merely a small coterie of Radicals,

The First Four Years

the latter a veritable "Cave of Adullam," to which flocked the irreconcilables from all political factions, attracted largely by the personality of Goto Shojiro. Prominent in the manifestoes of these two associations were demands for a responsible Cabinet and the immediate revision of the treaties.

As we have seen, the oligarchy paid no attention to the first of these demands—in the Constitution they had provided carefully against anything that savoured of responsible government—but Okuma was allowed to initiate a fresh project for treaty revision. Again negotiations proceeded successfully, and were almost concluded when suddenly the Cabinet deserted Okuma, and Inouye, who had returned to office in July 1888, with Ito, ousted Okuma once again from the Government.

In the history of these years immediately preceding the opening of the first Diet, the elements of greatest interest are these : the clan oligarchs were apparently firmly in power, their ranks purged of Radicals except for Mutsu and Goto ; the Radicals under the leadership of Itagaki and Okuma included Hoshi, Ozaki, Inukai, Shimada, Hatoyama, Hayashi, Komatsubara, Nakajima, and a host of able, if less conspicuous, debaters and writers. Some of them, like Itagaki, were without animus against the oligarchs and devoted to principles, but others were fired with a spirit of revenge. Okuma's hatred of Ito and Inouye was natural enough, considering what he had suffered at their hands, while Hoshi, Ozaki, Nakajima, and the others who had suffered oppression as a result of the Peace Preservation Ordinance might be pardoned if they harboured a grudge against the Government. Of all the questions which agitated the public mind in 1890, treaty revision stood out most prominently, followed, in order of their importance, by clan government, retrenchment of public expenditure, reform of the military services, increase of local autonomy in the Fu and Ken, etc. As for the first of these questions, progress toward a solution seemed hopeless, since the Radicals and oligarchs would not allow each other to benefit by the increased popularity which would accrue from successful revision. The question of clan government *versus* responsible government was impossible of compromise, while there was room for such serious differences of opinion on the other items of policy that successful adjustment was next to hopeless. The public had become so accustomed, throughout the four years immediately preceding 1890, to the noise and violence of political controversy that it was therefore little disposed to welcome a return to harmony and peace.

The process of wrecking the Constitution and the institutions it created was deliberately entered upon in 1890. Itagaki revived the Jiyuto and Okuma reestablished his connection with the Kaishinto, the two entering into negotiations the upshot of which was a temporary union of the main Opposition parties. The new combination contested the election in July 1890, and when the Diet opened in November it appeared in a solid phalanx, numbering nearly half the membership of the Lower House, to oppose the Government.

The first general election passed off with singularly little disturbance, considering the nature of the event. The electorate was composed of about half a million voters, one to every eighty of the population : that they were the substantial members of the population is certain, and the members elected should have been Conservative under any ordinary circumstances. That there was considerable interest taken in the election is shown both by the number of candidates who presented themselves, on an average three or four for every seat, and by the large proportion of the total vote polled, in some districts as high as 98 per cent. Classified according to occupation, the members of the first Diet represented a great variety of interests : agriculture, 77 ; administration, 48 ; no settled business, 36 ; law, 17 ; business, 14 ; journalism, 11 ; banking, 5, etc. Divided according to the old feudal ranks,

35 per cent. were of samurai and 65 per cent. of *heimin* (common people) origin. But most striking of all was the disparity between the rural and urban sections of the House, the former group including about 94 per cent., the latter 6 per cent., of the representatives. According to party allegiance, the Daido Danketsu claimed 60, the Jiyuto and Kaishinto 50 each ; the remaining 140 were Independents, from whose ranks, if from anywhere, the Government had to obtain its support.

The Upper House needs little comment, for during the four years under review its members played their parts faithfully and consistently as backers of the Government. The main articles of their creed were the maintenance of the Constitution and the supremacy of the oligarchy, and except for the vagaries of the two Princes, Konoye and Nijo, both members of the Sekke, that creed was never for an instant departed from. The Upper House was composed of 292 members, 146 of whom were peers of the realm, 45 representatives of the highest taxpayers in the Fu and Ken, and the remaining 101 Imperial nominees, mainly drawn from the ranks of the official class. Much solid ability and good sense were displayed in this Chamber. The most conspicuous failures were the representatives of the plutocracy. That body, insignificant in size and social position, found itself in a peculiarly difficult situation, and its members then earned for themselves the opprobrious title, which they still bear, of the " straw crows " of the Upper House. But even these failures were neither wantonly aggressive nor offensive. Ito's appointment as President of the Upper House during its first sessions undoubtedly did much to make its deliberations useful to the country and the Government.

The peculiarity of the situation which faced the first Administration under the Constitution when it met the Diet was its lack of the support of a political party, while opposed to it was a solidly organized union of politicians who had been the mainstay of the Opposition during the previous decade. Furthermore, the Administration was minus the services of two of the most trusted and influential oligarchs, Ito and Inouye. In fact, when Kuroda resigned the office of Minister President of State in October 1889 it was with the utmost difficulty that a successor could be found, for none of the members of the oligarchy were willing to head the Government during the first session of the Diet. Finally, after two months, during which Sanjo Saneyoshi, the former Daijodaijin who had been ousted by Ito in 1885, had been gazetted temporarily, Yamagata was persuaded to accept the post. With him were associated in the various Ministries Aoki, Matsukata, Oyama, Saigo, Yamada, Yoshikawa, Mutsu, and Goto. These men were influential and experienced administrators, but they belonged, as it were, to the second rank. With the exception of Mutsu, their chief qualification for their posts was that they were Satsuma and Choshu men, and all were true-blue oligarchs except Mutsu and Goto.

When the Lower House of the Diet settled down into working order, the Opposition launched its assault against the Government, which from the outset it had obviously resolved to make responsible to itself. The attack was directed against the Budget, and during the first three sessions and part of the fourth the Opposition efforts were concentrated upon that point. But the Cabinet, even without the support of a party, was so strongly entrenched on the side of finance that it could not easily be dislodged. Articles LXVII and LXXI of the Constitution made a practically impregnable defence, provided the Ministers were disposed to be defiant. By the terms of the 67th Article about three-fourths of the total annual expenditures were withdrawn from the action of the Diet, and the 71st Article provided that when the Houses had not passed the Budget the Cabinet should carry out the financial arrangements of the preceding

The First Four Years

year. In spite of these articles, the Opposition proposed a sweeping reduction amounting to some 10,000,000 yen in the estimates. The Ministers and their delegates protested that the motion was unconstitutional because it exceeded the powers of the Diet, but the Opposition remained noisily defiant, and rather than create a complete deadlock at the very outset of the Diet's history a compromise was effected, the Ministers yielding two-thirds and the Opposition one-third of their demands, and the estimates were cut by 6,500,000 yen. The session was a long one, marked by great violence of speech and continuous obstruction. The Lower House had forty-nine sittings, but accomplished little. There was, however, a great display of oratory, especially on the subjects of treaty revision and the reduction of taxation. Shimada, Ozaki, and Nakajima earned for themselves an enviable reputation as speakers and debaters. But on the whole the first session gave little comfort to the Administration, while it immensely strengthened the determination of the party men to persist in their tactics. Both sides braced themselves, as the Diet closed, for the serious struggle which was to ensue when the House met again toward the end of the year 1891.

But before it reassembled, new capital had been furnished the Opposition. To begin with, Yamagata, the Minister President, resigned, and was succeeded by Matsukata, the Finance Minister. The regularity with which the chief office in the Cabinet passed back and forth between Satsuma and Choshu—from 1885 to 1891 the order of succession being Ito, Kuroda, Yamagata, and Matsukata—was not lost sight of by the Opposition. Then on May 11 an insane policeman attempted to assassinate the Russian Czarevitch, at that time on a tour of Japan. Further, in October a disastrous earthquake devastated the province of Gifu, and tidal waves destroyed an immense amount of property in Toyama and Fukuoka. The consequence of the assault upon the Czarevitch was a series of harshly repressive police regulations, and of the natural calamities very considerable additions to the estimates, for the relief of the sufferers. As soon as the Diet opened on November 27 an acrimonious dispute arose over the means adopted by the Government to preserve the peace, the Opposition maintaining, with reason, that it was unnecessary to institute a reign of terror among the people because one crazy Government official had disgraced the nation by attempting the life of the heir to the Russian throne. To the Government's appeals for the sufferers in the stricken districts the Opposition paid no attention whatever. From this ominous beginning matters in the Diet grew rapidly worse. The Budget Committee recommended a reduction of 8,000,000 yen in the estimates, totally disregarding the provisions of the Constitution with regard to fixed expenditures. Upon every other matter brought into the House orators poured out floods of oratory or torrents of abuse. Speeches two hours long were a common occurrence, and they resulted in the total cessation of business. Finally, the Government's patience was exhausted, and it recommended that the Emperor should dissolve the Diet, which was accordingly done on December 25, 1891.

The members of the Opposition regarded the dissolution as a triumph. With the Government obstructed at every turn and compelled to fall back on the constitutional provision for the reapplication of the Budget of the previous year, the Opposition could claim that, save for the safeguards inserted into the Constitution by the oligarchy, it was at their mercy. Okuma, as was his wont, was interviewed by the Press, and stated that in general the policy of the Opposition was dictated by hostility toward a Government composed of Sat-Cho oligarchs : the monopoly of the administrative and executive offices by the members of the two clans was intolerable and must be destroyed. But aside from their general policy of obstruction, the Opposition was opposed to the financial and commercial

The First Four Years

policy of the Government, and especially to the prevailing corruption and favouritism. Okuma openly charged Inouye with venality in promoting the interests of the Mitsui family, and in a vague way affirmed that the various members of the Administration derived large sums from their connection with and the protection they afforded to other commercial houses. Needless to say, Okuma made no mention of, nor were his strictures upon Inouye modified in the slightest degree by, the fact that he himself during his term of office had served the interests of the great Mitsu Bishi Company, owned by the Iwasaki family. On the constructive side, the main items of the Opposition's policy, according to the same speaker, were the introduction of party Cabinets and the reduction of the land tax.

The election which followed the dissolution was held in February 1892, and proved very different from the orderly contest of 1890. The Government, convinced by its experience during the past year that official prestige and constitutional limitations carried no weight with the Lower House, determined to elect men who could be formed into an Administration party. With this end in view, candidates were put up in each district and the local Governors instructed to see that they were returned. This action was worthy of Matsukata, the new Minister President, as a member of the Satsuma clan—noted through all its history for its overbearing arrogance and disregard for the rights and interests of the nation—but the result was disastrous. Though every device known to the Government was brought into action—police power, repressive laws, bribery, intimidation, and violence—only ninety-five candidates of the official party were elected. On the other hand, the political feeling in the constituencies ran so high that in many of the prefectures violent clashes occurred. In Kagoshima, Shiga, Saga, and Ishikawa Kens there was much disorder, while in Kochi, Itagaki's native province, there were numerous pitched battles, with many killed and wounded. For the whole country the casualty lists totalled 25 killed and 388 injured. The disgrace of these shameful affairs rested directly upon Shinagawa, the Home Minister, and he resigned his office in March in response to the pressure of public opinion. For a very different reason Mutsu left the Cabinet at the same time, as a protest against the election methods of his colleagues. But apart from these results, which in themselves were not serious, for Matsukata took over the Home Office and Kono Hironaka was appointed to the Department of Agriculture and Commerce, the Government almost completely forfeited public confidence, and faced the Diet in May a discredited but defiant oligarchy.

The session began on May 6 and ended on June 14. The Budget of the previous year had been brought into force, and thus the most contentious legislation of any session was lacking. The only financial measure to be brought forward was a small supplementary Budget amounting to 2,750,000 yen. On this, however, the Lower House determined to exercise its assumed prerogatives, and struck out two of the items, the appropriations for shipbuilding and the study of earthquakes. In this abbreviated form the supplementary Budget was sent to the Upper House, which reinserted the items and sent the Bill back to the Representatives. A deadlock ensued, neither House being willing to compromise. Finally, it was decided to refer the question of the relative powers of the two Houses in the matter of finance Bills to the Emperor, who, after consulting the Privy Council, returned the following authoritative reply, fully recognizing the competence of the Upper Chamber to deal with questions of finance :—

" With regard to the right of consent to the Budget vested in the House of Peers and Representatives respectively, neither House is superior or inferior to the other except in one particular that, according to the 65th Article of the Constitution, the Lower House receives the Budget from the Government before

The First Four Years

the Upper. Therefore the House which deliberates subsequently is in no respect bound by the decisions of the House which deliberates previously, and it consequently follows that the restoration of any items which may have been excised by the House previously deliberating falls strictly within the right of revision vested in the House subsequently deliberating. The House subsequently deliberating has only to employ the method indicated by the Law of the Houses, namely, to seek the concurrence of the House previously deliberating."

This pronouncement had the effect of bringing about a conference of the two Houses, at which a compromise was agreed upon, one of the objectionable items being dropped, the other included. In this form the supplementary Budget became law. The result of this reference to the sovereign was not only to obtain a solution of the immediate difficulty but to destroy also the claim of the Representatives to exclusive jurisdiction over finance. It led also to the establishment upon a firmer footing of the Government's constitutional powers as defined in Articles LXVII and LXXI.

Though defeated, or at least only half victorious in its campaign upon the supplementary estimates, the Opposition found other grounds for an attack upon the Ministry in connection with the official interference in the elections. A strongly worded Address to the Throne on the subject was thrown out, after a violent debate, by only three votes in a House of 289. The failure of this effort to unseat the Cabinet was not due to any doubts in the minds of the members as to the justness of their accusation, but to unwillingness to harass the sovereign unduly with purely political and partisan questions, for when a representation to the Government upon the same subject was introduced it passed by a large majority. In part, the wording of the representation was as follows : " The Cabinet Ministers should consider their position, and, accepting their responsibility, should decide upon suitable measures. Otherwise the fundamental principle of representative government will be destroyed."

This plain-spoken invitation to resign and make room for a party Cabinet was ignored by the Government, except for an address which the Prime Minister made during the debate, in which he said : " Even supposing this representation be passed, I can assure you that the Ministers of this Empire do not propose lightly to resign their posts on account of such a careless and crude decision." During the remainder of this stormy session, brief as it was, the Government was attacked with such violence, not only in the House but outside of it, that shortly after the prorogation of the Diet the Matsukata Cabinet resigned, on August 4th.

Seldom, even in the history of the Japanese Diet, has there been a more unpopular Government than Matsukata's first Cabinet. Ordinarily, all Japanese Cabinets are unpopular, for the simple reason that they are not party Cabinets. But as for that accusation against a Ministry, it can always be refuted by saying that in the Japanese polity it was provided that the Emperor, and not the people, should exercise the right of choosing the Cabinet Ministers. This particular Cabinet, however, had earned the hatred of the populace by its conduct of the election of February 1892, and it would be difficult to say whether the people objected more to the manifest unfairness of using local officials and the police for the purpose of defeating the Opposition candidates or to the violence which resulted in a long list of killed and wounded on election day. In the estimation of the party politicians, the first two years of the Diet were almost completely successful. Though the principle of party government had not been recognized, it had been made fairly obvious that independent Cabinets would not run the Diet nor conduct the business of the Government in a satisfactory manner. Two champions of the oligarchy, Yamagata and Matsukata, had been driven

The First Four Years

from power, and the Opposition had little doubt that even when Ito and Inouye entered the lists the contest would end in their defeat and responsible government be realized. How completely Itagaki's and Okuma's expectations in the latter respect were disappointed may perhaps be best seen by the fact that twenty-two years later, in 1914, Okuma as Prime Minister found himself associated in the Ministry with such men as Oura, Saito, and other second-generation oligarchs, and his Cabinet overshadowed by Yamagata, Inouye, and Matsukata, the all-powerful Elder Statesmen.

In August 1892 Ito assumed the post of Minister President and the grave responsibility of making the system of government which he had imported from Prussia in 1885 and formulated in 1889 serve the purposes of the Japanese Empire. That Ito had confidence in his power to make the machine run smoothly was proved by his neglecting to take any section of the Opposition into his confidence and thus gain its support. Parties and party politics were deliberately avoided. On the contrary, he took into the Cabinet his old associate Inouye as Minister of the Interior, and Mutsu he secured for the Foreign Office. His other colleagues were mainly the Satsuma and Choshu oligarchs, Watanabe, Oyama, Nirei, Yamagata, Kono, Goto, and Kuroda. From the first, strenuous efforts were made to placate public sentiment. Inouye took up the question of undue interference in the elections of February, and after investigating the charges against the local Governors, dismissed eleven of the worst offenders. But the members of the Diet were not to be put off by any such measures, though the outside public might be ; their objection to the new Cabinet was rooted in the clan system, which had not been changed with the transfer of leadership from Matsukata to Ito. The temper of the Opposition was indicated by an ominous circumstance which occurred immediately after the opening of the session on November 25. In the absence of the Prime Minister, owing to illness, Inouye outlined before the Lower House the policy of the Government in an address which was distinctly friendly in tone, but a bitter attack was made upon him by some of the most fluent speakers of the House, merely because the Minister had *read*, not spoken, his address. From this purely factious insolence the attack shifted back to the old subject of interference with the elections, and from that to the financial measures of the year.

The Lower House carried an amendment to the estimates which reduced the ordinary expenditures by some 8,000,000 yen, and elided completely an item in the extraordinary expenditures providing 3,333,000 yen as the first annual instalment of a fund for the building of warships. The Ministers rejected both amendments, and thereupon the House carried by a vote of 181 to 103 an Address to the Throne and adjourned its sittings for eighteen days. This occurred on February 7. Just three days later the House was summoned to hear an Imperial rescript, and the upshot of the affair was the withdrawal of the objection of the Lower House to the Budget. How this result was achieved by Ito will repay closer investigation, since it displays some of the striking peculiarities of the Japanese system of government.

The Address to the Throne adopted by the Lower House on February 7 set forth the contentions of the Opposition. The following are the most important passages :—

" Humble reflection leads your Majesty's servants to conclude that the chief object of representative government is to promote concord between high and low, and to secure their co-operation in aid of the State. Hence there can be no profounder or greater desideratum than that the Legislature and the Administration should occupy toward each other attitudes of thorough sincerity, and should achieve the reality of harmonious co-operation. But ever since the opening of the Diet, the Legislature and the Administration

have been wanting in concord, all their projects have
been impeded, all their capabilities marred, so that
in the sequel they have failed to secure for the country
the benefits of progressive development in concert with
the advance of the age. Your Majesty's servants
acknowledge that the insufficiency of their own zeal
is in part responsible for these things, but they believe
that the chief cause is to be sought in the Cabinet's
failure to discharge its functions. If your Majesty's
servants have sought to reduce administrative expenditures and to economize the public outlay, it is because
they desire to reform the extravagant abuses of the
Government and to lighten the burdens of the people.
This House, when the Budget of the 26th year of
Meiji (1893) was submitted to it, subjected it
to the closest scrutiny, took careful count of the
nation's financial capacity, and with due regard to the
various administrative requirements introduced reductions of expenditure. With regard to the items of
Fixed Expenditures falling under the provision of
the 67th Article of the Constitution, the Government's concurrence was sought, in accordance with
the Constitution, no less than three times, but the
Government arbitrarily withheld its consent. Moreover, not only did it offer no statement of its reasons
or detailed explanation of the items to which it took
exception, but also it went so far as to declare positively that it could not reduce so much as one sen of
the amount. Thereupon this House suspended its
sittings for five days, and asked the Government to
reconsider the matter ; but the Government firmly
persisted in its former declaration and declined to pay
attention to the House's representation. Had the
Government, when announcing its dissent with reference
to the expenditure falling under the provisions of the
67th Article of the Constitution, given a detailed
statement of the various items and a clear explanation of reasons, it would have been acting in conformity
with the moral duty of statesmen under representative

institutions, and would also have adopted the path leading to harmonious co-operation. But to the deep regret of your Majesty's servants, the Cabinet did not adopt any such course. Further, with regard to the appropriations for building men-of-war, although the Diet rejected them, the Government declared its positive intention of devising some means of carrying out its policy within the limits prescribed by the Constitution. Your Majesty's servants, astonished at the impropriety of this declaration, immediately sought an explanation, but obtained no answer."

It took the Government less than three days to frame an answer to this bill of accusations, and by putting its answer in the form of an Imperial message it commanded a hearing in the Lower House. After a few preliminary paragraphs containing the usual hackneyed statements about the virtues of the Imperial Ancestors, the necessity of exhibiting the glories of the Empire before foreign nations, and the fulfilment of the Imperial determination to advance cautiously toward the establishment of representative government, the document in question struck at the root of the immediate difficulty in the following manner :—

" The items of expenditure referred to in the 67th Article of the Constitution are protected by the clear text of the Article, and cannot properly become a ground of dispute. Hereby We specially direct Our Ministers to bring all sections of the administration into good order, and, having due regard to essentials, to take such deliberate and careful counsel as shall secure freedom from error, under Our direction.

" With regard to the matter of national defences, a single day's neglect may involve a century's regret. We shall economize the expenditures of the Household, and shall contribute, during the space of six years, a sum of three hundred thousand yen annually. We direct Our military and civil officials, except in cases where special circumstances interfere, to contribute one-tenth of their salaries during the same period, which

sums shall be devoted to supplement the fund for
building men-of-war.

"We regard Our Cabinet and Our Diet as the
machinery of constitutional government, and We trust
that each, being careful to observe the due limitations
of its powers, will follow the route of harmonious
co-operation, so as to assist Us in this great undertaking, and continue to secure the beauty of successful
achievement."

From the first of the paragraphs quoted from the
Imperial rescript, an authoritative interpretation of the
meaning of the 67th Article was obtained, just as in
the previous year the question of the relative competence
of the two Houses of the Diet in financial legislation
was settled by a similar Imperial decision. While the
Diet was by no means blind to the device by which
there had been foisted on it the Government's own
reading of the Constitution, yet such was the extraordinary reverence in which the sovereign was held
that even the most outspoken Radical was debarred
from vocal dissent. As, however, the reverence of the
Japanese for their sovereign is largely the outcome
of his aloofness from the practical administration of
the affairs of state, the Government cannot safely continue to claim his authority for its measures without
gradually undermining the very power to the protection
of which it appeals.

The third of the paragraphs quoted from the Imperial
rescript reminded both the Diet and the Cabinet of
the necessity of following the "route of harmonious
co-operation," and thus furnished the two parties to
the dispute with a basis for mutual recrimination in
the subsequent sessions of the Diet. But the most
amazing of the three paragraphs was certainly the
second. It imposed as a special levy an income tax of
10 per cent. upon all officials, civil and military,
members of the Diet as well as of the bureaucracy.
Ito's *coup de main* provided not only for the success
of his naval expansion programme, but compelled the

members of the Opposition party itself to contribute to the fund. Apart from this really amusing side, the levy involved actual hardships for the official class. The Imperial Household with its immense resources could well afford the deduction of a paltry three hundred thousand yen a year—10 per cent. of the civil list—but the case was very different with the minor official struggling along on twenty or even ten yen a month. However, the very next year, during the war with China, the Diet, in a fervour of patriotism, voted 20,000,000 yen to the Imperial estates, as well as rewards for the officers of the Army and Navy.

As a result of the Minister President's adroit stroke of February 10, the Lower House patched up a compromise with the Cabinet, accepting a reduction of the ordinary expenditures amounting to 2,600,000 yen in lieu of its demand for 8,000,000, and the session closed after running its normal life of three months without any further untoward incident.

But the calm which brooded over the Diet during its closing sittings was merely that of a spell ; the demon of obstruction had been temporarily exorcised, but his place was shortly to be occupied by seven other devils, so that the last state of the Opposition was worse than the first. In this frame of mind the Diet met the Administration in November for the session of 1893-4. Ito was well aware of the attitude of his badly worsted opponents, and he had taken measures during the summer to strengthen the Government. An extensive programme for retrenchment of administrative expenses was carried out, over three thousand officials were dismissed, and by this and other means a saving of 1,700,000 yen was effected. By these measures he sought to dull the edge of the campaign against the extravagance of the Government. But he went further, for by arrangement with Itagaki and the Jiyuto he secured the support of that party in the Lower House, while by the same action he offended the Peers : to the Upper House any Cabinet was tainted as soon as it came to an agreement with any political party.

With these preparations, the Cabinet entered upon what was to prove a short and lively session of the Diet. The Lower House sat but twenty days, and never got as far as the discussion of the Budget, for a dissolution edict was issued on December 30.

The explanation of what occurred is to be found in Okuma's movements. His opportunity for revenge on Ito and Inouye had come, and he determined to improve it at all costs ; in this he was ably seconded by his brilliant coterie of young politicians. The first week was occupied by an attack on one of the Jiyuto leaders, Hoshi Toru, the President of the Lower House. Hoshi had been appointed in the previous year to the office, and by the terms of the Law of the Houses (Articles III and VIII) his tenure coincided with the life of the Diet, but between the close of the first and the opening of the second sessions Hoshi and the Jiyuto had swung over from the Opposition to support of the Government. This was the ground of his offence in the eyes of the Kaishinto. After the defection of the Jiyuto, Okuma, in order to preserve the Opposition majority, had entered into an agreement with the National Unionists (Kokumin-Kyokai), a party presided over by Shinagawa, a Choshu clansman, the very man who as Minister of Home Affairs, under Matsukata's direction, had been responsible for the interference of the local Governors in the election of February 1892, and who had subsequently been made the scapegoat of the Ministry. By means of this strange combination, held together only by resentment against the oligarchy, Hoshi was finally expelled from the House, after several days of confusion and uproar. The language of that week in the Diet was beyond description, culminating in the application to Hoshi of the epithet—one of the worst known to the Japanese—the Government's "beast," by a Kaishinto member. Hoshi was by no means a saint, it is true, but he afterward became one of the most influential personalities of modern Japan, brilliant, but it must be admitted utterly unscrupulous also. He was assassinated in July 1901, in the very zenith of his power.

Having driven Hoshi from the House, the Opposition then turned upon the Cabinet. Goto, the Minister of Agriculture and Commerce, and his Vice-Minister Saito were accused of improper relations with certain members of the Stock Exchange, and an Address to the Throne upon the subject of official discipline was carried. This caused Ito to resign, but the Emperor's reply to the address of the Lower House—that is, the reply of the oligarchy in the Privy Council—was to the effect that "the appointment or removal of Ministers of State is absolutely at the will of the sovereign, and no interference is allowed in this matter." Ito was at the same time bidden to resume his duties. Then the Opposition directed its attention to the subject of treaty revision, and proposed an Address to the Throne demanding a strict enforcement of the terms of the treaties against the foreigners resident in Japan as a means of forcibly securing from the Powers the desired changes. In formulating this address the Kaishinto found itself hand-in-glove with the followers of Oi Kentaro, a notorious *Soshi* who in 1889 had been mainly responsible for the popular hostility toward Okuma's revision proposals. It was indeed a strange crew —Kaishinto, Kokumin Kyokai and Oi Kentaro's near-*soshi*—which now fathered the "strict enforcement" plan for securing the revision of the treaties. The Cabinet, however, would not yield ; in fact, as afterwards came out, the Government had already almost completed the revision of the treaty with Great Britain, and was in no mind to have its work upset by the Lower House. Before the address could be carried, an Imperial order suspending the sittings for ten days was brought down on December 19. When the House met again on the 29th, Mutsu, the Foreign Minister, was put up to explain the Government's objections

The First Four Years

to the address. He denied that a policy of " strict enforcement " would secure revision, but on the contrary asserted that a successful issue of the project depended upon a display by Japan of those characteristics of enlightenment and justice which were demanded of all aspirants to the comity of nations, and he warned the House in the name of the Government that " we shall not hesitate to adopt any measure for that purpose."

When Mutsu descended from the rostrum, and before any further action could be taken, the President of the House announced the receipt of a second Imperial message postponing the sittings for a further term of fourteen days, and on December 30 the Diet was dissolved.

The General Election which followed in March 1894 was fought out on the issue of " strict enforcement," and the Opposition returned with a reduced majority. The Government did not interfere with the conduct of the election further than to apply the provisions of the Press Law and the Law of Public Meetings and Associations with the utmost severity. Scenes of great violence were enacted in Tochigi Ken, where Hoshi Toru was contesting a seat with a candidate put up by the Government : the casualty list included 1 killed and 117 wounded in Tochigi alone, the rest of the country adding to the toll only 36 wounded. The session opened on May 15, 1894, and on June 2 a dissolution was decreed by the Emperor. The history of this turbulent Diet need not be recounted, for in all essentials it was like its predecessor. The Government was impeached for its action in dissolving the Diet in December, and on May 30 an Address to the Throne was carried, in which the Diet complained, in no measured terms, that the Ministers neglected both reforms at home and national interests abroad. The Government's action in this crisis was at once dramatic and drastic. The Emperor refused to receive the address, and consequently the President of the Lower

House left it with the Household Department. On the following day, June 2, the President was summoned to the Palace and received a verbal message from the Emperor, through the Household Minister, which he reported immediately to the Diet. The message ran : " We shall not adopt the views contained in the address presented by the House of Representatives. A written communication will not be made with reference to the address." After presenting the message the President announced the receipt of an Imperial rescript, which he proceeded to read : " We, in accordance with the 7th Article of the Constitution, hereby dissolve the House of Representatives."

This third dissolution for the moment paralysed the Opposition. Ito's action was not entirely unexpected, and on the record of his opponents' factious and irresponsible conduct it was amply deserved. One of the Opposition papers came out in mourning, and another in half-inch type announced the dissolution.

Before the Opposition had quite recovered their breath, and just as they were beginning to launch a campaign for the adoption of responsible government, the Chino-Japanese War broke out and put an end for the time being to all domestic political squabbles.

CHAPTER X

THE CHINO-JAPANESE WAR

THE declaration of war checked all partisan political activities in Japan. A forward foreign policy had been at last adopted, and the Kaishinto agitation on that score ceased. The "strict enforcement" party had the wind taken out of its sails by the revision of the treaty with Great Britain. No grounds of opposition remained except "responsible Cabinets" and purely domestic questions of administrative and financial reform, and during a time of war such matters attract little or no attention. Hence it was that the General Election in July was as quiet as that held four years previously, and in the brief session of the Diet convoked in October 1894 at Hiroshima, the war capital, each section of the Lower House vied with the others in enthusiastic loyalty to the Emperor and the Government. Scarcely a murmur against the Cabinet was raised. A huge special Budget appropriating 150,000,000 yen was voted unanimously ; a loan of 3,000,000 yen to the Korean Government was sanctioned ; 20,000,000 yen were added to the Imperial estates, and thanks and rewards were showered upon the Army and Navy. Only one anxiety seemed to disturb the enthusiastic representatives of the people—lest the Cabinet should call a halt before Peking was occupied by their victorious troops and the Chinese Empire dismembered, or at least despoiled of its Manchu territories.

The clan oligarchy had played its trump card, and for the time being at least the game was won. During four years and a half, after the Diet had begun its sessions, the Government had struggled in vain against the Opposition. One after another of the clan oligarchs had assumed the responsibility of administration, not one of them with the slightest degree of success. Yamagata had adopted an attitude of indifference to the popular party in the Diet, Matsukata had tried to crush it ; Ito had coquetted with the Jiyuto, and thereby driven into opposition some of the previously loyal Government supporters among the Representatives and antagonized the Upper House as well. It is true that the oligarchy had provided against just such opposition as it encountered, by making the Constitution a veritable bulwark against popular government. The power of appointment and dismissal of Cabinet Ministers, by the 10th Article of the Constitution, was conferred upon the Emperor ; the 55th Article made the Cabinet independent of the Diet ; the 67th and 71st Articles reserved for the Government a sufficient control over finance. But, nevertheless, the Opposition, if it could not have its way, could at least prevent the Government from following its own course, with the result that all progress was stayed, and a veritable deadlock ensued. Development politically and economically was impossible, and the time was rapidly approaching when the abrogation or revision of the Constitution would be demanded. Just as the Chinese republic has in recent years been under the necessity of turning back to a dictatorship, or as Jamaica had its representative assembly taken away, so Japan in 1894 seemed to have reached a point from which further progress could be made only by some radical changes in her political institutions. The régime of *constitutional monarchy* had broken down. The clan oligarchy's arrangement for the government of the country had failed because it had yielded the *right of consent* to the Representatives of the people and withheld substantive powers over the Administration. The old dualism of the Stuart period or of the reign of George III was repeated in Japan, in spite of the plain teachings of

The Chino-Japanese War

English history. Ito and his colleagues, with the apparently successful experiences of Bismarck in their minds, disregarded the lessons of England's experience in the seventeenth and eighteenth centuries, and fastened upon their country a discredited and worn-out polity which had been discarded by the most advanced nations of the West. The immediate failure in Japan of the system adopted from Germany was due to the differences between Bismarck and Ito, between the Meiji Tenno and William II of Germany.

Whatever may be said of Ito's statesmanlike qualities previous to 1885, he will go down in Japanese history as a man of distinctly second-rate ability. He will be praised for the tenacity with which he upheld in the early years of Meiji a policy of domestic reform and reconstruction, but will be damned by the Constitution of 1889, as well as by his action in 1894 in distracting the attention of the nation from the problems of political progress by bringing on the war with China. It is true that he subsequently endeavoured to rehabilitate himself by his temperate policy in Korea after the Russo-Japanese War, but it was then too late. The Japanese had been swept into a militarist career in 1894, and it was ruled by the military party from that time onward ; Ito and his followers were unable to stem the tide of chauvinism, as he, Iwakura, Kido, and Okubo had done in 1873. By his tragic end at Harbin in 1909 he paid the price of his error in 1894.

The China War revived the militarism which had lain dormant since 1873. The ideas and teachings of Yoshida Shoin—that fiery patriot who had appeared in Choshu in the closing days of the Tokugawa régime—were now brought to light again. His programme, as we have already pointed out, included the acquisition of the Kurile Islands, Saghalien, Kamtchatka, Formosa, Korea, Manchuria, and large parts of Eastern Siberia—in fact, the expansion of the Japanese Empire into a great continental Asiatic Power. With this prospect, as gratifying to the vanity of the Japanese nation as any that Bismarck had ever held out to Prussia, Ito consented to quiet the political dissensions of the time. The effect was magical. The voices of the persistent critics of the Government were stilled, the hackneyed Opposition demands for responsible Cabinets, for the destruction of the clans, for financial and administrative reforms, gave place to the cry " On to Peking." Nothing less than the conquest of China, it appeared, would appease the appetite of the people for expansion. So unlimited were the pretensions of the chauvinists that when peace came, after less than a year of strife, the fruits of victory seemed all too few, and the popular acclaim of Ito's Government turned to revilings.

The immediate cause of the war was China's breach of the Tientsin Treaty of 1885. According to the terms of that agreement, both China and Japan had acknowledged the independence of Korea, and had exchanged mutual engagements to the effect that each should notify the other before sending troops into Korea for any purpose whatever. But in the spring of 1894, at the request of the Korean Court, China dispatched an expeditionary force to quell an insurrection which had arisen in the northern provinces. No notification was sent to Japan, and straightway the Japanese Government took steps to force on a war. There was a plain *casus belli* in the Chinese action, and Ito saw fit to use it as a means of escape from the *impasse* of domestic politics.

The progress of the war, on both land and water, was uniformly successful. The Chinese fleet, in spite of its superiority in armament, was swept from the sea, and the two expeditionary forces under Yamagata and Oyama cleared Korea and the Liaotung Peninsula of Chinese troops. At this point the Chinese Government sought peace, and sent Li Hung Chang to Japan as its plenipotentiary. By the Treaty of Shimonoseki, which resulted from the negotiations, the Japanese received assurances as to the status of Korea, an indemnity of 200,000,000 Kuping taels (305,717,000 yen), the island of Formosa, and the Liaotung. This latter grant, on the mainland of Asia, was only ceded by Li after he knew positively that Germany, France, and Russia would intervene and secure its retrocession to China. When this demand by the European coalition was made and the Japanese Government yielded, the amount of the indemnity was increased by 30,000,000 taels.

The terms of the treaty of peace were most unpopular in Japan. A plot was discovered against Ito's life in August, and in the same month Matsukata resigned his office as Finance Minister because he declared the amount of the indemnity insufficient. Mutsu, the Minister of Foreign Affairs, had withdrawn in June rather than face the storm which was certain to arise over the " surrender " involved in handing back the Liaotung to China. But the Government held the people firmly in hand. After an attempt on the life of the Chinese plenipotentiary—a murderous assault by some Japanese malcontents during the progress of the negotiations at Shimonoseki, not so much in protest against Li's terms as the fact that arrangements were being made to conclude peace before the Japanese troops had entered Peking—repressive measures had been at once applied. The Opposition journals were suspended, not on scores but hundreds of occasions ; the politicians who attempted to foment disturbances at political meetings were ruthlessly gagged and shadowed by the police. Ito, who had been the idol of the nation in October of the previous year, became the most unpopular public man in the Empire by the middle of 1895. The change in public sentiment must be explained solely on the grounds of the treaty of peace. What made that convention so distasteful to the Japanese was the disparity between the hopes raised in 1894 and their incomplete fulfilment at the end of the war. The arms of Japan had been uniformly successful, China had been compelled to sue for terms, then why let her off so leniently? was the popular logic. Ito and his Government, however, knew what the people did not, and what they did not dare to make public—that a coalition of three Great European Powers had been formed for the purpose of preventing the dismemberment of China by Japan. In the face of such a combination it was impossible to proceed —in fact, impossible to get a foothold in Asia.

If Li Hung Chang may be accused, as he often has been, of being misled by the domestic quarrels of Japanese politicians into regarding Japan as a negligible military power in Asia, if he mistakenly thought the time had arrived for reviving the ancient Chinese suzerainty over Korea which he had given up ten years previously, so, too, Ito and the Japanese Government, confident of their ability to conquer the Chinese, had also been mistaken in completely miscalculating the attitude of Europe toward China. Russia and France, at any rate, while not committed to the policy of preserving the integrity of China, had no intention of silently looking on while Japan proceeded to strip the Middle Kingdom of its northern provinces and entrench itself in Port Arthur, whence it could dominate the great province of Chili. Russia had ambitions in the Far East which precluded any such outcome of the war, and it was the influence of Russia, with that of her ally and of her German neighbour, which ousted the Japanese from Port Arthur in 1895. It was Russian pressure also that sent Li to Shimonoseki, and it was by Russian collusion that the Liaotung was originally ceded, partly that peace might be concluded, but largely for the purpose of providing the bitter pill which was subsequently to be forced down the Japanese Government's throat. If Ito knew any of these things, his policy did not indicate it. The terms of peace had not only soured and embittered the people and destroyed Ito's popularity, but had brought Japan face to face with Europe, especially Russia, in China.

The Chino-Japanese War

Financially, the war was a failure ; instead of improving, it demoralized the Government's fiscal arrangements. The actual cost of the various campaigns had been 225,000,000 yen, and though these expenses were more than reimbursed by the indemnity, the demands of the military services increased'; especially after the military party realized that a conflict later with Russia was inevitable did the outlays for armaments become so swollen that the whole of the Chinese indemnity would not have sufficed to liquidate the Government's new liabilities. The result was increased taxation, a policy which provided an opportunity of which the Opposition politicians were only too eager to make use.

Not only did the *post-bellum* programme lead ultimately to a revolution of the system of taxation ; its immediate result was a speculative boom, accompanied by a rise of prices, a temporary appearance of great prosperity, and finally a collapse. In the space of little more than a year the national finances were in disorder ; the elaborate programme of 1895 had to be readjusted and new sources of taxation tapped at the very time when the severest effects of the exploded boom were being experienced.

Politically, the war resulted not only in complete cessation of constitutional development, if the unseemly squabbling of the first four years of the parliamentary régime may be dignified by such an epithet, but it also gave the oligarchy the opportunity of acquiring new sources of power over the popular parties. The measures adopted by the clan statesmen were of the most disingenuous character. Against the oligarchs, who had entrenched themselves firmly behind the Constitution, as we have pointed out, no action of a strictly legal nature could be taken by the Opposition, with any reasonable prospect of successfully accomplishing the downfall of the Sat-Cho combination. Revolution was likewise out of the question, for the nature of the monarchy precluded any such eventuality. But

mere obstruction by the Opposition had served to destroy one Ministry after another, and Okuma was not likely to have overlooked the significance of the events of the Diet's history. If the Government was strong enough to stay in, it was at the same time powerless to carry out its own plans without the consent of the Representatives. The safety of the oligarchy lay in preserving its hold on the administrative offices, and yet that very monopoly of power was dangerous as well as futile. Some device was therefore necessary by which the clans could be strengthened in the popular estimation, but not weakened *vis-à-vis* the Opposition. It is manifestly impossible to thrust the Emperor constantly into the party arena without destroying his prestige, and seeking shelter behind the provisions of the Constitution must inevitably lead to a demand for the revision of that instrument. The simplest way out of the dilemma, as it appears to an outsider, would have been to yield the reins of office to the political parties. But such a course would have been unconstitutional, and, moreover, would only have transferred the hostility to the Cabinet from the Lower House to the Upper, for the Peers were more strongly opposed to party government than were the oligarchs themselves. At least, until a majority of the Peers could be brought to accept the principle of responsible government, such a simple expedient was impracticable, even if the constitutional point might be ignored.

The oligarchy's opportunity arrived when, as a result of the war, Japan became the possessor of colonies— Formosa and the Liaotung. Colonial government was a subject of which the people were ignorant, and the appointment of colonial Governors not a matter in which they were interested, so, unobtrusively, the Privy Council, under Yamagata's presidency, formulated certain rules for the appointment of Governors of colonies, and attached to the list of the offices those of the Department of the Army and Navy. As Formosa refused to be detached from China—or rather,

handed over to Japan—and set up as a republic on its
own account, a military occupation of the island became
necessary. Under such circumstances nothing was more
natural than that the Governor-General should be a
high officer of the Army or Navy in active service.
Similarly, the nation in its rampant chauvinistic mood
felt no inclination to dispute the propriety of having
high officers on the active service list of the Army
and Navy as Ministers of the Military Departments
of the Administration.

From the point of view of the militarist faction in
the Administration, the importance of these regulations
was that they brought under its control Formosa and
the various parts of the continent of Asia which were
about to be ceded by China to Japan. As more territory was acquired, each additional piece could be used
as a base for further encroachment. But that phase of
the subject does not interest us so much at present as
do the consequences for responsible government of the
regulations, in so far as they applied to appointments to
the Departments of the Army and Navy. So long as
a Lieutenant-General or some higher officer in active
service held the chief post in the War Office would
the General Staff be in control of that department,
and similarly with the Navy. Each Minister President
of State in the future would be under the necessity of
applying to the General Staff and the Supreme Naval
Board for officers to complete his Cabinet. Arrangements could then be made by the military party for
the support of its policy by the Cabinet. If the Prime
Minister refused to comply, then no officers could be
obtained to head the military departments and no
Cabinet could be formed, or if a Cabinet, once formed,
were unwilling or unable to carry out its covenant with
the Army and Navy, the Administration could be
destroyed by simply ordering the resignation of the
Ministers of those services. As Satsuma and Choshu
men, even if they did not completely monopolize the
high offices in the two military services, constituted

a majority of the members of the General Staff and the Supreme Naval Board, the oligarchy was invincible. With this regulation in force, the Sat-Cho combination, in response to popular demands, could well afford to allow party politicians to hold Cabinet offices, and, in fact, create what appeared to be a party Cabinet, and yet control the policy of the latter through the two non-party members, the Ministers of the Army and Navy.

As time went on, a steadily increasing proportion of party men has been found in the successive Cabinets. Itagaki as Home Minister in 1896, Okuma as Foreign Minister in 1897, and the Okuma-Itagaki Administration of 1898 are examples of the process. But, whatever the outward appearances, no Cabinet has ever been free from the control of the Sat-Cho oligarchy— a control provided for in the Constitution and strengthened by the regulations for the appointment to high offices which date from the Chino-Japanese War.

As a result of that war, Japan emerged as a nation distinct from the general welter of Orientals. Western nations acknowledged that a Power on a level with themselves had arisen in the Far East, and recognized the fact that the Japanese could no longer be regarded as belonging to the group in which they included indiscriminately Chinese, Siamese, Tibetans, Indians, Turks, *et al.* They were a nation apart. Both by her military prowess and her careful adherence to all the principles of humanity in time of war [1] Japan had raised herself to the rank of a great nation.

The first result of her changed status was the revision of the treaties, though it must in fairness be said that the British Treaty was revised before the war broke out. According to the terms of this new treaty with Great Britain, which formed a model for nearly all

[1] The massacre of the Chinese coolies at Port Arthur has been cited as an atrocity, and it undoubtedly was, but the conduct of the Japanese on that occasion may be partly excused by the nature of the provocation under which they acted—the finding of many of their own wounded with their throats cut, or otherwise mutilated.

the others, extra-territorial privileges were given up by Great Britain, and the right of mixed residence and freedom to travel anywhere in the Empire were accorded to British subjects. These provisions did not, however, come into force immediately. It was stipulated that after five years, provided the Japanese Government gave one year's notice of its desire, extra-territoriality was to be abolished. The reason for this delay, and for the still more curious provision that Japan should give one year's notice of its desire to bring the revision into force, was to give the Japanese Government time to get its new codes compiled and enacted into law. As it turned out, the five years were barely sufficient for the completion of the task and the year's notice that it had been accomplished. Inouye's and Okuma's revision projects had been wrecked by popular opposition, and the members of the Lower House of the Diet on more than one occasion had postponed the consideration of the new codes on the ground that the country did not want laws which had been dictated by European Chancelleries. It was in consideration of this hyper-sensitiveness on the subject of judicial autonomy that the year's-notice provision was inserted, to make it appear that the initiative had come from Tokyo, and not from London.

The other main provision of the treaty related to the tariff of Customs duties on imports, and it was in this article that the British secured their *quid pro quo* for the abandoned extra-territorial rights. The Conventional Tariff provided that about forty articles of merchandise, including the chief British exports to Japan (cottons, woollens, iron and steel, and machinery) should enter under low rates, ranging from 5 per cent. to 15 per cent., average about $7\frac{1}{2}$ per cent., for a period of seventeen years. Of similar import were the treaties with other countries, and by means of the most-favoured-nation-treatment clause practically all the Western countries secured for their merchants and manufacturers the continuation for a considerable period of reasonable Customs duties upon their chief exports to Japan. In addition to the Conventional Tariff there was a Statutory Tariff upon all commodities not included in the conventional list, and the rates to be charged upon such goods were to be determined by the Japanese Government from and after the date of the ratification of the treaty. It was not to be wondered at, perhaps, that before the expiration of the seventeen years the Conventional Tariff became as unpopular in Japan as the extra-territorial provisions had been previous to 1894. The Japanese of 1911 referred to the provisions of the tariff treaty of 1894 as " unilateral," forgetting, of course, that in the minds of the Japanese and British Governments in 1894 the Conventional Tariff had been the price paid for the abolition of extra-territoriality.

In 1894, however, the new treaty was welcomed by every one, with the exception of the foreigners resident in the treaty ports. To them it seemed that their interests had been sacrificed, and their criticisms of their home Governments, as well as of the Japanese authorities, were virulent, to say the least, and injudicious to the last degree. It did not favourably predispose Japanese officials to read in the English papers of Yokohama and Kobe diatribes against their inefficiency and dishonesty, or attacks upon the Japanese administration of justice, directed against both the codes and the procedure of their courts. Whatever may be said in justification of this outburst in the foreign Press in Japan, and in a real sense it expressed the by no means groundless fears of the residents of the Settlements, the Japanese justly took umbrage at such slurs upon their nation and its Government, and to the present day speak disparagingly of the foreign inhabitants of the original treaty ports. By a curious process of psychology the cities of Yokohama, Kobe, and Nagasaki are held in more or less contempt, by official Japanese, at any rate, merely because they happen to contain the former foreign Settlements.

The Chino-Japanese War

That there remains still much of the animosity against the foreign resident which was generated in 1894 and previously may be seen by the diligence with which distinguished European and American visitors to Japan are taught by the officials, who conduct them about, to regard their respectable fellow-countrymen in Yokohama and Kobe as a crew of tax-dodging, carousing, dishonest merchants.

If the treaty was the immediate cause of much misunderstanding between the resident foreigners and the native official Japanese, the circumstances of the years immediately following intensified their mutual dislike. The almost complete monopoly of the import and export business of the country by the foreigners in 1894 aroused the jealous anger of the Japanese, and the latter's mostly unsuccessful propaganda for " direct trade," supported by the Government by bounties upon the export of raw silk by Japanese houses and other less open means, only intensified the dislike of the foreign merchants for the Japanese. As the competition between foreigners and natives in the foreign trade grew, ill-feeling increased. Mutual recriminations became the order of the day, and by 1900 the situation was about as unfortunate as it could be.

When mixed residence was inaugurated in 1899, as a result of the treaty of 1894, and the foreign Settlements were merged in the Japanese municipalities, the question of perpetual leases and taxation came to the fore. These new and specific causes of difference between the Japanese and the foreign residents in the Settlements remain to the present far from adjusted, and are a constant source of annoyance and ill-feeling. But an account of the various stages through which the controversy has passed would occupy far too much space here for a topic which is, after all, of only local interest.[1]

[1] For the literature of this question consult the official versions of the British and Japanese cases as presented before the Hague Tribunal in 1906, and the pamphlets issued by the Committee of the Foreign Land Owners, Yokohama.

A Political History of Japan

In summing up the gains and losses of the Chino-Japanese War, it is necessary to look at both the immediate and ultimate results. As to territory, Formosa was the only gain, though China was forced to acknowledge Japan's paramount influence in Korea, a claim which was at once disputed by Russia, the inevitable sequel to that dispute being the war between Russia and Japan over Korea in 1904-5. The indemnity received from China exceeded the expenses directly incurred in the various campaigns by over 100,000,000 yen, but the importation of so much money into Japan threw the domestic monetary arrangements into disorder, and furthermore furnished the main incentive to the adoption of a wildly optimistic *post-bellum* programme for the increase of armaments and the encouragement of trade and commerce. Though regarded in 1895 as a signal evidence of their triumph over China, as it was, the indemnity caused an enormous rise in prices in Japan during the boom, and indirectly was responsible for the crisis and period of depression which ensued. . The elevation of Japan to the rank of the great military Powers of the earth was a source of legitimate satisfaction and pride to the nation, but the new state of affairs involved heavy financial responsibilities upon the people. The change in the nation's status likewise changed the tenor of the people's thoughts. The continent of Asia, not the island Empire, from that time became the focus of the national ambition. When the revision of the treaties had removed the objective of the Government's foreign policy, Asia and continental Asiatic empire took its place. In the patriotic enthusiasm for war the constitutional struggle was abandoned, and before it was renewed the oligarchy had succeeded in adjusting its arrangements for carrying on an aggressive warfare against the popular party in the Diet by framing a series of regulations limiting appointments to the ministerial posts in the Army and Navy Departments to high officers in the active service.

The Chino-Japanese War

When the Diet was convened on December 25, 1895, the former struggle against the oligarchy was immediately renewed. The Ito Ministry was weakened by the loss of Matsukata in the Finance Department, for, whatever else might be said against him, Matsukata was the most trusted financier of the time, and his public criticism of the Government's proposed disposition of the indemnity carried weight with the country. The financial measures of the year were included in an elaborate *post-bellum* programme which was to be carried out in seven years. These long-term financial arrangements, or programmes as they were called, giving the figures for revenues and expenditures down to the last fraction of a sen not only for the current but for some years in the future, seem to have a fascination for the Japanese ; even though they have never been carried out to the letter, at short intervals during the last two decades long-time programmes have been published and accepted as a prophecy of the future. What is still more strange in the light of their usually favourable reception, a continuous increase in the total to be raised by taxation, if not in the rate of the taxes, is generally foreshadowed in such arrangements ; though as an exception to the rule in this respect may be cited the announcement made by Yamamoto Tatsuo, the Finance Minister in the second Saionji Cabinet, in 1911, providing for an increase of taxation during the first five or six years and then a steady decline until 1922. The Ito programme of 1895 proposed to spend 190,000,000 yen on productive enterprises and 325,000,000 on the Army and Navy, in addition to the ordinary expenditures of the Government. To raise these vast sums the remainder of the Chinese indemnity was to be supplemented by the receipts from increased taxation and by domestic loans. It was argued that the distribution among the people of the sums which were to be spent on public works and for the encouragement of industry would enable them to pay more taxes and to subscribe

generously to Government loans. Speaking at a
meeting of the Seiyukai [1] in 1902, Ito stated that
the Government had disbursed between 1896 and
1901 nearly 600,000,000 yen on productive or unpro-
ductive enterprises, and that more than half of the
total had been spent on the Army and Navy. Such
an astonishing financial programme was certain to
furnish numerous occasions of dispute between the
Government and the Opposition. In addition, the retrocession of the Liaotung peninsula and the murder
of the Korean Queen in 1895—of the suspicion of com-
plicity in which the Japanese Government never
succeeded in clearing itself—supplied weapons to the
popular party for their attack on the Ministry.

As a preparation for the session, Ito had abandoned
the principle of " independent Cabinets " and allied
himself with the Jiyuto, which after the election of
July 1894 controlled 108 seats in the Lower House.
Likewise he took precautions to retain the allegiance
of the Kokumin Kyokai with its thirty-four members,
and these two parties, along with the twenty-six staunch
supporters of the Government in the Dainihon Kyokai,
assured him of 168 votes in the House of Representatives. Despite the vehement opposition of the Kaishinto
the Cabinet was able to carry through its financial
measures and tide over one of the most critical sessions
of the Diet.

Nevertheless, before the Diet assembled again at
the close of 1896, the Ito Ministry had resigned and
Matsukata had begun his second administration. In
the forefront of the events which led up to this change
must be placed the Government's financial policy. The
programme did not inspire confidence, especially as
Watanabe, the Finance Minister, was indiscreet enough
to present to the Diet a Budget which showed in the
ordinary revenue a deficit of 40,000,000 yen, which had
subsequently to be arranged by means of reductions
in the expenditures and a draft upon the special Navy

[1] A political party formed in 1901 under Ito's leadership.

Fund created out of the Chinese indemnity. If the Budget offered one opportunity for an attack on the Cabinet, numerous others were found in the mismanagement of affairs in Formosa and Korea. The Administration in the new colony was undoubtedly faced by most difficult problems, which arose out of the disturbed state of the island, only about half of which had been wrested from the Chinese, the other remaining in the possession of the savage aborigines. But the " Formosan scandals," as they were called in Tokyo, arose mainly in connection with the civil administration, though the military officials were accused by the Opposition Press in Japan of pursuing a policy which would lead to the complete extermination of the natives, both Chinese and aborigines. The civil officials were in many cases drawn from the worst class of Japanese, and were bent only upon making money by the exploitation of the island's resources, and the clearance which was effected a few years later by Lieut.-General Kodama, who was appointed Governor-General in 1898, was sufficient proof of the appalling corruption of the early administrators, literally thousands of Japanese being deported from Formosa as undesirable officials and citizens. But even these failures of the Administration in Formosa, complete as they had been, were surpassed in Korea, where Baron Miura, the Japanese Agent in Seoul, was so far implicated in the murder of the Queen that he and several of his associates were recalled, and though they were subsequently acquitted of the crime by a Japanese court, Ito's Cabinet for the time being was held responsible for the actions of its agents.

The boom of the winter of 1895-6 exploded during the following summer, and the public laid the blame upon the Administration's *post bellum* finance. To add to the Ministry's embarrassment, Okuma succeeded in March 1896 in forming a new party, the Shimpoto (Progressives), which included his old followers in the Kaishinto and about fifty members from the other

Opposition groups. The strength of the Shimpoto was about equal to that of the Jiyuto ; the Cabinet had still a fighting chance in the Diet, at least until April, when Itagaki was taken into the Ministry as the successor of Nomura in the Department of Home Affairs. While this action guaranteed the support of the Jiyuto, it drove the Kokumin Kyokai into an alliance with the Shimpoto against the Cabinet. No better illustration of the motives which animated the parties in the Japanese Diet could be found than in the history of the Kokumin Kyokai. It was formed by a reactionary member of the Choshu oligarchy, Viscount Shinagawa, ostensibly for the support of the Government. But the first article of the party's creed was " independent Cabinets," and whenever the Administration sought the alliance of a political party, the Kokumin Kyokai turned against the Government. It was nothing to them, apparently, that by so doing they united their strength with that of the Ishmaelites, the party politicians, to oust the Government, and in the spring of 1896, after Itagaki had become a member of the Administration, Ito could no longer retain the support of the ultra-Conservatives of the Kokumin Kyokai : they evidently did not desire office themselves, but insisted that the Cabinet posts must be retained as the perquisites of the clans.

With nearly half of the members of the Lower House arrayed against him and the country clamouring for his downfall, Ito resigned in the closing days of August. Owing to the war and an alliance with the Jiyuto, the life of his first Administration in the parliamentary régime had been prolonged to the unheard-of length of four years and one month.

The Ito who emerged from that period was not the confident oligarch who in 1885 had set out upon a Bismarckian career by becoming the virtual Chancellor of the Japanese Empire, nor the triumphant architect of national institutions who had promulgated the Constitution in 1889. Even in 1892, when he stepped forward as the champion of the clan system, he was regarded as the only man who was capable of handling the Diet, but the short and unruly sessions of the winters of 1892 and 1893 were proof of his failure in this respect. He likewise stood convicted in the eyes of the nation as the author of a system of government which was defective and impracticable. In the confusion of mind and depression of spirit which followed upon his abortive resignation in 1894, he had been persuaded into sanctioning the war against China, and thereby committed the blunder of departing from the policy of peaceful development of the national laws and resources which he had inherited from Iwakura, Kido, and Okubo. He had been discredited by his framing the "immutable laws" of 1889 and by his unsuccessful administration in the constitutional régime, and after 1894 he could no longer claim the confidence of the nation as the consistent exponent of civil progress ; though his power was by no means broken, it had begun to decline. For two brief periods, marked by the bitterest political strife, he subsequently occupied the office of Minister President of State ; later still he was the Resident-General of Korea, but on each and every one of these occasions his failure was conspicuous.

Ito's was a strange career. It began and ended in violence, and during the greater part of its course he was the recipient of honours and rewards that were far out of proportion to his services, conspicuous as they undoubtedly were. He was possessed of a genuine desire to perfect the laws and institutions of his country, but he lacked the necessary patience and consistency, and, as he grew older, receptivity to new ideas and the capacity to act upon them.

CHAPTER XI

MILITARISM AND CLAN GOVERNMENT

WHEN the Ito Administration resigned in August 1896, Okuma was undoubtedly the greatest figure in Japanese politics, and the people demanded that he should be placed in charge of the Foreign Affairs of the Empire. But Okuma stood outside of the official coterie : he was the acknowledged head of the Shimpoto, the strongest of the Opposition parties, and he was committed to the cause of responsible government. His admission to the Cabinet was therefore a matter not easily arranged, especially as the bankers and manufacturers desired the return of Matsukata to the Finance Ministry.

Negotiations occupied more than a fortnight. On the one side, Matsukata had a rooted objection to all political parties. He had never truckled to any of them, and he resigned in 1891 rather than violate the strict principles of the Constitution with regard to the " independence " of the Cabinet. On the other, Okuma could not afford to enter a clan Cabinet unless he could make terms acceptable to his party. The programme of the Shimpoto, as set forth in a manifesto issued in March 1896, included the following : " Our party intends to introduce the system of responsible Cabinets by the steady pursuit of progressive principles ; to assert the national rights by remodelling the Empire's foreign policy ; to manage the national finances in such a manner as to encourage the development of industry and commerce ; in short, to obtain the reality of constitutional government." It was the

Militarism and Clan Government

first article in this confession of faith of Okuma's party which was the stumbling-block. However, even that obstacle was surmounted. According to the terms of the *rapprochement*, Okuma agreed to enter the Cabinet and guarantee the support of his party for the Administration, upon the understanding that the Ministers should be collectively responsible to the Lower House, that a thoroughgoing reformation of the administrative and financial systems should be undertaken, and that the rights of the people should be respected and their wishes receive more consideration. The compromise was regarded as a triumph for the popular party, and the new Ministry was acclaimed as the realization of " constitutional government."

On September 18 the Cabinet was sworn in, the Finance Office as well as that of Minister President being occupied by Matsukata, the Foreign Office by Okuma, and the other Cabinet posts distributed among the second rank of the Sat-Cho oligarchs. In this company Okuma soon began to find himself isolated ; the fine promises he received at the outset were not fulfilled, and after a little more than a year he resigned his office, in November 1897.

By Okuma's defection and the withdrawing of the Shimpoto's support in the Diet the Government was forced to resign. Other causes contributed to the Cabinet's fall ; during the session of 1896-7 it had steadily grown more unpopular, and became the object of constant attack both in and out of the Diet. The session opened on December 25, and the Speech from the Throne emphasized the necessity of improving the national defences. After the New Year recess, an Address to the Throne impeaching the Cabinet was introduced by the Jiyuto, now the main party in the Opposition, but it was thrown out by a large majority. The Budget was passed into law, and provided for an increase of the ordinary revenue amounting to 62,000,000 yen. The *post-bellum* programme inherited from the late Ito Administration was extended from

247

seven to ten years, thus reducing the annual charges involved, though not the total of the expenditures contemplated. All these measures were carried through with the support of the Shimpoto and the members of the Kokumin Kyokai, who abandoned for the time being their policy of opposition to any and every Government which entered into relations with a political party. In connection with the action of the Kokumin Kyokai, as well as with that of other members of the Diet, in deserting the Opposition for the Government, open charges of bribery were made. The *Jiji Shimpo*, the most responsible paper in Tokyo, voiced the suspicions of the country by declaring editorially that " the only programme for a Government desirous of commanding a majority in the House is to take steps to secure the goodwill of the members. Hence it is not strange that the Cabinet should adopt the easiest method of obtaining the support of its members, namely, bribery, which is said to be the most efficacious and the simplest weapon available."

Not only was corruption of the members of the Diet by the distribution of money charged against the Administration, but it was accused of having introduced the " spoils system " into Japan, since places had been made for party men in the Audit Bureau, and even in the Department of Education. These appointments threatened the existence of the bureaucracy, and not only earned for the Government the hostility of the official classes, but provided the Opposition Press with a new weapon of attack. In connection with this phase of the Government's policy, the case of a certain Judge Takano, of Formosa, became notorious. The judge was dismissed from office, but refused to accept his *congé* on the ground that the Constitution (Article LVIII) guaranteed his tenure during life and good conduct. The Government replied that the Constitution had not yet been enforced in Formosa, and consequently his plea was invalid. Nevertheless, the judge proceeded to Formosa to resume his duties, only to find himself unable to obtain access to his office. Therefore he resigned, and, returning to Japan, enlisted the services of the Press, and with the first-hand information thus supplied them the editors made out a sweeping indictment of the Government's administration of Formosa as having produced a " virtual state of anarchy " in the island.

To further embarrass Matsukata, the leaders of the Shimpoto appointed a committee to approach the Prime Minister and present a programme of reforms. At first he refused to receive the delegation, but afterwards admitted it, having exacted from its spokesman a promise of secrecy. In violation of that promise, the very next day the Press contained an account of the interview and the main items of the Shimpoto's programme. The result was Matsukata's rejection of all the suggestions and the consequent loss of the Shimpoto's adherence, shortly followed by Okuma's resignation.

Baron Nishi was appointed to the vacancy thus created in the Foreign Office, and the Government proceeded to secure the support of the Diet by a wholesale distribution of money among the independents as well as the members of the Jiyuto. But the efforts of the Cabinet in this direction failed, for at a general meeting of that party held on December 15 it was decided to oppose the Government. The session opened six days later, and on the 25th a vote of want of confidence in the Ministry for causing dissatisfaction at home, loss of prestige abroad, and confusion in the national finance was carried through the Lower House. The Diet was dissolved forthwith, after sitting but two days more, and before any administrative business was transacted. The Cabinet resigned on the same day.

Upon the fall of the second Matsukata Ministry, by the Emperor's personal intervention Ito was again thrust forward into the breach, and on January 12 the new Cabinet took up office. It included Inouye, in the Department of Finance, three of Ito's personal following—Saionji, Ito Miyoji, and Suyematsu—while the other members, except for Katsura, were the usual second-generation scions of the two clans. Katsura's elevation to the War Office, it is to be noted, marked the first appearance on the Cabinet stage of the man who was destined to become the champion of the military party during the remainder of Meiji. The Government acknowledged no affiliations with any of the parties and disclaimed any hostility toward them. Its attitude was proclaimed as one of "benevolent neutrality," a phrase which was to become historic.

In the General Election which followed on March 15 there occurred the usual kaleidoscopic changes in the smaller factions and groups within the two main parties. There was no particular issue to be presented. Neither the Jiyuto nor the Shimpoto could consistently pose as being entirely opposed to clan government, for both had been allied with clan Cabinets, and it was well known that before the election the Jiyuto had tried to effect an alliance with the new Ito Cabinet, but that its advances had been spurned, mainly because the party was not strong enough to control the Lower House. As the Cabinet which had been responsible for the recent dissolution had resigned, the Opposition parties were unable with even the smallest show of consistency to charge against the new Ministry the arbitrary conduct of the former Administration. It was therefore an issueless fight, or, as it was described in the contemporary Press, "a struggle in the dark," and the outcome was to leave the parties with much the same numerical strength as that with which they had entered. The Jiyuto secured 99 seats, the Shimpoto 105, the Kokumin Kyokai 32, and the Independents 40; the remaining 24 were divided up amongst five small factions.

The session which followed, beginning on May 14, 1898, was "Extraordinary," and was limited by Imperial ordinance to twenty days' duration. The Government's programme was embodied in three principal measures—the enforcement of the Civil Code, a new Election Law, and an increase of taxation of 35,000,000 yen—and from the outset the Lower House was in an exceedingly hostile mood. Various attempts were made to get a vote of want of confidence through the House by Ito's enemies within the ranks of the oligarchy, but the party politicians were not to be distracted from the main issues. The Bill for enforcing the Civil Code was passed, but only after the Cabinet pointed out the necessity of the measure if the revised treaties were to come into force in 1899, as a year's notice was necessary, according to their terms. The Land Tax Bill was then taken up. According to the provisions of the Bill, the rate of taxation, which had been 3 per cent. of the assessed valuation in 1873 but was subsequently reduced to $2\frac{1}{2}$ per cent. in 1877, was to be raised to 3˙7 per cent. on agricultural land, 3 per cent. on rural, and 5 per cent. on urban building sites. This Bill was reported from a committee on June 7 with a contrary recommendation. The Government immediately suspended the sittings for two days, and tried to negotiate, but without avail, for on June 10 the Bill was rejected by an overwhelming majority. The other Bills relating to finance and the project for revision of the Election Law did not reach a division. In consequence of the defeat of its measures the Government resigned, but not before it had dissolved the House. That Ito had no support in the Representatives was shown by the division— 27 ayes and 247 nays—on the Land Tax Bill, for he had refused to make any effort to secure adherents for the Government. It would almost appear as if he had been deliberately riding for a fall in order to demonstrate incontestably the impracticability of " independent Cabinets."

The action of the two chief sections of the popular party furthered his scheme. Immediately after the dissolution on June 10, Okuma and Itagaki began to concert measures for a combination of the Shimpoto and the Jiyuto. On June 16 a preliminary meeting was held, and six days later a new party, the Kenseito (Constitutionalists), was organized. The principles for which the party stood were stated in the nine articles of its manifesto as the establishment of party government and responsible Cabinets, protection of national interests, extension of trade and commerce, development of means of communication and transportation, maintenance of the Army and Navy in proportion to the national strength, improvement of the educational system, and balancing of revenues and expenditures.

The remarks of the two leaders at the various meetings held between June 16 and 22 reveal the thoughts which were uppermost in the minds of the politicians. Speaking at a meeting of the Jiyuto, Itagaki said to his followers : " Each party has tried the experiment of co-operation with the clan statesmen, and each has found it a failure, because the Government attaches no real importance to political parties, but merely consults its own convenience in taking them up and casting them off." Okuma, addressing the new party, described the Sat-Cho oligarchy as a " virtual Tokugawa regency, which, acting in the name of the Emperor, really prosecuted its own designs and increased its own powers." The Kenseito therefore turned its face against the oligarchy, and Ito, taking his cue from the new party, resigned along with his Cabinet on June 25.

Previous to this action a meeting of the Elder Statesmen—Ito, Yamagata, Saigo, Oyama, Kuroda, and Inouye—had been convened for the purpose of discussing the situation created by the formation of the Kenseito. It is said that at this meeting Ito maintained that the Cabinet must ally itself definitively with the party and must give up the fiction of independent action, whereas Yamagata argued that such a course would involve a violation of the Constitution and therefore must be avoided. As neither Yamagata nor any of the other members of the narrow circle was willing to assume the responsibilities of administration, Ito thereupon handed back the seals of office to the Emperor, recommending at the same time that Okuma and Itagaki be called upon to form a party Cabinet.

The precipitancy with which one event followed another left the leaders of the Kenseito dumbfounded, and Okuma and Itagaki were disposed at first to plead incapacity, since their party had been in existence only five days and their plans were far from matured, but upon Ito's representations they finally agreed to serve. Their favourable decision was regarded as marking the end of clan government, and great popular rejoicing ensued.

It is difficult to explain these events by any other hypothesis than that Ito had availed himself of the formation of the Kenseito, the most powerful party numerically that had been organized in Japan, to bring about the fall for which he had been preparing since the beginning of the year. He had perceived that the power among the oligarchs was passing out of his hands into those of Yamagata, or, to put it in other words, from the civil to the military faction. The fruits of his war policy in 1894 were beginning to ripen, and already one had been gathered, for in January 1898 the Supreme Military Advisory Council had been set up, under the presidency of Yamagata, with Saigo, Oyama, and Komatsu as members. The conduct of Yamagata at the meeting of the Elder Statesmen on June 25 had further incensed Ito, and he resolved to make an effort to defeat the military party by throwing the Government into the hands of the Kenseito. Even if that party had been able to hold together in office, however, Ito's plans would have necessarily miscarried, for Yamagata had in 1894, as we have pointed out, provided a lever with which he could oust any Cabinet from office, no matter how great the numerical strength of its supporters in the Lower House.

R

A Political History of Japan

By June 30 the first so-called party Administration was organized. Okuma became Premier and Minister of Foreign Affairs, Itagaki Home Minister ; the other non-military posts were distributed in such a way as to provide for three members of the Shimpoto section, Ogihashi, Oishi, and Ozaki, and two of the Jiyuto, Matsuda and Hayashi Yuzo. Katsura and Saigo, the Ministers of the Army and Navy in the former Cabinet, were reappointed to their respective posts.

Having seen his project launched, Ito proceeded to China to study the situation there, and to strive to effect a peaceful settlement of the questions in Chino-Russo-Japanese relations in Manchuria and Korea. Before his return domestic politics had passed through a crisis, and the Okuma-Itagaki Cabinet had been replaced by the military section of the oligarchy, with Yamagata in the position of Minister President. That incident marked the final rupture between Ito and Yamagata ; from that time onward Ito fought the rising power of militarism with every weapon in his possession, but always unsuccessfully. The collapse of the Kenseito Cabinet had been assured from the beginning. The party was an ill-assorted collection of quondam Liberals and Progressives, held together only by the flimsy bond of common enmity to clan oligarchy, an enmity which had not been deep enough, however, to keep its members from joining hands with a clan Cabinet whenever it was possible : otherwise the two sections in the party were enemies rather than friends. Hoshi Toru, the real leader of the former Jiyuto, could hardly have been expected to forgive the men who had hounded him from the presidency of the Lower House in December 1893. The rank and file of the two factions, also, had been involved for the past three years in a series of rancorous political disputes. Elements of discord made their appearance in the General Election in August. The Jiyuto section accused the Shimpoto of unfairly applying the election regulations so as to exclude or defeat candidates other than their own, these charges resulting in a lawsuit and the resignation of the Vice-Minister of the Department of Home Affairs. As far as the results of the election were concerned, the Kenseito won 259 out of the 300 seats in the Lower House. But the party was not united. In the election returns the separate factions were enumerated as follows : Shimpoto, 112 ; Jiyuto, 96 ; Independents, 51. That this method of reporting was not merely accidental was proved by the constant party bickerings upon any and every subject which disgraced the summer. But the most serious cause of difference among the members of the party was the " balance of power " theory maintained by Hoshi. According to that theory, Cabinet offices were to be equally divided between the two factions, and similarly the patronage, but in the original distribution the Okuma faction had obtained five offices and the Itagaki section only three. This dispute reached a climax toward the end of October, when Ozaki Yukio, the Minister of Education, resigned, as the result of pressure from the Court and the clan Press. The Itagaki section demanded that the office should be filled by one of their number, but Okuma as Minister President nominated one of his own faction, Inukai Ki, to the vacant post, and received the Emperor's sanction to the appointment. Itagaki, Matsuda, and Hayashi thereupon withdrew, and two days later, on October 31, Okuma and his three followers handed in their resignations. Katsura and Saigo did likewise. Thus ended the experiment from which so much had been expected, the attempted substitute for clan government.

It is hardly necessary to look for any hidden causes for the fall of the Kenseito Cabinet : the plain fact seems obvious enough—that the Kenseito as a party lacked homogeneity and co-ordination. Its leading men were not in sympathy with one another, and the characteristics of the two groups of which it was composed were radically different. The past history of the two factions had been such that it was impossible for them to forget their differences. Nevertheless, the clan oligarchs can hardly be acquitted of participation in the overthrow of this unfortunate coalition. The agitation against Ozaki, for a trivial blunder, which had developed in August and September, is incredible as a spontaneous demonstration. Speaking, as Minister of Education, against the evil tendency in the country to set money gain above other considerations, he was led in a flight of oratory into making a comparison between the United States and Japan. He said : " Even in America, where the plutocracy is all-powerful, the people do not elect a millionaire to the Presidency, whereas, if Japan were a republic, the people would be sure to place the richest·man in the office." This peroration was seized upon not only by the members of the Jiyuto faction, but by the official Press as well, and Ozaki was accused of sedition, and even treason. In vain he pointed out the difference between a mere supposititious case advanced for the sake of illustration and a straightforward advocacy of republican institutions, for, in spite of indications that he would have been able to weather the storm, there came an intimation from the Court that his resignation would be acceptable to the Emperor.

That blow came from the oligarchs, who saw in the situation the means of immediately overturning the Government and the possibility of getting safely into the saddle before Ito could get back from China, and inside of eight days a new Cabinet was gazetted. It contained no representatives of either the political parties or the Ito faction in the oligarchy.

It is scarcely necessary to point out the significance of the events of 1898. The party politicians' failure was of no great importance, nor was the fact that they were actually given a chance to make their experiment. It had sometimes been held that the entrance of party men into the Cabinet under Okuma and Itagaki was a " great landmark in the development of constitutional government in Japan." [1]   But that landmark had already been passed before 1898. Itagaki had been a member of the first Ito Ministry in 1896, and Okuma of the second Matsukata Administration in 1896-7, and both of the great parties had been ranged on the side of the Administration at various times, as well as in Opposition.   It is difficult to see, therefore, wherein lay the importance of the political convulsions of 1898 for constitutional progress.   Their cause was rather the growing predominance of the military section of the oligarchy, led by Yamagata and Katsura, over the civil section, under Ito and Inouye.   This view is supported by Ito's action in bringing about the fall of his own second Administration at the end of June, and in handing over the reins of power to the political parties, as well as in Yamagata's assumption of office immediately after the fall of the Okuma-Itagaki Cabinet in October, while Ito was in China.

Further confirmation of this interpretation is supplied by the policy of the Yamagata Cabinet.   Before the Diet met the Kenseito was disrupted by Hoshi, who dissolved the party at a general meeting from which Okuma's followers absented themselves.   Immediately a new party organization was formed out of the former Jiyuto faction and the name Kenseito was readopted.   The Okuma section reorganized as the Kensei-honto (Real Constitutionalists).   Yamagata entered into negotiations with the new Kenseito, and secured their support in the Diet for the measures which were necessary to enable the military party to carry out its projects, but as soon as the Cabinet had concluded its main business it turned against the Kenseito, and went out of office on September 26, 1900.

The terms upon which the Kenseito, now under the virtual dictatorship of Hoshi Toru, allied itself with the Yamagata Cabinet are interesting in the light of

[1] See Uyehara, G. E., *The Political Development of Japan, 1867–1909.* London, 1910, p. 241.

what was to follow. Yamagata conceded the principle of "independent Cabinets," and promised to adopt certain measures advocated by the politicians, such as the reform of the electoral system, extension of the franchise, and nationalization of the railways, and further, it was understood that the patronage should be divided between the oligarchs and the politicians. In return for these concessions Hoshi guaranteed the support of his party for the Cabinet's Budget proposals, which included an increase of the income, *saké*, and land taxes, in order to carry out the *post-bellum* programme of military and naval expansion.

The chief drawback from the Government's point of view in this alliance was the paucity of members in the Kenseito. Even when combined with the Kokumin Kyokai the Government was in a minority in the Lower House. That defect, however, was overcome by corruption, for the military party felt the absolute necessity of securing new sources of revenue. Hoshi was a past master of the art of managing his supporters, and his services were secured by the Government. At that time he held the government of Tokyo City in the hollow of his hand, and had secured the sanction of the City Council to a project for uniting under one management the three systems of street-railways in the capital. The Home Ministry had persistently refused its assent to this merger on the ground that the creation of a monopoly of the transport facilities would be injurious to public interests, but the matter was finally compromised on the basis of sanction of the amalgamation project in return for Hoshi's support of the Land Tax Bill. The large fee received by Hoshi for his services in connection with the amalgamation was distributed among the members of the Kenseito. But other funds provided directly by the Government were supplied, and with these sums the support of a majority of the Lower House was purchased.

Thus the session, which began on December 31 and continued till March 10, passed off successfully, in spite of the efforts of the Kensei-honto to obstruct the conduct of business. The Budget provided for appropriations amounting to 220,000,000 yen, the increase in expenditures being met in the main by the increased taxation on incomes, *saké*, and land. One-third of the ordinary and five-eighths of the extra-ordinary expenditures were devoted to the Army and Navy.

During the interval between the close of the Diet in March and the opening of the winter session, the alliance of the Kenseito and the Cabinet almost broke down. Hoshi proved a hard task-master, his demands for the spoils of office becoming increasingly insistent, and Yamagata, who hated all party connection, was with difficulty restrained from an open break with Hoshi's followers. The Kokumin Kyokai was dissolved during the interval between the sessions, and reconstructed under the title Teikokuto (Imperialists), but without any change in either principles or membership. In the same interval an attempt was made to enter into an alliance with China, for the purpose of checking Russian aggression in Manchuria. A Chinese Prince visited Tokyo for the purpose, but was compelled to return without accomplishing anything, the Tsung-li-Yamen, as a consequence of Russian pressure on Peking, recalling its envoy in August. The Russian menace, especially where the independence of Korea was concerned, furnished the *pièce de résistance* of the daily pabulum provided by the Press. An alliance with Great Britain was persistently advocated, as it had been in the previous year, when even Great Britain's occupation of Wei-hai-wei had not created unfavourable comment in Japan, though the German occupation of Kaio-chau had been deeply resented.

The session of 1899-1900 was convened on November 19. The Cabinet was supported by the Kenseito and the Teikokuto, the Kensei-honto being in Opposition. The principal measures introduced, apart from the Budget, were the Election Law Revision

Bill and the Religions Bill. The Budget; though it provided for a further increase of expenditures, the estimates amounting to 255,000,000 yen, was passed by both Houses without amendment. The Religions Bill, which concerned mainly the Buddhist organizations, was accepted by the Lower House, but rejected by the Peers on February 19 by a vote of 121-100 ; the action of the Upper House was a serious blow to the Administration, not so much because the Bill failed to pass, as that its rejection by the Peers was a plain intimation of their revolt against the Cabinet on account of its affiliation with the Kenseito. But the main interest in the session was in the project for amending the Election Law. The provisions of the original " Law of Elections " promulgated along with the Constitution in 1889 were still in force, but the experience of the first decade of parliamentary institutions had led to a general desire for their revision. On the one hand, the Government found that the immense predominance of the representatives of the agricultural class impeded any increase of taxation, especially on land, and on the other, that in the single-member electoral districts established by law, corruption and violence were engendered during each campaign. The politicians likewise objected to the under representation of the urban communities and to the signed ballot. As we have seen, one of the Bills introduced by the Ito Cabinet during the extraordinary session of May and June 1898, had been a project for the revision of the Election Law. But the shortness of that session and the absorbing interest of the Land Tax Bill had precluded the discussion of the measure. During the first session of the second Yamagata Administration the question was not brought up in the Diet, though electoral reform and extension of the franchise had been among the Prime Minister's promises to the Kenseito in November 1898. In this session, therefore, a Government Bill for the revision of the Law of Elections was introduced into the Diet for its sanction.

Militarism and Clan Government

The Bill was finally enacted into law, after being amended by both Representatives and Peers and made the subject of a conference between the two Houses. The result of the measure, as finally approved in 1900, and subsequently amended in 1903, was to increase the membership of the Lower House from 300 to 381 and to obtain a more adequate representation for the urban communities ; to increase the electorate from approximately 500,000 in 1890 to 967,000 in 1902 by a reduction of the property qualification from 15 yen annual national taxes to 10 yen ; to secure a secret unsigned ballot, and to enlarge the boundaries of election districts by making them coterminous with those of the Fu and Ken.

During the session the Kensei-honto attempted to impeach the Cabinet on the ground of corruption during the previous year, but its Address to the Throne was defeated, as was also a private Bill introduced by Ozaki for the trial by the ordinary law courts of members of the Diet charged with corruption. The failure of the Opposition in the House made its criticism of the Government and the Kenseito all the more violent.. Its Press, led by the *Mainichi* under the editorship of Shimada Saburo, published daily the most scurrilous attacks upon Hoshi and his party. The charges in nearly every issue were the same—robbery, pilfering, and piracy. So sweeping were the condemnations of the morals of the party politicians hurled back and forth in the newspapers during the session and after its close, that the public grew apprehensive, and many sober writers declared themselves convinced that Parliamentary Government had failed in Japan. As convincing proof of the correctness of their conclusions it was pointed out that the last Diet had met infrequently, the debates on the Budget had been listless, and no attempts had been made by any section of the Houses to curb the ever-increasing public expenditures ; many of the Representatives were corrupt and the majority showed no desire to eradicate venality. As an example of the depravity of the party politicians, the case of Koyama Kinnosuke was cited ; he was a self-confessed recipient of bribes, and yet neither the Government nor the Opposition would institute disciplinary proceedings against him, the former because he had been bribed in its interest, the latter because he was a member of their party. The *Jiji Shimpo* alone championed the cause of the Diet. There was a certain amount of corruption, it admitted, but the members of the Lower House were not more dishonest than the oligarchs. The Elder Statesmen had all begun life in poverty and were now prosperous, having accumulated fortunes which were certainly not saved from their meagre official salaries. This was certainly faint praise for the Diet, but it was all that it was entitled to.

Seizing what seemed to be a favourable opportunity, Ito turned to avenge himself on the military faction, particularly Yamagata. During the late spring of 1900 he toured the provinces, speaking everywhere in favour of party government, and his campaign aroused the interest of the leaders of the Kenseito, who were upon the point of breaking with Yamagata. When the prospect of securing Ito's allegiance seemed assured, Hoshi approached the Prime Minister with the demand that several of the members of the Cabinet should join the Kenseito, and that the Ministry be reconstructed so as to admit to office some of the members of the party. To the first of these proposals Yamagata correctly replied that the matter of joining the party must rest with the individual Ministers, to the second that it was impossible, because the Constitution provided that appointments to ministerial posts were the Emperor's prerogative. This decision served as an excuse for the party to withdraw from its alliance with the Government.

The next step toward the downfall of the Ministry was taken forthwith. A committee of the Kenseito waited upon Ito and preferred the request that he should

Militarism and Clan Government

become their leader. Harking back to the burden
of his recent political speeches in the provinces, he
pointed out that he could only accept their invitation
on his own terms, which he intimated were hard. He
must be the real leader and every member of the
party "must absolutely obey his mandate." No objection was raised to these terms, and finally, on July 8,
Ito assumed the presidency of the proposed party.

During the next six weeks preparations for the new
party were hurried forward : the Kenseito was dissolved, even the factions in it being disbanded, and
on September 15 the preliminary organization of the
Rikken Seiyukai was completed. Ten days later the
public ceremony of inauguration was held in Tokyo,
one hundred and fifty-two members of the Lower House
signing the roll. Ito's remarks upon the occasion and
the manifesto of the party are so interesting that we
quote verbatim from the translation which appeared
in a contemporary issue of the *Japan Times* :—

"Ten years' experience of constitutional government
has not been unattended by some noteworthy results,
but much still remains to be done in the way of so
guiding and educating public opinion as to render it
a help and assistance to the conduct of the affairs
of state. To speak frankly, it has for some years been
a source of profound regret to me to observe a
tendency on the part of the existing political parties
to be betrayed into words and deeds that are at variance
with the principles laid down in the Constitution, which
indicates a proneness to sacrifice national for private
interests, and which, moreover, are antagonistic to the
fundamental national policy decided upon by His
Imperial Majesty at the time of the glorious Restoration
in unison with the requirements of the progress achieved.
The lamentable consequence is that the conduct of
these parties leaves much to be desired in regard to
the maintenance of the honour and good name of the
Empire abroad and to the acquirement of the confidence
and trust of the people at home. Being now called

263

upon to collect around me men of similar views with myself and to submit to the candid consideration of the public a general statement of the lines of this policy which I intend to pursue in common with these my friends, I shall avail myself of the present opportunity of briefly setting forth some of the principles which, in my humble opinion, ought to guide the actions of a political party.

" The appointment and dismissal of Cabinet Ministers appertain, under the Constitution, to the prerogative of the sovereign, who consequently retains absolute freedom to select his advisers from whatever quarters he deems proper, be it from among the members of the political parties or from circles outside of those parties. When once Ministers have been appointed and invested with their respective functions, it is not, under any circumstances whatever, permissible for their fellow party-men, or their other political friends, to interfere in any manner with the discharge of their duties. Any failure to grasp this fundamental principle would be fatal to the proper and efficient management of the important matters of state, and might lead to unseemly struggles for political power, thus engendering evils and abuses unspeakable. In inviting my political friends and sympathizers to rally around me, it is my earnest wish that we keep ourselves free of these evils and abuses.

" In view of the duties which it owes to the State, a political party ought to make it its primary object to devote its whole energies to the public weal. In order to improve and infuse life and vigour into the administrative machinery of the country, so as to enable it to keep up with the general progress of the nation, it is necessary that administrative officials should be recruited, under a system of definite qualifications, from among capable men of proper attainments and experience, irrespective of whether they belong to a political party or not. It is absolutely necessary that caution should be taken to avoid falling into the fatal mistake of giving posts to men of doubtful qualifications, simply because they belong to a particular political party. In considering questions affecting the interests of local or other corporate bodies, the decision must always be guided by considerations of the general good of the public and of the relative importance of those questions. In no case should the support of a political party be given for the promotion of any partial interests, in response to considerations of local connections or under the corrupt influence of interested persons. It is my earnest wish to sweep away, with the help of my friends, all these evil practices.

" If a political party aims, as it should aim, at being a guide to the people, it must commence with maintaining strict discipline and order in its own ranks, and, above all, with shaping its own conduct with an absolute and sincere devotion to the public interests of the country. Convinced of this truth, I venture, unworthy as I feel myself for such an important task, to organize, in concert with my political friends, an association under the name of Rikken Seiyukai, and offer to use my humble endeavours for the rectification of the standing abuses and evils connected with political parties ; my only wish in so doing being to contribute what little is in my power to the future success of constitutional government in this Empire, and thus discharge what I owe to my august sovereign and my country.

" Actuated by the desire to discharge the duties which every loyal subject owes to the Imperial house and the State, I now propose to organize a political association under the name of the Rikken Seiyukai, and hereby announce the general principles by which, in common with the other members of the association, I propose to shape our policy. These principles are as follows :—

" 1. We propose to strictly observe the Constitution of the Empire, and, in accordance with its provisions, to secure the successful operation of the sovereign power, so that the important affairs of state may be properly conducted, and further, that the rights and liberties of individual subjects may be efficiently preserved and safeguarded.

" 2. We make it our aim to advance the prosperity and position of the country and promote its civilization, in strict obedience to, and in whole-hearted support and furtherance of, that grand Imperial policy inaugurated at the time of the Restoration.

" 3. Desirous as we are to secure the harmonious working of the administrative machinery and to preserve the equity and justice of its action, we propose to use scrupulous vigilance in the appointment of officials ; to avoid useless formalities in the transaction of official business ; to clearly define and rigidly exact the performance of the duties and responsibilities attaching to the various official positions ; to maintain strict discipline among the public functionaries, and to secure such dispatch and precision in the conduct of business as are required by the country.

" 4. Attaching as we do high importance to the foreign intercourse of the Empire, we will use our best endeavours to cultivate good relations with the Treaty Powers and guard the welfare of all foreign sojourners in the country by extending to them the benefits of such enlightened government as is necessary for every well-regulated community.

" 5. Recognizing, as we do, the necessity of completing the defences of the country in accordance with the march of events both at home and abroad, we propose to secure, within the limits of the national resources, effective protection for national rights and interests.

" 6. Being desirous of placing the strength of the country on a sure and solid basis, we propose to encourage and promote education and to foster the personal character of the people, so that their moral and intellectual qualities may be so developed as to enable them to fulfil satisfactorily the duties they owe to the State in their private and public capacities.

" 7. We make it our object to strengthen the

economic basis of national life by encouraging agricultural and industrial enterprises, by promoting navigation and commerce, and by completing the various means of communication.

" 8. We propose to direct our efforts toward the realization of the object of local self-government, so that the communal units may be knit together in such a way as to secure social and economic harmony among them.

" 9. Keenly aware as we are of the serious responsibilities that a political party owes to the State, we will strive to shape our actions in accordance with the requirements of public interest, and always endeavour, in the spirit of self-admonition, to guard ourselves against falling into the old evils and abuses."

The inaugural address afforded little comfort to the Radicals, who hoped to find the new party adopting the principle of responsible Ministry. The opening paragraphs stated plainly that the prerogative of the sovereign included the appointment and dismissal of Cabinet officers, and it is only fair to interpret Ito's words as a repetition of the Imperial pronouncement in 1893 [1] upon that subject. But the harshness of his dictum upon the main constitutional question of the day was largely mitigated by the nature of the appointments to Cabinet offices which followed about a month later.

Further, Ito's dissatisfaction with the achievements and the conduct of the parties in the past was boldly stated, but his diagnosis of the disease affecting the Opposition was fundamentally inaccurate—that sectional or personal interests had been preferred to those of the Empire—for behind such abuses it must have been evident, even to Ito's mind, that the irresponsibility and the obstruction of the parties throughout the parliamentary régime were based upon their inability to assume office on the basis of a popular mandate at a general election. Nevertheless, Ito was too much of

[1] See Chapter IX, p. 224.

an oligarch to acknowledge the point, though he hoped that under his guidance and in the enjoyment of the fruits of office the members of the new party might acquire habits of moderation, honesty, and disinterested loyalty to the State. It is difficult to imagine Hoshi or Matsuda or Hayashi listening with satisfaction to this address, or to understand why Ozaki should forsake Okuma and his colleagues in the Kensei-honto and join the Seiyukai, unless they were already in possession of information which enabled them to discount Ito's strictures against the parties, to reconstruct in accordance with their own desires his extremely orthodox views of the sovereign's prerogative, and to overlook any expression of principles for the sake of the promised office.

Without some such key to his meaning, Ito's remarks upon that occasion completely baffle the understanding. As one paragraph follows another the reader gets merely the impression of the staunchest of the clan oligarchs, presiding over a meeting of the party politicians, announcing the strictest principles of constitutional orthodoxy and denouncing his audience for their evil conduct in the past. Now, such was not the case ; if it had been, the Seiyukai would never have been organized. Every one present knew that Ito was there for the purpose of joining hands with the Opposition in an attempt to overthrow his enemies, the military clique. In Ito's mind, the object was to be accomplished by leading the people back to an interest not so much in constitutional progress as in the material and intellectual development of the country, while his audience undoubtedly had in mind the consummation of• these hopes and the destruction of the power of *all* the oligarchs, whether military or otherwise, by the gradual adoption of responsible government. Thus the President and the rank and file of the party were working at cross purposes, a fact which was soon to become apparent, and which caused, after a few years, Ito's resignation.

Militarism and Clan Government

The manifesto represented Ito's ideas, not those of the great majority of the members of the party. The emphasis was laid upon promotion of education, encouragement of agriculture, manufactures, and commerce, extension of local autonomy, reform of the conduct of business in the administrative departments, and the preservation of the Imperial house and the Constitution. Foreign relations and military expansion, the two topics which the innate chauvinism of the people exalted to places of first importance, were mentioned in terms of the greatest moderation.

Ito named as the twelve members of the General Committee Saionji, Watanabe, Honda, Kaneko, Suyematsu, Hoshi, Matsuda, Hayashi, Haseba, Watanabe Koki, Ooka, and Suzuki, whom the *Jiji* facetiously dubbed the " Twelve Apostles of Marquis Ito."

The reception accorded to the new party was flattering in the extreme, even its opponents in the Kensei-honto speaking well of it. Okuma welcomed the entrance of " his old friend " Ito into the ranks of the party politicians, but did not offer to co-operate with the Seiyukai. The more Radical section of the Press saw in the party the promise of responsible government, and declared that nothing of such importance had occurred since the Restoration.

Secretly, the Kensei-honto was greatly disturbed by the increased prestige of the former Kenseito, the more so because their own party was torn by internal dissensions, and even threatened with dissolution. Ozaki, Mochizuki, and Kurabara were read out of the party in August because they attempted to swing the members across into the Seiyukai. To strengthen their position, it was decided to install Okuma formally [1] as leader of the party. He was consequently elected President

---

[1] We have been referring constantly to Okuma and Itagaki as the leaders of the Kensei-honto and the Jiyuto, which as a matter of fact they were, but both being members of the nobility, they were excluded from membership in the Lower House ; consequently they were not openly acknowledged as leaders of any party. Usually a Business Committee represented the party on formal occasions.

and Kusumoto Vice-President at the general meeting on December 18. Speaking at this meeting, Okuma announced that the party, in order to purge the politics of the time, must oppose the Seiyukai and the Government because both harboured " rogues and thieves." The reference was undoubtedly to Hoshi and the members of his former Kwanto Club.

The summer of 1900 not only saw the birth of the Seiyukai but also that of a very different kind of political party, the Kokumin Domei-Kai (National Union Association). The promoters of this association were Prince Konoye, President of the House of Peers, Inukai Ki, and Sasa Tomofusa. Its object was to create a body of opinion in the country for the support of the Government's policy of preserving the integrity of China. After the Boxer Rebellion, Russia had been disinclined to withdraw her troops from Manchuria, and Prince Konoye and his associates were perturbed over the success of Russian diplomacy in Peking and the apparent indifference thereto in the Japanese Foreign Office.

This small party, composed of about twenty-five members of the Diet, had the sympathy of the Kensei-honto, but was regarded with displeasure by the Seiyukai and the Court. Its life was short—it was dissolved in 1902—but it was an example of what is not uncommon in Japan, the formation of a party to promote or discourage action upon some specific measure. The significance of this temporary association lay in the main in showing how Japan was being antagonized by Russia, and was allying herself with England and the United States where Far Eastern questions were involved.

With the organization of the Seiyukai, the position of the Yamagata Cabinet became untenable. There was no prospect of surviving another session of the Diet, nor was there any great need for the military party to cling to office, since during the past two sessions the immediately necessary financial legislation had been obtained. Yamagata resigned on September 26, having been in office nearly two years. There was great difficulty in finding a successor, though Ito was the only feasible candidate in sight. No one realized that fact more clearly than Ito himself, and he intended to assume the office from the beginning, but he hoped by hesitating to exact such terms from both the oligarchy and his party as would make his tenure of office secure. He provided against interference from the former by securing a promise to that effect from Yamagata, and against insubordination of his followers in the Seiyukai by keeping them on tenterhooks for a month. The Seiyukai resembled in some measure the original Kenseito, as it included in its membership a variety of hostile elements, and was a new organization with no background in history, no traditions to hold it together. To placate the various factions of the party was Ito's main consideration in distributing the offices in the Cabinet, which was finally gazetted on October 19. All but three of the offices, the two military posts and the Department of Foreign Affairs, were given to members of the Seiyukai. Suyematsu, Matsuda, Hayashi, and Hoshi —four members of the original Jiyuto—and two personal followers of Ito—Viscount Watanabe and Baron Kaneko, representatives of the new elements entering into the formation of the Seiyukai—were exalted to Cabinet rank. The three outsiders were Kato Takaaki, the Foreign Minister, and Katsura and Yamamoto, the nominees of the oligarchy for the military offices. Outside of the ministerial posts, Saionji was made President of the Privy Council and Kataoka the President of the Lower House. Hoshi, who resigned his portfolio in December, was appointed parliamentary leader of the party with almost dictatorial powers, and Ozaki replaced Viscount Watanabe on the general committee. The minor offices in the Administration, as far as they were political, were distributed among party men of secondary importance.

A Political History of Japan

But even with these arrangements the Seiyukai remained a hotbed of dissension and the object of violent denunciations in the Opposition Press. The presence of Hoshi in the Cabinet was made the ground of the Kensei-honto's opposition. During the whole of the year the *Mainichi* had never for a day ceased to fulminate against him as the fountain-head of corruption in national and local politics. Various scandals in connection with the administration of the city of Tokyo were connected with his name, but though the courts pronounced him not guilty, the attacks were kept up, and he finally brought suit for libel against Shimada Saburo, the editor of the *Mainichi*. Having successfully vindicated his reputation in the courts, he resigned his portfolio in December, and was succeeded by Hara Kei. Ito, as we have already mentioned, completely whitewashed Hoshi by making him the parliamentary leader of the party. If this appointment was an exhibition of generosity, it was also a fatal mistake on Ito's part, for an alliance with Hoshi, even though he was the most influential politician in Japan, could not help but bring upon the party the condemnation of the oligarchy, the Court, the Opposition, and a large section of the general public.

The case of Viscount Watanabe, the Finance Minister, was entirely different. He had joined the Seiyukai with reluctance, for at heart he was opposed to party government. Notwithstanding, he was appointed Chairman of the General Committee of the party on August 25, but was soon deposed by the members of that Committee, whereupon Ito removed the entire Committee and reappointed the members, with the substitution of Ozaki for Watanabe. When the Cabinet was gazetted, Watanabe's appointment to the Finance Office was greeted with an outburst of hostile criticism, and as time went on his relations with the party grew more strained. Watanabe's unpopularity with the members of the Seiyukai, even more than the popular distrust of Hoshi, contributed to the overthrow of the

Militarism and Clan Government

Ito Cabinet in May 1901.   With that event Ito's career as a parliamentarian ended.   His attempt to stem the rising tide of militarism by a return to the former policy of civil progress under the ægis of a great political party had ended in a failure even more complete than had his previous effort in 1898.

CHAPTER XII

THE RUSSO-JAPANESE WAR

WHEN the Diet met on December 22, 1900, to organize
for its fifteenth session, the Seiyukai commanded 155
seats, the Kenseito 101, the Teikokuto 14, and the
Independents 30. The Government had a small
majority in a House composed of 300 members.
On December 25 the formal opening was held.
The Emperor attended in person and received
the Speech from the Throne from the hands of the
Prime Minister, the two main topics referred to being
the Boxer Rebellion and a project for an increase of
taxation. The next day the reply to the Speech was
drafted, and the House rose for the New Year
recess, having previously agreed to reassemble on
January 20.

The Budget was brought down to the Lower House
immediately after the recess ; the estimates provided
for the balancing of the revenues and expenditures at
approximately 255,000,000 yen, of which amount
88,000,000 yen was to be devoted to the military
services ; but the total figures in the estimates were
of far less interest than the new taxation Bills, by
which it was proposed to increase the levies on sugar,
saké, beer, tobacco, etc. A large section of the
Seiyukai opposed the new tax proposals, and a general
meeting of the party was held on January 28 to
arrange a compromise. Ito made his attitude clear
by threatening to resign from the party if the Bills
were not passed. Accordingly, on February 7 the

Budget Committee reported favourably, and the Lower House adopted the report.

In the Upper House the taxation Bills were rejected, only three votes being recorded in their favour. It was obvious from such a division that the measures were not being considered on their merits, and the Diet was prorogued in order to effect a settlement. Okuma, as the head of the Kenseito, attributed the deadlock to Ito's party connection, and the Kenseito Press renewed their attack upon Hoshi, likening him to a Tammany boss. The *Jiji* stated that the situation was the result of the Peers' objection to a party Cabinet. During the régime of the " independent Cabinets " the Government had mainly depended upon the Upper House, but now that the Seiyukai had been formed the Ministers turned to the House of Representatives for support. It was a case of jealousy between the two Houses. The Seiyukai Press talked loudly of the necessity of reforming the Peers, abolishing the life tenure of the Imperial nominees, and reducing the seven-year terms of the representatives of the lower orders of nobility and the highest taxpayers to four years. The deadlock was finally broken by an Imperial message to the Upper House requesting their assent to the Bills. This bolt from the blue brought the Peers to terms, but it also put Ito in a difficult position. Though he disclaimed all knowledge of the Imperial action—probably with truth, for the message was not countersigned either by him or any responsible Minister—he accepted responsibility for it, and stood condemned before the country for having resorted to an Imperial message to overcome the Peers' opposition to his programme of taxation.

Behind these events it is not difficult to see the military clique at work. It was highly improbable that the Emperor had acted on his own initiative, and if it was not with Ito's consent that the message to the Peers was dispatched, then the Elder Statesmen must have suggested it. Yamagata knew that the results would be, on the one hand, the passage of the new tax Bills, to which he was not opposed, and, on the other, the discrediting of the Ito-Seiyukai Ministry. In this forecast the military clique had been correct, for after much discussion the Press almost unanimously concluded that, according to the Constitution as interpreted in an Imperial message in 1892, the powers of the two Houses in financial legislation were equal, and that therefore violence had been used against the Peers to prevent them from exercising their undoubted constitutional powers.

So great was Ito's chagrin over the Emperor's action that he resigned his office, and, doubtless to arouse public sympathy, begged to be stripped of all his titles and allowed to retire into private life as plain Ito Hirobumi. But the Emperor refused to sanction either of his petitions, and ordered him to continue in office. The session came to an end on March 24, 1901, without further mishap, the Peers in high dudgeon voting *nem.-con.* all Bills sent up to them.

After the close of the session the Seiyukai returned to its squabbles, Watanabe being the storm centre. Early in April the Finance Minister, with Ito's sanction, announced the postponement of certain undertakings provided for in the Budget because of the impossibility of obtaining the necessary funds by domestic loans. This action was criticized severely by his opponents in the Cabinet, and finally, on April 20, the five party members of the Administration presented an ultimatum to the Minister President, requiring him either to dismiss Watanabe or accept their resignations. Compromise proving impossible, on May 2 Ito resigned, his action being imitated by the rest of the Ministers with the exception of Kodama, who had succeeded Katsura in the War Office in December 1900.

The fall of the third Ito Ministry, after eight months in office, was proximately due to party dissensions ; but even if the Seiyukai had been a homogeneous association it could not have saved Ito from the hostile power of the military oligarchy operating through the House of Peers and the Court. His policy of opposition to the designs of the militarist clique, initiated in 1898 by setting up the Okuma-Itagaki Cabinet and continued in 1900 by allying himself with the Seiyukai, brought on a definitive struggle between the civil and military sections in the oligarchy. In that strife Ito stood almost alone, and knowing his weakness in the Council of the Elder Statesmen, he turned to the people for support, and found little or none. During the first decade of the parliamentary régime the interest in constitutional progress had flagged, and the struggle for commercial development and military expansion absorbed all attention. For the change Ito was mainly responsible, as the Constitution which he fathered made political progress impossible, and his policy in 1894 had turned the nation's thoughts towards conquest.

It was not until June 2 that a new Administration was formed, with Katsura as Minister President. The month which elapsed between the fall of Ito and the rise of Katsura was spent in a series of manœuvres eminently characteristic of the Japanese system. It was reported that Ito had recommended Yamagata as his successor, but if this is to be credited Ito must have had some sinister object in view ; Yamagata was not to be enticed into office again—at least, not so long as the Seiyukai remained a solid phalanx in opposition to the oligarchy. Then the premiership was offered in turn to Inouye, Katsura, and Ito, and finally to Katsura again, who accepted it. This hawking of the highest political office from door to door, unseemly as the performance was, had an object. The military party desired to completely humiliate their opponents, not only Ito, but also the politicians of all parties. As evidence of the incompetency of the civil party in the oligarchy, Inouye was compelled to confess his inability to form a Government, and Ito was similarly treated ; then Katsura was led forward by Yamagata, and installed in office at the head of the

Administration. With him were associated a number of the younger members of the oligarchy—Kodama and Yamamoto in the Army and Navy Departments, Komura, Utsumi, Sone, Kiyoura, Kikuchi, Hirata, and Yoshikawa in the civil departments. It was a second-generation Cabinet throughout, not a single member of the original group of Meiji statesmen having been included, though Yamagata, Oyama, and Saigo stood by to lend their assistance if necessary.

The Minister President immediately announced his attitude toward the parties, for though the politicians could not form an Administration, it was in their power to obstruct. Katsura declared that he would remain neutral, neither dependent on the parties nor independent of them. The Teikokuto announced their support ; the Seiyukai decided to remain neutral and the Kenseito independent. In this attitude of mind the Government and the parties came together in the Diet on December 7, 1901. The organization of the two Houses having been completed, the formal opening ceremony was performed on December 10, and immediately afterwards the Budget was introduced by the Finance Minister. The estimates provided for revenues amounting to 278,000,000 yen and for expenditures of three million less. Opposition immediately developed in the ranks of the Seiyukai, which by its control of 160 seats was in a position to block the passage of the Finance Bill. The chief objection of the party was to the proposed inclusion of the Boxer indemnity in the Budget, on the ground that the value of the bonds was uncertain. The Government proposed to sell them to the Deposit Bureau at 80 per cent. of par, while the Seiyukai wished to create a separate account and segregate the bonds until it became evident exactly how much they were worth. The point of the whole dispute, as far as the Government was concerned, was obvious. If the Boxer indemnity bonds were not to be included in the Budget, then a loan would have to be floated in order to balance the year's account, or else new taxes would have to be imposed. Upon this question the Kensei-honto, seeing a possibility of getting into the good graces of the Government, opposed the Seiyukai, but its support was not sufficient to carry the measure. There was nothing for Katsura to do but approach the Seiyukai leaders. Ozaki and Matsuda were invited to a conference at the Prime Minister's residence, and though both sides remained obdurate for a week, at last the terms of an *entente* were arranged. The party agreed to the inclusion of the indemnity bonds in the Budget at the rate of 70 per cent. of par, but the Budget was to be withdrawn and redrafted. The Government further agreed to revert to the old method of redeeming its bonds, by drawing lots and paying at par, instead of buying in the open market. From this promise the House of Peers absolved the Government, for when the Bill providing for the change was sent to the Upper House it was unanimously rejected.

With the support of the majority party in the Lower House, and strengthened by that of the Upper, Katsura was able to carry through his measures. The relations between the two Houses were, however, more strained than ever. Following immediately upon their action during the previous session in rejecting Ito's tax Bills, the Peers threw out the Seiyukai's bond redemption measure. Various violent speeches against the Upper Chamber were made in the Lower, in one of which Nemoto Sho compared the House of Peers " to a city inhabited by old-fashioned persons with obsolete views," and declared that it was " not of the slightest use to the State." Matsuda Masahisa warned the Peers that the Seiyukai would not submit to any modifications of the Budget, and intimated that the blame need not be placed upon the party if it did not pass. The Upper House, however, held firmly to the view that party government was an abomination, and it was disposed to range itself against the Representatives upon principle, independent of specific measures, and undoubtedly the hostility of the Peers to the parties had been a substantial obstacle to the smooth operation of parliamentary institutions in Japan.

The session closed on March 11, and the parties turned to make their preparation for the General Election, the first to be held under the revised election law. The Seiyukai could claim to have supported the Government and carried through a programme of legislation, and Ito even went to the length of announcing that a Ministry must be respected and supported as long as it enjoyed the confidence of the sovereign. Okuma and his followers, having given up their rather clumsy party name, had reverted to their former title of Shimpoto (Progressives). During the latter part of the session, after the Government alliance with the Seiyukai was effected, the Shimpoto had adopted the policy of assailing the Cabinet, mainly by means of interpellations, with a view to attracting the attention of the country. Thus on January 25 Oishi Masami presented a list of questions relating to the Government's foreign and domestic policy ; the failure to float a foreign loan ; the Australian policy of excluding Japanese immigrants ; the Korean and Manchurian problems ; the Saghalien fishery dispute with Russia, and the Chinese loot scandal ; the defects in the arrangements for local government and the abuses of party politics in local elections.

In the main, the Shimpoto canvassed the country with their old slogans against clan government and in favour of responsible Cabinets, and their motto was " Peace with honour abroad, progress with order at home." The election resulted in the return of 190 Seiyukai members, 105 Shimpoto, 18 Teikokuto, 56 Independents, and 7 Sanshi Club.

During the campaign a flood of eloquence was poured forth in reviling the dishonesty of the times, especially by the speakers serving the interests of Seiyukai candidates. In the instructions issued in April to the branch

The Russo-Japanese War

offices of the Seiyukai, Ito had adjured his followers to abstain from all "unlawful or questionable acts." But his attempts to conduct an honest election, if the accounts in the contemporary Press are to be believed, failed. The *Nippon*, while it admitted that violence and bloodshed had disappeared and that expensive entertainments to constituents had been discontinued, maintained that election expenses remained heavy, ranging from about 2,000 to 6,000 yen per seat. This was attributed to the practice of purchasing votes. Each candidate had a regiment of canvassers who were sent about among the electorate to obtain the signatures of his supporters, and the *Nippon* stated that all the books of signatures thus circulated in a district often contained more names than the total number of voters, from which state of affairs it deduced the conclusion that the voters were "selling their wares in more than one market." The *Asahi* confirmed this report, adding that the candidates announced no principles and discussed no national problems on a public platform, but appealed to sentiment and personal favour, and were, moreover, so persistent that they and their canvassers had become a public nuisance. In many places signs bearing the inscription "No Admittance to Election Candidates" were posted at the outer gates of houses. Seats in the Diet were held in high esteem, even though the sessional allowance was only 800 yen and the cost of an election at least as great as the remuneration received for attendance on four annual sessions.

As was now the custom, the political parties held their general meetings just previous to the opening of the Diet and decided upon their course of conduct during the session. The Shimpoto announced that its members would strive to establish party Cabinets ; to secure administrative and financial reform ; to reduce the land tax ; to oppose all naval increase not consistent with the country's financial position ; to develop Japan's trade in Asia. The Seiyukai determined to oppose naval expansion and the continuance of the existing land tax, and Ito accepted the policy, though with the proviso that he would support naval increase if funds could be obtained without further increase of taxation—i.e. by cutting down administrative and other expenses.

The Diet assembled on December 6, 1902, and organized for the session. Kataoka Kenkichi and Motoda Hajime were elected President and Vice-President of the Lower House, and the various Standing Committees were appointed. The official opening occurred on December 9, and on the following day the Budget was brought down by Sone, the Finance Minister. On December 13 Katsura outlined the policy of the Government as including naval expansion, the increase of the land taxes, administrative reforms, and general postponement of all enterprises undertaken by the Government except those dictated by military necessity. This declaration, along with Sone's explanation of the Budget, elicited little comment, and the financial programme was handed *pro forma* to the Budget Committee for consideration.

The Land Tax Bill introduced by the Government provided that the old rates as adopted should be changed to $3\frac{1}{3}$ per cent. and 5 per cent. upon the assessed valuation of rural and urban lands respectively, and that the proportion of the national land tax collected by prefectures and cities should be reduced from one-third to one-fourth and in the towns and villages from one-fifth to one-seventh. On December 16 the Bill was reported by the Committee with an adverse recommendation, and after some debate, in which the parliamentary leaders of both the Seiyukai and the Shimpoto opposed the measure, the sittings of the Lower House were suspended for five days. As no compromise was reached by December 20, a further suspension for seven days was decreed by Imperial order. On Sunday, December 28, the House resumed the sitting, and, having voted against the

Bill, the Diet was dissolved by Katsura, and the Budget of 1902-3 was subsequently reapplied.

The motive for this dissolution was certainly not to be found in the Cabinet's desire to refer the question of the land tax to the electors. It could scarcely be expected that the people would support the Government in a project for increasing taxation, as against the Representatives who had opposed it. Katsura did not look forward to the election of a Diet which would pass his measures, but he did assume, and quite correctly, that a dissolution as a disciplinary measure would bring the parties to their senses. The cost of an election was so great that the outlay upon a seat could only be recouped by allowing the Diet to run the limit of its natural life. During four years the sessional indemnities would amount to 3,200 yen, which on the lowest estimated average of election expenses would just repay the outlay incurred in securing a seat. Further, if any profit was to be made out of the business of sitting in the Lower House, it must come by way of bribes received from the Government. In the main, though there were exceptions, this was the general view of the matter in 1902. Frequent elections meant financial ruin to members of the Lower House, and an unyielding opposition to the Government destroyed all hope of profit. In a system of government like Japan's, no party can hope by its mere numerical strength to come into office, and if it does do so by accident, as in 1898 and 1900, it cannot long remain there. The appointment and dismissal of the members of an Administration are the prerogatives of the Emperor, not of the people.

In the political crisis at the end of 1902, Ito was not consulted by the members of the Seiyukai's General Committee, and his influence with the party of which he was the nominal leader practically vanished. After the elections in March, he read his followers a lecture on the subject of fruitless opposition to the Government, and threatened to resign his leadership if they persisted in their hostility to the Katsura Cabinet. He intimated also that he had modified his views on the increase of the land tax, and regarded naval expansion as essential to the country's safety. This change in his attitude towards militarism may be set down to his anticipation of the Russo-Japanese War, which he regarded as practically inevitable after the failure of his efforts to bring about an understanding with Russia and the conclusion by the military party of the Anglo-Japanese Alliance in January 1902.

The extraordinary session of the Diet which was convened in the spring of 1903 sat from May 12 to June 5. The Seiyukai had been returned by the country with 193 seats, the Shimpoto with 191, the Teikokuto with 18, and the Independents with 74. Kataoka and Motoda were re-elected President and Vice-President of the Lower House, and forty out of the sixty-three members on the Budget Committee were Seiyukai men. An arrangement had been made in April by the representatives of the two chief parties to oppose the Cabinet, but as the Government had not disclosed its policy the details could not be settled. On May 11 a conference of the representatives of the two parties was held, and resulted in the virtual breaking up of the agreement between them. The Shimpoto wished to impeach the Cabinet by carrying an Address to the Throne, but the Seiyukai would only consent to a resolution of want of confidence by the Lower House. An Address would of necessity call upon the Emperor to take sides with his Ministers or against them, whereas a mere resolution involved no action whatever.

The Government introduced the Budget, which had been trimmed in order to meet the objections taken against it in the previous session except in the case of the Tax Bill, the reintroduction of which once more precipitated a crisis ; Ito was, however, able to swing his party into line with the Cabinet. The Shimpoto was furious at the outcome. Okuma declared that his party had been left in the lurch and that Ito had deserted his principles, and recommended that the Seiyukai should repudiate its leader. Nevertheless, the short session ended in a triumph for the Government. The Shimpoto Address to the Throne, introduced on May 30, was defeated, the Budget was enacted into law, and as far as the military party was concerned their main object was gained, funds having been provided for naval expansion, though not as generously as they had desired.

With the close of the session, and even before the end, Ito's party began to disintegrate. Ozaki had seceded in May, with twenty-two others, on the ground that Ito had committed the party to the *entente* with the Government without consulting the General Committee. On June 6 the Tosa section, headed by Kataoka Kenkichi and Hayashi Yuzo, withdrew. When Ito resigned from the leadership of the party in July it had been reduced to 123 members, and had lost its control of the Lower House.

Saionji, at Ito's recommendation, was chosen as the new head of the party, a position which he continued to occupy until the close of the Meiji Era. His claim to the position was twofold. In the first place, he was a Liberal and a believer in party government, some years of his boyhood and early youth having been spent at school in France, whence he had returned to Japan in the 'seventies a convinced Republican. He started a small paper to propagate his views, but after a few issues it was discontinued at the request of the Court. He was thereafter drafted into the bureaucracy, and had spent his life in honourable if inconspicuous services for his country. With the formation of the Seiyukai in 1900 he was appointed a member of its General Committee, and when Ito came into power toward the end of the year, Saionji was made President of the Privy Council. In the second place, he was a nobleman of the very highest rank, descended from one of the few Kuge families which had followed

T

the Emperor Go Daigo into exile at Yoshino in the fourteenth century, for which reason the Court had always looked upon his house with favour. The Japanese, for whom a romantic story has an extraordinary attraction, had for centuries regarded the Saionji with admiration, not only because of their loyalty to the Court but also for their adherence through more than two hundred years to the vow of perpetual celibacy made by one of the early ancestors of the house. That such a vow did not result in the extinction of the family is to be explained by the fact that it applied to the taking of legal consorts only, and not to concubinage, extensively practised in Japan during the feudal period. The present Marquis Saionji was therefore, by reason of his Liberal opinions, his exalted rank and lineage, his favour at Court, and the romantic history of his house, fitted to become the head of a great political party.

It is unnecessary to comment upon Ito's elevation to the Privy Council immediately after his resignation from the Seiyukai, except to draw attention to the most probable explanation of it. The Emperor called him to the post and he obeyed the Imperial command. But in Japan, as elsewhere, such posts are not filled or vacated at the Emperor's order except upon the advice of the Government of the day. Katsura and his master Yamagata were therefore responsible for the Emperor's summons. They were not averse to humiliating Ito by compelling his desertion of the Seiyukai, nor to disrupting the party by removing its leader. The employment of such violence against an opponent was not without precedent in Japan : for example, in 1874 Itagaki had been ordered into the oligarchy by the Emperor. Saionji, as we have related, had been diverted from a career of opposition to the oligarchy into the bureaucracy by the exercise of the same authority. The weapon is still made use of, for in January 1913, at the very beginning of the present reign, Saionji's connection with the Seiyukai was broken by his appointment to the Genro, as Ito's had been ten years before by his elevation to the Privy Council.

Towards the close of the year the Diet assembled once more, but was dissolved before any business whatever was transacted. The Lower House had met on December 5 and completed its organization for the session, Kono Hironaka being elected President of the Lower House. On December 10 the Emperor attended and read the Speech from the Throne. The Representatives, having returned to their Chamber, proceeded to pass the usual formal reply. It was at this point that Kono launched a *coup* unprecedented in Japan, and precipitated a dissolution of the Diet. The reply to the Speech from the Throne had become so much a matter of routine that the Lower House had adopted the practice of leaving its composition and presentation entirely to the President and Chief Secretary of the House, and for some years the formality of reading and voting the reply had been dropped. On this occasion Kono received the reply from the Chief Secretary, put it into his pocket, and drew forth and proceeded to read a document of his own preparation, which was an impeachment of the Cabinet in the following terms :—

" The present is a time when the fortunes of the country have reached a unique and unprecedented stage, yet the measures taken by the Ministers of State are not in keeping with the situation, since at home they pursue a policy of opportunism and abroad they forfeit opportunities. We, your servants, cannot but regard these things with profound solicitude, and we earnestly pray that your Majesty will bring your enlightened judgment to bear on the situation."

This reply, which he read twice in a loud voice, was passed without dissent ; he withdrew immediately, resigned both his office and his membership in the House, and awaited the consequences. The House assembled on December 11, but before any business was taken up an Imperial rescript was read dissolving the Diet.

This extraordinary incident, the result of Kono's strategy, was an illustration of the peculiarities of the Japanese mind. If Kono foresaw the results of his dissolution *coup*, he did not allow himself to be deflected from his purpose. It was nothing to him that the outside world should regard another dissolution of the Diet as a proof of lack of harmony between the governed and the governors in Japan. For years he had been a staunch supporter of a strong foreign policy, and his quarrel with the Government was based not upon its militarist programme but the weakness of its foreign policy. To call public attention to the encroachments of Russia in Manchuria and Korea and the apparent indifference thereto of Japan's Ministers was his purpose. He shared his plans with no one, but, utilizing his position as President of the Lower House and his knowledge of the carelessness of its members in dealing with the reply to the Speech from the Throne, he carried his project single-handed to a successful issue. The public, though startled, approved Kono's action, and lauded his loyalty and indifference to personal consequences, much as it had applauded the murder of Ii Kamon no Kami in 1860, that of Mori Arinori in 1889, or Hoshi Toru in 1901. The suicide of General Nogi in 1912, on the day of the Meiji Tenno's funeral, as evidence of his grief and as a protest against the luxury and corruption in the Army, is the most recent example of this peculiarity of the Japanese psychology. Kono Hironaka, far from ruining his political career, continued to sit in the Diet, and was given the portfolio of Agriculture and Commerce in the Okuma Cabinet of 1914.

But the temporary excitement over Kono's action was soon overshadowed by the war with Russia, which broke out in February 1904. At once the interminable dissensions in the Diet ceased. As in 1894, all parties vied with one another in loyal support of the Government, and the nation threw itself into the struggle in the whole-hearted way of a homogeneous people. As Li Hung Chang in 1894 had misinterpreted the early dissensions of the Japanese Diet, so Alexieff in 1904 had underestimated the loyalty of the nation to its Government.

It is not possible to explain the Russo-Japanese War, as the Chino-Japanese War can be explained, as a diversion of the popular interest from domestic to foreign politics. It is true that in 1903 Katsura begged the Emperor to accept his resignation on the ground that the Diet had rejected the financial measures necessary to complete the national defences, but that course was taken mainly for the purpose of warning the Diet against further obstruction. He knew only too well that he could control the Diet by corrupting its members, and he had no personal scruples against such a course, nor was he impressed by the high-sounding phrases of the Imperial utterances during the whole reign, " the grand purposes of the Restoration," " the consummation of the constitutional system," " the Constitution, which maintained the immemorial polity above, and admitted those below to a share in the administration on the basis of the people's welfare." Katsura cared for none of these things. His interests had been and were in the Army and Navy, and he consented to play the rôle of the Minister President of State to further the military party's designs, not those of the civil party. The war with Russia was to him, therefore, not connected with domestic politics ; it was undertaken with strictly militarist ambitions, not as a means of producing harmony at home. It was a national policy in the sense that Yoshida Shoin's had been, the extension of the Empire to include large portions of the continent of Asia. " On to Lake Baikal " was the plan of the General Staff, which gradually filtered down to the people and became the national ambition. Korea, Manchuria, Mongolia, and all Siberia east of Lake Baikal were to be absorbed.

A Political History of Japan

The causes of the war are to be looked for in the weakness of Korea and China, and in the ambitions of Japan and Russia. We have already pointed out the source of Japan's policy in Asia, a policy still pursued because still unaccomplished. The direction of Russian ambition in the Far East, once the colossus of Europe reached the Pacific, was perforce south, and in turning south Russia encountered China, Korea, and Japan. As early as 1885, while Ito and the civil party were still supreme, Japan sought to check the encroachments of both China and Russia by raising Korea to the rank of an independent kingdom, and by starting her upon a career of economic, civil, and military reform and reconstruction. The failure to accomplish any results in Korea was primarily due to lack of men and capital, for if suitable immigrants with money enough could have been poured into Korea, that country might have progressed sufficiently to frighten China off. But Japan had neither men nor money to spare. The policy of peaceful development of Korea having failed, Ito in 1894 had been driven by pressure at home to consent to a war with China over Korean independence. The result of that war was the overthrow of the civil party in the Japanese oligarchy, the galvanizing into life of the inherent chauvinism of the people, and the appearance of Russia as Japan's rival in Asia.

From 1895 until the outbreak of the war with Russia, Japan was a nation preparing for an inevitable conflict, the issue being predominance in the Far East : the various shifts of Russian and Japanese policy which fill that decade are to be explained as the preliminaries to the struggle. The only Japanese efforts to avoid the conflict emanated from anti-Government sources. An alliance with Russia on the basis of Korea for the Japanese, Manchuria for the Russians, and the Middle Kingdom for the Chinese, was advocated by Ozaki Yukio and a small circle of his friends. Okuma thundered against Russia and China. The Government

The Russo-Japanese War

sparred for time, as its military preparations could not be completed before 1904 at the earliest, and Russia was waiting for the completion of the Siberian railway. By the alliance with Great Britain, signed January 30, 1902, Japan enlisted the services as well as the capital of one of the great European Powers, as an offset to the Russo-French *entente*. Great Britain's advantage from the alliance was not so apparent at the time, and if her action is to be understood it must be regarded as the beginning of a sweeping change in her traditional foreign policy, dictated in 1902 by Russian designs on India.

But the most interesting, if not the most important, feature of Japanese policy during the decade preceding the war was its acquiescence in the American Note anent the integrity of China. Japan did not desire, either before or after the war, the integrity of China. The national ambitions of the Japanese were incompatible with such a policy. If their Empire was to expand in Asia, not only Russian and Korean but Chinese territory as well must be absorbed. According to Yoshida's book, to which every militarist member of the oligarchy subscribed, Manchuria and Mongolia must be wrested from China. Nevertheless, in 1899 the Hay proposal was accepted as a bid for the sympathy of England and America in a war the object of which was to secure a foothold in Asia. When Russia was cleared out of Manchuria in 1906, the policy of China's integrity and the " open door " were repudiated, not publicly, except where Korea was concerned, but quietly and unostentatiously. In 1910 Knox's plan to neutralize the Manchurian railways with a view to restoring them ultimately to China, checking in the meantime the extension of Japanese and Russian influence in the three Eastern provinces, was burked by Japan's scandalous breach of diplomatic etiquette in immediately publishing the contents of the note. When two years later the Chinese Republic was set up, the Japanese looked with great disfavour upon Yuan Shi-kai's appointment to the

Presidency, not only because he was China's strongest man, but Japan's implacable foe as well, and the counter-revolution which followed was planned and led by Japanese military officers, with or without the consent of the Government, but certainly with its connivance. In 1915, when all the great European Powers who had interests in Asia were otherwise absorbed, the Japanese Government under Okuma, the lifelong exponent of a forward policy in China, took occasion to begin an encroachment not only in Manchuria and Mongolia but upon the Middle Kingdom itself, thus beginning a new chapter in Chino-Japanese relations.

Japan's ambitions for predominance in the Far East were at the root of the conflict with Russia in 1904-6, but her militaristic demand for a " place in the sun " was not something with which the Powers were likely to sympathize, hence Japan's rôle as the defender of China's integrity and Korea's independence was advertised abroad in 1904, as well as the plea of national defence. These were objects which Europe and America could understand, and doubtless the United States and Europe, outside of France perhaps, were willing enough that Japan's should be the hand to check Russia's Asiatic pretensions. The English, for instance, could perceive from their own policy in Belgium and the Netherlands the necessity for Japan's insistence upon an independent Korea, for with Russia dominant in that peninsula Japan's position would be perilous in the extreme. When the conflict began, Japan had therefore not only the sympathy of the Anglo-Saxon world, but its active support.

The immediate causes of the war were similar to those of the Chino-Japanese conflict a decade before. Apart from the nonfulfilment by Russia of the terms of the Manchurian Agreement—a convention between Russia and China signed in April 1902, by the terms of which Manchuria was to be evacuated by the former within eighteen months—Korea proved the proximate *casus belli*. In the spring of 1903 the Korean Govern-

The Russo-Japanese War

ment granted a concession to a Russian timber company to exploit the forests on its northern frontier, and this was interpreted in Japan as a move against the independence of Korea. After seven or eight months of fruitless negotiation with Russia, during which that Empire's Viceroy of the Amur, Admiral Alexieff, displayed a disregard of ordinary diplomatic courtesy that must have been galling in the extreme to the Japanese Foreign Office, Japan presented an ultimatum, and began hostilities in February 1904.

On sea and land, the Japanese were successful in all engagements, but though Port Arthur was captured and the Russians were driven back as far as Mukden, they were by no means beaten. In 1905 Japan, realizing that it had accomplished all that could be expected under the circumstances, made the first move towards the conclusion of peace.

The situation, as far as Russia was concerned, when President Roosevelt invited the two belligerents to a meeting on American soil with the object of composing their differences, was far from desperate. Her field armies were still intact, and her generals were convinced that the initial difficulties of the war had been overcome and a successful offensive might soon be entered upon. But the position of the Tsar and the war-party at home was beset with the gravest difficulties. The peace party clamoured for the end of the war, and serious internal disturbances were taking place. Moreover, Russia had lost—for reasons which we have already referred to—the sympathy and encouragement of the world, with the exception of her ally France. To refuse to participate in the proposed peace convention was impossible, and to take part in it offered at least the prospect of satisfying the peace party, and perhaps of winning the good will of the Powers. The Tsar's decision to send representatives to Portsmouth was taken as a result of the widely circulated and presumably accurate report that the Japanese Government would demand an indemnity as the *sine qua non* of peace, Russia believing that the indemnity could be made the rock upon which the negotiations might be wrecked, for it was obvious that with her armies still in the field and in no danger of ultimate defeat, and her territory not invaded seriously, it was manifestly unnecessary for her to agree to reimburse Japan for the expenses of the campaigns. This explanation of Russia's entrance into the negotiations was given immediately after the conclusion of peace, and presumption of its truth is strengthened by the subsequent disgrace of the two Russian envoys, Witte and Rosen.

The situation in Japan in the spring of 1905 can be fairly accurately deduced from an interview given by Yamagata to the *Nichi Nichi Shimbun* in September of that year, even if the matter of the personal letter from the Emperor of Japan to President Roosevelt, intimating that his good offices as mediator would be welcomed, be ignored. As far as we know, this letter has never been published, though Colonel Roosevelt has affirmed categorically that it is in his possession. In this interview, Yamagata stated that " peace was made because in the unanimous opinion of the Genro and Cabinet Ministers such a step was wisest, having regard to the Empire's financial resources, to the sequence of its expansion, to the difficulty of striking a decisive blow at Russia in East Asia, and to the opinion of the world."

As in 1895, the Government, by the terms of peace to which it agreed, made itself so unpopular with the people that it was forced to resign. Komura, the Japanese plenipotentiary and Minister of Foreign Affairs, was made the scapegoat, and his life was threatened. Serious riots broke out in September 1906 in Tokyo, and the city was put under martial law, a virtual state of siege lasting for three months as a consequence. Rioting on a somewhat smaller scale occurred in other cities, as a protest against what the populace called a " disgraceful peace." The significance of these demonstrations against the terms of the Portsmouth Treaty was not clear at the time, and they were explained by the contemporary Press as a natural, though disturbing, reaction on the part of the lower orders. But sufficient time has elapsed to view the events surrounding the Treaty of Portsmouth in approximately their true historical perspective.

Considering the Russian and Japanese views of the situation in juxtaposition, the Tsar's Government as decidedly opposed to peace, the Japanese as decidedly in favour of it, the interesting question arises, How did the Portsmouth Treaty eventuate? Why was it regarded by the Japanese nation on the one hand, and by the Russian Government on the other, as a disgraceful surrender?

Various theories to explain the successful conclusion of the treaty have been propounded. One widely circulated in America attributed the event to the pressure exerted by President Roosevelt upon the Japanese envoys ; to his powers of persuasion Komura's waiving of the indemnity at the eleventh hour has been attributed. An elaboration of that theory has recently been published by the President of the Associated Press, Mr. Melville Stone, in which he claims that it was to his—Mr. Stone's—untiring energies, his intimate friendship with the envoys of both Powers, and his ability to dictate to President Roosevelt, that success was at last achieved when failure seemed absolutely certain.

Theories of this sort, however flattering they may be to the makers, lack even the remotest semblance of historical truth. They represent that the Japanese envoys arrived in America to attend the Conference bearing terms of peace which included, as an irreducible minimum, the payment by Russia of a substantial indemnity, and that the Russian plenipotentiaries came with instructions to conclude a peace if the claim for an indemnity were not insisted upon, and that finally, after matters had reached a deadlock and many telegrams

had passed between Portsmouth and Tokyo, the
Japanese members of the Conference withdrew their
demand for money compensation. Every one of these
assumptions is erroneous. It is now quite evident that
the Japanese envoys did not go to Portsmouth with
instructions that the indemnity should form part of
the irreducible minimum of the Empire's demands.
Japan was already, in 1905, beginning to feel seriously
the strain of the war. While she had won a notable
victory at sea, in her operations on land, though they
were uniformly successful as far as they went, she had
not succeeded in obtaining any such superiority over
the opposing force as to warrant the belief that the
Russian armies could be crushed within a measurable
time. If the war was to be proceeded with, it was
evident that the huge loans already raised abroad would
not be sufficient to prosecute the campaign with the same
vigour as in the past. It would be necessary to enter
foreign markets again as a borrower, and it seemed
probable that some hesitation would be shown by
investors in taking up the bonds of a nation involved
in a war of exhaustion with a Power of enormous
strength and resources, against which it was impossible
to deliver a crushing military blow. Finance was therefore the great difficulty which loomed up in the future.
It was realized in Tokyo that without unlimited funds
further progress in Manchuria would be impossible,
and at the same time it was obvious that to terminate
the war at the stage then reached would preclude the
recognition of any claim for an indemnity. The
decision faced by the Japanese military oligarchy was
therefore either to end the war as soon as possible
without an indemnity, or to continue it at the price
of ruinous financial sacrifices, with no prospect of an
indemnity when a later peace was concluded. Faced
with this choice, there is no doubt whatever that the
Government sent Komura to Portsmouth with instructions to demand an indemnity, but at the critical
moment to abandon the claim and conclude peace on the

best terms possible. The Yamagata interview made it evident that before the Japanese plenipotentiaries left for Portsmouth the position had been fully considered and a determination to waive the indemnity arrived at, despite the sacrifice thereby involved, because of the pressure of the financial situation in Japan. If this fact had been known, or even suspected, before the Conference, the chances for peace would have been remote. The Russian envoys frankly stated that they had come, in response to President Roosevelt's invitation, to hear the terms suggested by the Japanese, and they let it be understood that they had little faith in the possibility of concluding a treaty at the juncture then reached. The Japanese had repeatedly given to the Press assurances that an indemnity formed part of their minimum demands. Correspondents at Tokyo, Japanese newspapers, and even the Press agent attached to Komura's suite, all were agreed that peace could be concluded only if Russia paid the expenses of the war. It was natural under the circumstances, therefore, that Witte and Rosen should have adopted a liberal attitude as regards the general terms proposed by Japan, while refusing absolutely to entertain the proposition upon which Komura and Takahira laid the most stress, the indemnity. At the same time, Russia was unwilling that the onus of continuing the war should rest upon her, and if the Conference should break up as a result of Japan's insistence upon compensation, then all her envoys had come for would have been gained.

That that was the course actually followed by Count Witte is obvious from the official report of the proceedings at Portsmouth issued by the Japanese Government. Japan's demands were comprised under twelve heads. To three of these—first, the surrender to Japan of Russian warships interned at various neutral ports; second, the limitation of Russian naval strength in the Far East; third, the reimbursement to Japan of the actual expenses of the war—the Russian plenipotentiaries offered unqualified opposition, and after a little discussion the Japanese withdrew the first two as being incompatible with Russia's national honour and prestige. On some other points, also, Russian opposition was offered, with the result that Japan agreed to Chang-chun, not Harbin, as the northern terminus of the South Manchurian Railway, and to the partition of Saghalien, instead of its cession. But on the indemnity claim the Conference reached a deadlock. At this point Witte considered that the negotiations were at an end, for he reported to that effect to his Government, and awaited his recall, confident that Russia would gain applause for the very liberal concessions she had already made and that Japan would be universally condemned for her insistence upon an indemnity. When the plenipotentiaries met on August 29, 1905, it was believed by the Russians that the session would be the last and that they had won. Business being taken up, to show their magnanimity, the Russian delegation intimated that their Government would be willing to cede the whole of Saghalien, when to their consternation the proposition was met by Komura with the sudden withdrawal of the Japanese claim for compensation for the expenses of the war. A greater sensation could not have been created if a bomb had been thrown into the Conference chamber, for the terms of peace already agreed upon now became binding on both parties, and Witte, outmanœuvred, could not refuse his signature.[1] Some hours later he wired his sovereign : " I have the honour to report to your Majesty that Japan has agreed to your demands concerning the conditions of peace, and that consequently peace will be established, thanks to your wise and firm decision, and with strict conformity with the instructions of your Majesty."

[1] For this account of the negotiations I am indebted to Mr. Robert Young, the editor of the *Japan Chronicle*, Kobe, Japan.

CHAPTER XIII

JAPAN ON THE CONTINENT OF ASIA

THE news of the peace was received in Japan at the end of August with the utmost dissatisfaction, and on the first day of September the Japanese papers expressed themselves in terms of the greatest hostility. The *Jiji* made no pretence of being satisfied. The *Nichi Nichi* said that profound discontent would spread to all classes, because the concessions made by the Japanese envoys amounted to a " craven and discreditable surrender," the *Asahi* and *Niroku* that the Government had lifted the crown of victory from the nation's head, the *Hochi* that ratification ought to be refused, the *Yomiuri* that the people must pursue all legal methods to demonstrate their objection to the treaty ; the *Nippon* thought the terms of peace would be useful in reducing Japanese conceit, while the *Shogyo Shimpo* and the *Kokumin* declared that the objects of the war had been attained. The next day the expressions of discontent grew louder. Reports from the provinces showed that everywhere the peace was being denounced. On September 3 the *Niroku*, *Yorodzu*, and the *Hochi* openly advocated the assassination of the members of the Cabinet and the Genro, and hardly a newspaper rose above the level of the most virulent abuse of the authorities. On September 4 the *Jiji* demanded the resignation of the Government, while the *Hochi* and the rest of the Yellow Press teemed with the vilest aspersions, both in text and cartoons, on the personal morality of the members of the Cabinet, especially the Prime

299

Minister. Finally, the *Yorodzu, Niroku, Miyako, Hochi, Jimmin,* and *Nippon* were suppressed. The political parties, the Seiyukai and the Shimpoto, had held general meetings on September 2 to discuss the peace. Saionji addressed the members of the former, and presented the Russian and foreign views of the situation at Portsmouth in an attempt to create a calmer mood among his followers. The meeting adjourned, however, without formulating any definite expression of opinion, though the terms of the peace were characterized as " unsatisfactory." The next day the non-parliamentary members of the party held a meeting, at which resolutions were passed calling upon the Cabinet to resign because the peace was " dishonourable and calculated to work lasting evil to Japan." The Shimpoto's resolution was brief but drastic : " The peace concluded . . . loses sight of the objects of the war and is contrary to the interests of the nation. Therefore we consider it an unprecedented disgrace to the country."

On September 5 a mass meeting of the citizens of Tokyo was called to take place in Hibiya Park, but when the people assembled they found the gates closed by order of the Home Minister and guarded by the police. A fierce riot ensued, and the mob, headed by Kono Hironaka, broke through the iron fence and gained admittance to the park. As evening approached, the rioters attacked the residence of the Home Minister and almost succeeded in setting fire to the building. At this juncture the Guards were called out, and the mob moved off, burning police-boxes as they went. During the night the police-stations in five wards of the city—Kyobashi, Fukugawa, Shitaya, Asakusa, and Yorodzuyabashi—were burned ; the next day the station in Nihonbashi was destroyed, and on September 7 martial law was proclaimed in the capital. Altogether the dead numbered 11, the wounded among the citizens 547 and among the police 471. Persons arrested numbered over 300. The responsibility for all this violence was fastened upon the police, and in consequence the Home Minister, Viscount Yoshikawa, resigned his office.

By September 8th or 9th the military authorities, who had taken over the government of the city, had restored order, and a few days later the Yamagata interview, part of which we have already quoted,[1] was published by the *Nichi Nichi*. This statement had the effect of silencing the demands of the Press for the resignation of the Ministry, for it was obvious that the Peace of Portsmouth was not the blunder of the Cabinet, at any rate. On October 14 the Emperor ratified the treaty thus : " Having carefully examined the various clauses of the peace treaty . . . We find them in full accord with Our wishes and in no respect defective. Therefore, We ratify the said treaty." Two days later, upon the return of the peace mission, Imperial messages congratulating Komura and his colleagues were published.

Nevertheless, Komura's reception at Yokohama was far from a popular demonstration, and the greatest precautions were taken to ensure his personal safety, even his landing-place being kept secret. A great gathering of officials came down from Tokyo and assembled on the Customs quay as if to welcome him, but he was taken ashore direct to the Detached Palace at Benten, where a few of the highest officials awaited him, his staff landing at the Customs House. From the Palace he was driven in a closed carriage, through streets lined by the police, to the station, and proceeded by special train to Tokyo. For many months there was no more unpopular man in Japan.

The crux of all this hostility to the peace and the plenipotentiaries was the failure to exact an indemnity from Russia. In 1895, even though China had not been brought to her knees or Peking captured, the expenses of the war had been more than recouped, and the nation could not see why relief from the

U   [1] See above, p. 294.

financial burden of the war had not been secured in 1905. The debt had enormously increased, and taxation had jumped to a new high level. But the gains were great—Japanese predominance in Korea, the lease of the Liaotung peninsula, Port Arthur, Dalny, and the Chinese Eastern railways south of Changchun, the cession of half the island of Saghalien, and equal rights for Japanese and Russian fishermen on the Siberian littoral. Though the Russian menace had been removed and a foothold in Asia secured—the ostensible and the secret object of the war—the financial burden remained. As debt and taxation were more the concern of the people than of the Government, the people accused their rulers of sacrificing the nation's interests.

At the end of 1905 the debt of the country was in the neighbourhood of 2,000,000,000 yen, divided in the proportion of 12 to 8 between foreign and domestic loans, and the annual interest charge was 90,100,000 yen. The *per capita* debt in 1903-4 was 11·3 yen, in 1905-6, 36·9 yen, and the taxes *per capita* had increased from 5·1 yen to 8·3 yen. Knowledge of these facts partly accounted for the popular uproar against the Cabinet for its failure to include an indemnity in the arrangements for peace. In a certain sense, the Cabinet had been responsible for raising the nation's hopes for reimbursement, since, as we have seen, it was necessary in order to outwit the Russian envoys to give the Japanese demand for an indemnity the greatest publicity. Even though the Governmental Press Bureau was extremely efficient in controlling news coming into and leaving Japan, the danger of the envoys' secret leaking out was too great to warrant even the slightest official intimation of the Government's decision in the matter of the indemnity. The Administration, therefore, foreseeing the inevitable storm, was compelled to read, day after day, the calculations in the newspapers of the amount to be exacted from Russia, knowing full well the strength of the popular indignation which would burst upon their heads when peace was signed. But it was not unaccustomed to such displays of popular hatred and knew its rôle thoroughly.

How the first fury of the storm was weathered we have already seen. Martial law was enforced throughout the country ; thousands of rioters were arrested ; then the Imperial voice spoke and the people were cowed into submission. The Government held on until the end of the year, and then resigned to make room for Saionji and the Seiyukai. The two war sessions of the Diet, held in March 1904 and November 1904 to February 1905, were uninteresting. The various parties loyally supported the Administration, and voted supplies and addresses of confidence in the Army and Navy. The first *post-bellum* session began December 25, 1905. The Speech from the Throne referred to the peace as " honourable " and to the Anglo-Japanese Alliance with " profound satisfaction," and intimated that a convention with Korea had been arranged. The reply from the Lower House was purely formal, but that from the Peers was couched in astonishing terms. Referring to the operations of the Army and Navy, the Upper House attributed the victories to the sovereign thus : " The influence of your Majesty's almost supernatural wisdom then extended to the field," the reply concluding, " Your Majesty's prestige extends to all quarters and the glory of the nation shines over the four seas. We, your Majesty's servants, whose happiness it is to witness these great things, dance with joy and cannot contain our delight."

But if the replies to the Speech from the Throne were extravagant in their expressions of loyalty, the attitude towards the Government of the parties in the Lower House was extremely hostile. Okuma's ideas as to the terms of peace, embodied in a resolution of his party, had been disregarded, and as a consequence the Shimpoto had condemned the Government's policy as a " thousand years' disgrace to

Japan." Ozaki's small following was also consumed with rage over the peace, for which it held the Cabinet responsible. It had adopted a resolution on August 30 to the effect that the object of the war had been forgotten and the honour of the country tarnished. The Seiyukai was like-minded. In the face of all this opposition Katsura wisely withdrew, and announced on December 21 that Saionji had consented to form a Cabinet. On January 6, 1906, the new Ministry was gazetted, with the Cabinet posts widely distributed among the members of the Seiyukai, the oligarchy, and the Independents. Kato Takaaki entered the Foreign Office ; Sakatani, a son-in-law of Baron Shibusawa, the intimate of Inouye Kaoru, the Finance Department ; Terauchi and Saito the military and naval offices; Makino, a son of Okubo Toshimichi, the Department of Education ; Yamagata, a son of the Marquis, the Communications Department ; Matsuoka the Department of Agriculture and Commerce ; and two Seiyukai men, Hara and Matsuda, the Departments of the Interior and of Justice respectively. The *Kokumin* described the new Ministry as a blow to the pretensions of the Seiyukai. The *Jiji* and *Nichi Nichi* made no comment except to praise Saionji's courage in taking up office at such a time. The Yellow Press denounced the new Government, the *Asahi* referring to it as a " hybrid," and the *Hochi* raising the old cry of clan government (Hambatsu Seifu).

The situation was undoubtedly critical, especially on the side of finance. Saionji sent a message to his party on the eve of the reassembling of the Diet, on January 20, pointing out that the whole future of the country depended on the success of the Government's financial measures, and urging the members to co-operate with the Ministry. Throughout the country there was a general feeling that the war had imposed a crushing and inescapable burden of debt and taxation.

Japan on the Continent of Asia

The Diet met on January 22, and appointed Sugita Teiichi President of the Lower House, and on January 25 the general policy of the Government was outlined and the Budget presented. The Prime Minister, after referring to the war and its conclusion, to the Anglo-Japanese Alliance, and the Korean Convention, turned to the items of domestic policy, saying : " At home we have to make the finances firm, to restore the Army and Navy, to contrive the growth of industry, to provide for the extension of education and the progress of learning. . . . This is the time for all classes, with one heart, to face the great problem of the *post-bellum* undertaking." To give effect to this policy eight Government Bills were introduced, as follows :—

1. A Bill relating to the payment of extra-ordinary events expenses—viz. for withdrawing the troops, pensions and rewards, military and naval restoration, and military preparation in Manchuria and Korea, the amount required being 363,000,000 yen.

2. A Bill for establishing a capital fund for the adjustment of the national debt—viz. for amortization, conversion, etc.—110,000,000 yen annually.

3. A Bill to amend the Extraordinary Special Tax Law, in the sense of making it continuing.

4. A Bill to abolish the Naval Maintenance Fund.

7. A Bill to provide for the expenses of experiments and instruction in connection with productive enterprises, 200,000 yen annually.

8. A Bill to provide for the establishment of compulsory Government conditioning of raw silk.

The fifth and sixth Bills in the list were of no interest and therefore are not given in detail.

This programme was generally applauded by the Press, but the *Jiji* took exception to the third Bill in the list, on the ground that all the war taxes were not equally sound, and therefore discrimination must be exercised. The Shimpoto objected *in toto* to the second of the Bills, and demanded that a limit should be set to the continuance of the war taxes. The Seiyukai and the Daido Club, a Katsura party of which Kiyoura and Oura were the leaders, decided to support the whole programme. In spite, therefore, of the opposition of the Shimpoto, the Budget was passed by both Houses, and the session closed on March 28, 1906.

Among the measures not connected directly with the Budget passed during this session was the Railway Bill. The project of railway nationalization was not an entirely new one, for in 1900 the Yamagata Cabinet had introduced a Bill for the purpose, which had been rejected on the ground that compulsory sale involved a violation of the property rights of private individuals. At that time Sakatani, who was the Government delegate in charge of the Bill, admitted the validity of the objection. The proposal was put forward in 1905 by the Katsura Government, which was evidently desirous of finding new sources of revenue and regarded the State management of railways as a promising venture. The project, however, drew from the Press little but hostile comment. Okuma, whose opinions never failed to obtain the widest publicity, declared that his party would oppose the measure on the ground that it would only add to the existing burdens of the State. The official view presented by the Director of the Railway Bureau was to the effect that either the railways must be nationalized or made to combine into one system, in order to aid in the development of commerce and industry by granting rebates to importers and exporters. The rates for ocean transport had already been determined upon this basis, and the Government desired to complete the arrangements in so far as railway rates were concerned. From these official expressions it was obvious that the Government had thoroughly studied the methods in vogue in

Germany as to the uses to which the facilities of transportation should be put.

In 1906, on March 6, a Government Bill to nationalize the private railways, with a total mileage of 3,200 miles, was introduced in the Lower House. The immediate effect was the resignation of the Foreign Minister. His objections to the measure were as follows : It was a contravention of the Constitution (Article XXVII), for by forcing the sale of private property individual rights would be seriously impaired ; it would involve another domestic loan and thus complicate the problem of finance ; it assumed the capacity of the Government to operate the railways economically, an assumption not warranted by history. The Press opposed the measure with the greatest vigour and unanimity, but, nevertheless, in the Lower House the Bill passed its first reading on March 16th, and, upon the motion of Haseba Junko, was carried, the other stages of its progress being omitted. On March 19th the Bill as passed by the Lower House was taken up by the Peers, and handed over to a Committee with instructions to report by the 27th of the same month. On that date the Committee reported the Bill with certain amendments, the most important of which were to extend to ten years the period during which the purchase was to be completed and to reduce from thirty-two to seventeen the number of railways to be purchased. In this form the measure passed all three readings and was sent back to the Lower House. The Government accepted the Peers' amendments and asked the Lower House to do likewise. In a sitting full of exciting incidents and disgraced by a free fight, quelled only by the interference of the police after a number of the members had been injured and the furniture around the rostrum broken, the Bill was passed unanimously, its opponents having retired from the Chamber.

The railway nationalization law involved the purchase of about nine-tenths of the total mileage under

A Political History of Japan

private ownership, the cost to the Government being estimated at 420,000,000 yen. In order to obviate the necessity of floating a loan, it was determined to pay the owners of the railways in Government bonds, bearing 5 per cent. interest annually. To protect the bond market, it was further decided that the actual bonds should not be handed over to the owners until the expiration of a period of five years. If these arbitrary provisions with regard to payment constituted a real basis for opposition on the part of the owners, the same could hardly be said of the total compensation. The selling price was arrived at by the Government by taking the average profits of each railway company for the three years previous to June 30, 1904, and capitalizing them at twenty years' purchase. The cost of construction of the railways thus taken over was estimated at 230,000,000 yen, which was 190,000,000 yen less than the purchase price paid by the Government. The excess of almost 100 per cent. was paid for unexpired franchises or to satisfy the owners.

The disbursement of immense sums of borrowed money owing to the reckless financial policy of the Government, in conjunction with the reaction from the extreme disappointment over the terms of peace in 1905, started an industrial boom. In the thirteen months between the conclusion of peace and October 1906, some 900,000,000 yen was subscribed for the promotion of new or the expansion of existing enterprises. These subscriptions were not fully paid up, but it was estimated that nearly 400,000,000 yen in cash had been invested in the new securities. The *Kokumin* in September 1906 stated that 183 new companies with a capital of 248,000,000 yen had been started, and that the capital of existing enterprises had been increased from 214,000,000 to 400,000,000 yen. Among the promotions of this period was the Dai Nippon Seito Kaisha (The Japan Sugar Refining Company), formed by the amalgamation of the Tokyo **and**

Osaka Refineries, with a capital of 12,000,000 yen. This company a year or two later was implicated in one of the greatest political scandals of the Meiji Era. The stock market became the centre of interest, and a mania for speculation in securities became universal. The prices of shares rose rapidly during the second half of the year, the bubble bursting in January 1907, the bottom being reached in June. The prices of a few well-known stocks serve to illustrate the extent of the inflation. Bank of Japan shares, par 200 yen, paying a dividend of 12 per cent., yielding 6 per cent., rose to 585 in September and to 1,000 in December. At that price the yield was 1·2 per cent. Specie Bank stock, par 100, dividend of 12 per cent., rose to 229 in September and 360 in December ; yield 3·3 per cent. Among the industrials, Kanegafuchi Cotton Spinning, par 50 yen, dividend 16 per cent., was 125 in July, and rose to 299 in January 1907 ; yield 2·6 per cent. After the boom exploded, prices tumbled in a ratio equal to their previous rise. Tokyo Gas fell from 191 in January to 90 in June, Kanegafuchi from 299 to 140, Fuji Cotton Spinning from 244 to 88, and Tokyo Stock Exchange from 780 to 123.

But even these astonishing figures do not begin to represent the extent of the mania. Not only were the shares of established corporations margined, but rights to shares (*kenri kabu*) in wild-cat companies, which never came into existence, were eagerly bought and sold. By the middle of 1907 the fever of speculation had burned itself out, and the nation, except for the few who had made fortunes, settled down into a state of financial depression which has lasted practically until the present day.

It was in the midst of the boom that the Diet opened in December 1906. The Government in preparing the Budget evidently had been in a very optimistic frame of mind, for the estimates of revenues and expenditures were balanced at 611,000,000 yen. When the financial programme was introduced into the House on January 22, the Finance Minister stated that "the general condition of the revenue is excellent and shows an increasing tendency." Nevertheless, not one of the influential newspapers defended the Budget, and the *Nippon* drew attention to the fact that before the war the State's expenditures had been 275,000,000 yen. The enormous increase it attributed almost entirely to the charges for the debt services and expansion of armaments. While the interest on the national debt and the funds required for its gradual liquidation were proper charges on the revenues, the case was different with the funds expended by the military party on the Army and Navy. In the Budget Committee, Oishi Masami, while he welcomed the " positive " financial policy of the Cabinet, inquired as to the sources of revenue out of which the Government proposed to defray the continuing expenditures on armaments in the years to come. He likewise wanted to know what enemy the Government was preparing to meet by its " expansionary " military programme. This point was brought up again and again, but the Government through the various Ministers combated vigorously such an interpretation of the purpose of the expenditures on the Army and Navy. Terauchi, the Minister of War, assured the Diet that the money spent on armaments was not a threat against any foreign Power, but merely an insurance against attack. Sakatani explained it as a policy not of military expansion but of renewal of military stores depleted by the war.

In the Diet the only opponents of the Budget were the eleven members of the Yukokai, headed by Shimada and Ozaki. When the Budget Committee reported the estimates on February 12 in the form presented by the Government, Miwa, a member of the Yukokai, moved that it be returned for redrafting and the excision of 100,000,000 yen. The motion was lost, as it was supported by only thirteen votes, and the report of the Committee was adopted. Similarly, the Peers voted the whole programme on March 15. The attitude of the parties to the Government's financial policy was on the whole favourable. The Seiyukai on January 19th adopted a resolution which committed the party to support a " positive " policy in the development of industry, the extension of education, the completion of the national defences, the protection of Korea, and the exploitation of Manchuria. The Shimpoto being in one of its periodic disruptive fits, Oishi's faction having gained the upper hand and ousted Okuma from the leadership of the party, it condemned the Budget because " expenses and revenues were not balanced," but in other respects it approved of the " forward " policy of the Cabinet. The Daido Club, a small Katsura party under the nominal leadership of Oura, was solid for the militarist Budget.

In respect to other parts of the Government's programme of legislation, especially to the *Gun* Abolition Bill, there was great diversity of opinion among the parties. The members of the Daido Club ranged themselves in opposition to the Cabinet, and Katsura came out openly in the *Hochi* with the accusation against the Seiyukai that certain promoters had corrupted the party in the interests of a project to establish a rival stock exchange in Tokyo. Thus, while the session resulted in the enactment into law of the main Bills presented by the Government, and while it resulted particularly in the voting for another year at least of immense sums for the Army and Navy, it was not difficult to see that the military party was perfecting its plans for a return to power, in order to carry through the annexation of Korea and incidentally to reap the rich harvest of spoils from office.

Immediately after the close of the war the Government had made a beginning upon the task of consolidating Japan's position on the continent of Asia. By a reconstruction of the Anglo-Japanese Alliance, which was signed in London in August 1905, the terms of the original pact were materially altered. The new treaty provided that in case of unprovoked aggression against either Power, the other should come to its assistance, instead of making such assistance dependent on a third Power's joining the aggressor, Great Britain recognizing also Japan's paramount interests in Korea and her right to take special measures to protect them. The original treaty had limited the scope of the engagement to China and Korea, but in the revised version of 1905 its scope was widened to include "the consolidation and maintenance of the general peace in the regions of Eastern Asia and India." The main gain for Japan by the revision was in the free hand she secured in Korea.

That freedom was immediately exercised. In November the control of Korea's foreign affairs, subject to existing treaties, was taken over by Japan, and provision was made for the appointment of a Japanese Resident-General in Seoul. In return for this concession, the Japanese Government undertook to "maintain the welfare and dignity of the Imperial house of Korea." The "independence" of Korea, which had figured so largely in the Tientsin Treaty of 1885 and in numerous subsequent engagements, dropped out of sight. The new treaty, which practically involved the extinguishing of Korea as an independent State, was not willingly signed by the representatives of that unfortunate kingdom ; in fact, it was asserted that the Korean Emperor's signature had been attached by the Japanese envoy. Whether true or false, the story gained wide currency. Frantic efforts were made by the Koreans to secure the assistance of the Powers, especially the United States, in preserving their independence. Two of the Korean Ministers of State committed suicide rather than face the disgrace of the treaty, and rebellion broke out in various parts of the country. The Powers, however, were in no mood to live up to the terms of their treaties with Korea in the face of Japan's determination to subvert the independence of that decadent State, for Korea's weakness had been a menace to the peace of the Far East

Japan on the Continent of Asia

for years. Two wars had been fought by Japan in a decade partly because of Korea's inability to protect herself from the encroachments of China and Russia. As we have pointed out, the policy of guaranteeing the independence of Korea initiated by Japan in 1885, in which she was followed by the Western Powers, was devised for the purpose of securing the safety of that State until Japan was prepared to carry out her design of absorption. Both the time and the circumstances seemed ripe in 1905, and Japan moved in the direction of her ambitions. Great Britain's acquiescence in the Japanese policy had been assured by the Treaty of Alliance in 1905, while that of the United States was plainly signified by the withdrawal of her diplomatic representative in Seoul.

On December 22, 1905, a treaty between Japan and China relating to Manchuria was signed in Peking, by the provisions of which the transfer to Japan of Russia's Chinese concessions stipulated for in the Portsmouth Treaty was confirmed. Permission to build a railway from Antung to Mukden and the exemption from taxation of the necessary railway materials was obtained, as was also a concession for a joint Chino-Japanese timber company to operate in the Yalu valley. Japan covenanted to withdraw her troops from Manchuria, except such as were necessary to guard the railways in Japanese hands.

Such was the position of Japan in Asia at the beginning of 1906. Plainly she was the predominant Power of the Far East, firmly established in Korea, in possession of the Liaotung—though by leasehold, it is true—and by her railways dominating the trade and industry of Manchuria. The only treaty stipulations by which she was bound were her undertakings to respect the integrity of China and the " open-door " in Manchuria, the policy of Chinese integrity being dictated by a kind of Asiatic " balance of power " theory. No peace in the Far East would be possible during any predictable period in the future if China were

313

dismembered. If China were successfully absorbed—by Japan, let us say—temporary peace might be secured, but the balance of power in Asia would be destroyed. However, as no Power or combination of Powers has ever been able to absorb China in the past, there is no reason to suppose that Japan could do so, and any attempt would only throw the Far East into endless turmoil. But the traditional ambition of the Japanese for dominance in Asia, revived in 1894, and grown more vigorous than ever during the Russian War, is fundamentally opposed to a strong China. Nevertheless, from 1905 to 1914 the Japanese Government openly espoused that policy in concert with the other Great Powers. In 1915, when a convenient opportunity presented itself, the Japanese Government, under the guidance of Okuma, and supported by stalwarts like Oishi Masami, Kono Hironaka, Inukai Ki, and by the bulk of the nation, initiated a policy the object of which was not to dismember China but to convert her into a second Korea, a dependency of Japan. We know that the attempt failed, but whether through Kato's efforts or no remains for the future to disclose. It is certain, however, that the grounds for a great struggle between Japan and China are always in existence. As Okuma said in 1896, the Chinese problem is for Japan a permanent one, and it will not be solved until China strengthens herself to the point of making further aggression impossible, for to expect that the Powers who have agreed to respect the integrity of the Middle Kingdom would do more than they did in Korea's case is quixotic, to say the least.

The second of the general treaty stipulations which control Japan's action in Asia, the maintenance of an " open door " for the commerce of all nations, is likewise inherently distasteful to Japan, and fundamentally opposed to the most deeply-rooted characteristics of the national mind. " Equal opportunity for all " as a guide to the conduct of commercial dealings is in flat contradiction of the principles which underlie all

Japan on the Continent of Asia

competition, and when applied to the business competition of nations the rule is as likely to be broken as in the case of individuals. Japan's immediate closing of the door upon the commerce of all outsiders, when she secured Formosa, showed that similar action might be expected in Korea and Manchuria. In the case of Korea her action was not without precedent, since practically all continental European nations have acted in this way with regard to the trade with their outlying possessions, such markets being supposed to be the monopoly of the merchants and manufacturers of the nation acquiring the territory, but with regard to Manchuria the circumstances were different. Those great provinces were not Japanese possessions, though occupied in part by Japan's troops, yet there was a general belief among the people of Japan that Manchuria was to all intents a Japanese colony, and that consequently special facilities should be afforded her merchants in exploiting the resources of her territory. That belief was naturally shared by the Government, hence the double-faced policy which contributed so largely to the alienation of the world's sympathy for the new Power in the Far East. In 1905 the Japanese had gained universal admiration ; by 1910 they had come to be as widely disliked and distrusted, especially in the Anglo-Saxon world.

Following rapidly upon the so-called Korean Treaty, Japan took steps to consolidate her rule over that country. On December 30 an Imperial Ordinance (No. 267) was issued, setting forth the "Regulations on the Composition and Duties of the Residency-General and the Residencies in Korea," and appointing Marquis Ito Hirobumi to the office of Resident-General. Ito outlined his policy in a speech made in Tokyo in January 1906, on the eve of his departure for Seoul. He began by referring to the treaty of November 1905 as settling the fundamental relations between Japan and Korea, but went on to say that as that convention was brief, it constituted merely a founda-

315

tion, and his efforts would be directed to working out the details of the structure to be erected thereon. Korea's foreign relations, her treaties with the Powers, would require revision so as to become consonant with the changed circumstances of the country. Reform of the internal administration would be difficult because of the antiquity of Korea's corrupt traditions, and only a slow and gradual improvement was to be hoped for in that direction. The universal poverty of the Koreans would have to be removed, both for their own happiness and in order that the country's financial strength might soon become sufficient to bear the expense of its own defence. To bring about this desirable end he proposed to institute improvements in agriculture, forestry, and means of communication. Japanese emigration to Korea was to be strictly supervised, and all evil-minded persons were to be deported. Ito had in mind the experience of a decade earlier in Formosa.

After more than a year of office, during which time immense strides had been made in improving the facilities for transportation, Ito once more spoke in Tokyo on Korean affairs. He said, in substance, that Japan's policy was to guide Korea into the haven of progress and enlightenment, but if Korea refused to be so guided, Japan had plans for the future which might bring serious consequences upon all Koreans. This threat was interpreted to mean nothing less than annexation in event of Korea's continued contumacy. The basis of the threat was the state of insurrection necessitating hostilities on an extensive scale which had marred Ito's régime through practically the whole of the year 1906.

The position of the Resident-General was one of extreme difficulty. In Korea the Japanese régime was unpopular, not only with those who suffered from its reforming activities, but with the nation generally because the people feared for their independence. From the time of Hideyoshi's unwarranted and ruthless invasion of the country at the close of the sixteenth century Japan had been regarded in the peninsula as the " accursed nation." In Japan itself popular sympathy with Korea had died out, as a result of the insurrection, and even the moderate papers in Tokyo demanded that fuller powers be given to the Resident-General in order that the interference of the Korean Government in the work of reconstruction might be curbed. In answer to this insistent popular clamour the Japanese Minister of Foreign Affairs, Hayashi Tadasu, visited Seoul in June 1907, and shortly afterwards the successful negotiation of a new treaty was announced. By this convention the Resident-General became a virtual Regent. It provided that Japan should undertake the protection, guidance, and control of Korea ; that the Resident-General should be empowered to veto Korean legislative and administrative ordinances and to appoint Japanese subjects to official positions. Hayashi, upon his return to Tokyo, ascribed the negotiation of the new treaty not only to the violation of the former convention by the Korean Government's dispatch of two delegates to The Hague for the purpose of submitting their case to arbitration before that tribunal, but to the long series of difficulties encountered by the Japanese in attempting to promote the welfare of Korea. He hoped that, as a result of the enlarged powers conferred upon the Residency-General, Japan would soon be exercising as beneficial an influence in Korea as Great Britain in Egypt. Speaking for the people as well as the Foreign Office, the *Jiji* commended the treaty because it gave the Resident-General complete control of the situation. The outward semblance of annexation had been avoided, but the substance had been secured.

It is in the light of the new convention that Ito's remarks, summarized above, must be interpreted. He was probably not unwilling that his powers in Korea should be increased, for, after all, he was a bureaucrat. From 1877 until 1889 he had been in a position to dictate the course of the reconstruction of his own country, and his short connection with the Seiyukai between 1900 and 1903 had proved that he still retained his dictatorial disposition. But however much of an oligarch he may have been in 1907, however gratified by the position he occupied in Korea, Ito was still guided by two fixed ideas—that of the superiority of civil over military progress and an inveterate hatred for the Yamagata military clique in Tokyo. In 1907 Saionji, his protégé and successor as leader of the Seiyukai, was Premier, and he had little fear of the Government's interference with his plans for Korea. His threat of September 13, 1907, which was generally regarded as foreshadowing annexation if the Koreans did not settle down to peaceful co-operation with him, might have been interpreted as a mere warning to the Koreans themselves of a worse fate to befall them if they made his continuance in the office of Resident-General impossible. His subsequent course, as we shall see, goes far to justify such a reading of his words. What Ito wished to avoid was the annexation of Korea, not because he objected to such a policy in itself but because he knew that once the measure was decreed it would involve the appointment of a military Governor and the inception of a militarist régime.

In July 1908 the Saionji Cabinet collapsed, and Katsura at the head of the military party returned to power. Before a year had passed Ito's rule in Korea came to an end, for on June 14, 1909, Sone, who had been the Minister of Finance in the former Katsura Cabinet, was gazetted Resident-General. Ostensibly the policy of the Ito régime was continued. Sone was reported by the *Asahi* as deprecating immediate annexation, but the *Jiji* continued to advocate the completion of the process of absorbing the protectorate on the ground that the Ito system, which divided the power and responsibility between Japanese and Koreans, made a satisfactory administration impossible. Sone's views as to Korean needs were plainly those of an official

who regarded his tenure as limited, his régime a mere
interregnum. The Cabinet's hesitation in taking the
final step undoubtedly was due to Ito's opposition, for
though out of office he was still a member of that
inner circle of the oligarchy, the Genro, and the
Emperor clung to him as the faithful adviser of his
early manhood. His ideas on the subject of the
regeneration of Korea remained unchanged, and until
he was out of the way the Government could not move
forward. At this juncture, so a story which was widely
current in Tokyo runs, the military party arrived at
the conclusion that Ito must be sacrificed in the interests
of its policy. In old Japan, when it became advisable
to remove some one highly placed he was given the
privilege of committing *hara-kiri* as a means of serving
his country. As such a course was out of the question
here, Ito was sent on a tour of Korea and Manchuria,
and at Harbin, on October 24, 1909, he was assassinated by a supposedly fanatical Korean. The story
has it that his guards were withdrawn, or at least
that the assassin's access to him was not interfered
with, and that Ito himself had a foreknowledge of
his impending fate. However that may be, his tragic
taking-off served the double purpose of furnishing a
pretext for annexation and of silencing the chief
opposition thereto.

On May 25, 1910, Sone resigned on the plea of
ill-health, and was succeeded by Terauchi Seiki, who
had been Minister of War in all the Administrations
since 1902. The appointment of this formidable
militarist was the cause of grave concern to the
Koreans, as well as an indication to the Japanese
people that the policy of immediate annexation had
been decided upon. The final stages of the process
may be described by quoting from the official statement issued by the Japanese Foreign Office on
August 29 :—

" Viscount Terauchi, upon his arrival at Seoul, was
convinced that the situation did not permit any further

delay in effecting the contemplated annexation, and on the 16th of this month he opened discussion on the subject with the Korean Government, by giving detailed explanation of the views of the Japanese Government. Subsequently, several conferences were held for the exchange of views, and in the course of each conference the Korean Government expressed their concurrence as to the necessity of annexation. Viscount Terauchi, having found that the Governments of Japan and Korea were in complete accord regarding the proposed arrangement, telegraphed to the Japanese Government on the evening of the 20th the final draft of the Treaty of Annexation, and requested that it be submitted to his Majesty the Emperor of Japan for approval. His Majesty referred it to the Privy Council, which specially met on the 22nd, and Imperial sanction was then given with the advice of the Council. Accordingly the Japanese Government at once telegraphed to the Resident-General on the same day, authorizing him to sign the treaty. The Korean Government also submitted to his Majesty the Emperor of Korea for approval the draft of the treaty on the 22nd, and his Korean Majesty in full appreciation of the general situation and recognizing that the annexation of Korea to Japan would contribute to the promotion of the welfare and interests common to both nations, gave prompt approval to the treaty. Thereupon the Treaty of Annexation was signed on the afternoon of the 22nd by the Resident-General, Viscount Terauchi, and Mr. Ye Wan Yong, Minister President of State of Korea.

" The Japanese Government then communicated the treaty to all the Powers concerned, at the same time declaring the rules to be followed by Japan in dealing with the external affairs of Korea. The treaty is thus promulgated to-day, and takes effect from this date."

The treaty contained eight articles. The first two announced the " complete and permanent cession " to the Emperor of Japan of " all the rights of sovereignty over the whole of Korea," and the acceptance of that cession by the Japanese Emperor. Articles III, IV, and V provided for the bestowal of titles and rewards upon the Korean Imperial family and high officials of the Court who should accept the new status of their country with equanimity. By the terms of Article VI the Japanese Government assumed entire control of the administration of Korea, and undertook to afford full protection for the persons and property of Koreans who obeyed the laws and to promote the welfare of the whole people. Article VII provided that the Government of Japan should " employ in the public service in Korea those Koreans who accept the new régime loyally and in good faith and who are duly qualified for such service." The final article concerned only the date on which the treaty should come into force.

A general amnesty was proclaimed by Imperial order, arrears of taxes were waived, and the land tax for the year 1910 was reduced. Seventeen million yen were distributed among the people, and everything possible was done to placate the feelings of the nation. The dreams of the Japanese Imperialists were realized and a firm foothold in Asia was secured, a base for any future operations in the interests of expansion.

Japan's new position as a first-class Power with special interests in Asia, coupled with the changing foreign policy of Europe, had resulted in new conventions with France, Russia, and Great Britain. The French *entente* of 1907 stipulated for the preservation of the *status quo* in the Far East, and guaranteed the independence and integrity of China and pledged the contracting parties to the open-door policy. In July 1907 a convention with Russia secured the mutual recognition of the territorial integrity and independence of China and of the principle of equal opportunity in whatever concerned industry and commerce ; likewise it was agreed that each party should respect the actual territorial integrity of the other and acknowledge all rights accruing to the other from treaties and conventions with China. In the same year a Treaty of Navigation and Commerce was concluded between Russia and Japan. In 1910 the Russo-Japanese Convention of July 1907 was superseded by a further convention, according to the terms of which the contracting parties agreed to abstain from railway competition in Manchuria, to maintain the *status quo* in Manchuria, and to exchange communications in case anything threatened the existing arrangements in Manchuria. In 1911 the Anglo-Japanese Alliance was modified once more, the annexation of Korea making the Korean clause in the instrument of 1905 no longer necessary ; the *rapprochement* of Britain and Russia removed the necessity for the clause which referred to India, and the Arbitration Treaty between Great Britain and the United States necessitated the deletion of the article which bound the contracting parties to come to each other's assistance in case of an unprovoked attack on either by another Power. The emasculated Alliance, which provided for the maintenance of the peace in the Far East, was regarded with little favour in Japan. It was called " unilateral " by the *Nichi Nichi*, and the *Hochi* declared that " Japan is now America's slave and India's policeman."

The net result of these various treaties and conventions was to consolidate and strengthen Japan's position in Asia. But if the European Powers with interests in Asia were, for reasons of their own, not unwilling to recognize and even further Japan's ambitions, the United States regarded the paramountcy of the Island Empire in the Far East with some anxiety. But it is doubtful if any open conflict of interests would have arisen had it not been for the action of the State of California in raising the so-called " school question," which developed into an agitation against the admission of Japanese labourers into the United States. The problems created by California's hostility to Japanese coolie immigration in 1906 still remain

Japan on the Continent of Asia

unsettled, and their adjustment is not likely to be accomplished in the near future. Canada and Australia have also had their agitations against the admission of Japanese labourers. The hostility on the American continent to the Japanese is confined largely to the Pacific Coast, and it is undoubtedly due in part to a feeling of distrust and fear of Japanese designs. A militaristic nation pursuing methods which are not easy to understand is likely to be an object of suspicion, with or without reason, to its nearest neighbours.

CHAPTER XIV

THE END OF THE MEIJI ERA

In May 1908 a General Election was held, the Diet having completed its full term of four years for the second time in succession. Various predictions were made as to the probable fate of the Seiyukai. The *Asahi* pointed out that the campaign would differ from all previous ones, not only because of the enlarged electorate due to the high taxes and the consequent increased expenses entailed upon the candidates, but also because of the uncertain state of politics, which would render the life of the next Diet insecure. The general feeling was that the outcome would depend upon the size of the party's election fund. Immediately preceding the polling the local Governors issued to the police strict orders to suppress bribery and corruption, and how thoroughly these injunctions were carried out was indicated by the extraordinary number of prosecutions for infraction of the election laws. Nevertheless, the Seiyukai returned from the country with 189 members, a gain of 8 seats, and the Shimpoto with 77, a loss of 12. The result constituted a signal victory for the Seiyukai, for not since 1903 had the party commanded a majority in the Lower House of the Diet.

Under such circumstances it might have been supposed that the Saionji Cabinet would continue long in office, for with the support of the Seiyukai its position seemed secure. Nevertheless, in the first week of July the Ministry resigned, ostensibly because of the Premier's illness. The collapse of the Government was accepted in Japan with little comment, nor did the fact that Saionji recommended Katsura as his successor seem out of the way, yet every feature of this crisis runs counter to the preconceived notions of the student of parliamentary institutions outside of Japan. The Emperor, heeding Saionji's recommendation, installed Katsura as Minister President early in July. This sequence of events, mysterious as it may seem to the foreigner, was in perfect accord with precedent in Japan, and constituted a fresh evidence of the peculiarities of the political system of that country.

The Seiyukai, even with Saionji as its President, was not Saionji's party while he was in office, for according to Japanese constitutional practice the appointment to office in the Cabinet is the prerogative of the Crown, as it is in England, but with this difference, that the Emperor's selection of his Ministers is not limited by any considerations of party strength in the House of Representatives. When Saionji accepted office in 1906 he did not fill the Cabinet offices with members of the Seiyukai. The oligarchy, as we have seen, had provided in 1894 against any such contingency, but even if the Privy Council's rules governing appointments to high offices had not been adopted, the hostility of the House of Peers to party government would have discouraged the Prime Minister's attempting to form a strictly Seiyukai Cabinet. There is therefore no clear connection between the Administration and the dominant party. Even though the Seiyukai was strengthened by the General Election in 1908, that fact alone did not secure the continuance in office of the Saionji Ministry.

The triumph of the Seiyukai at the General Election was not the result of its connection with the Cabinet, but was due primarily to the expenditure of its immense funds in corrupting the electorate, though doubtless, also, its prestige as a great political organization closely allied with the Government carried weight in the country.

But if the analogy between a General Election in Japan and a similar event in England be maintained, the Seiyukai should have been defeated in 1908, since the Government, with which it was allied, had been completely discredited as early as the end of 1907, its financial programme broken down, and its popularity lost, especially with the business community. The looseness of the bond uniting the party to the Government and the universal venality of the electorate not only explain the success of the party in May, but made possible Katsura's return to power in July.

But there were other forces at work in this political crisis. Toward the end of 1907 the Elder Statesmen had determined to get rid of the Ministry on the ground that its *post-bellum* financial programme had not satisfied the nation. The Government had not been able to raise funds to defray its immense expenditures without recourse to increased taxation, or additions to the national debt in the form of loans. The attack upon the Ministry was begun by Inouye, who without any apparent reason, unless it be that he represented the huge moneyed interests of the Mitsui family, had for years been regarded as the Nestor of Japan's public finance. Inouye determined to remove Sakatani from the Finance Department, ostensibly because of his incompetence, but really, as the *Jiji* stated, to satisfy a private grudge. Although it was their policy of expansion of armaments that had been mainly the cause of the Government's financial embarrassment, the military members of the Genro threw themselves into the project, knowing that if Saionji stepped down he would certainly be succeeded by Katsura. The intrigue against Sakatani was carried through at the earliest opportunity: Yamagata's son, who was Minister of Communications, was instructed to demand a huge appropriation for the development of State railways. Sakatani refused to include such a large sum in the estimates, and as the result of a compromise the amount was reduced. Here Inouye stepped in and publicly

The End of the Meiji Era

condemned the arrangement, not because the estimates of the Department of Communications had been cut too much, but because they had not been reduced enough, whereupon the Ministry resigned. The Emperor, however, was advised by the Genro to allow only Sakatani and the younger Yamagata to retire, and to order the rest of the Cabinet to remain in office.

Such was the first step toward ousting the Saionji Cabinet. Inouye, having satisfied a grudge against an opponent and vindicated his reputation as a public financier, retired into the background, leaving the field to Yamagata and Katsura, who in July completed the wreck of the Administration. The process by which this result was accomplished, though the actual steps remain as yet a mystery, is not difficult to conceive. The Emperor, at the suggestion of the Genro, has merely to intimate to his Ministers that they no longer enjoy his confidence, and their resignation is the immediate consequence. In this case, even though Saionji's party was supreme in the House of Representatives—in fact, having only a few months before been returned in increased strength by the country—his Cabinet was unpopular, and the people welcomed its downfall. Yamagata and Katsura were not the men to be deceived by the outcome of a General Election in which money had counted for more than either men or policies ; they easily dissociated the election returns from the popularity of the Ministry, and did not hesitate to ask the sovereign to overturn the Administration, their judgment being sustained by the general acquiescence of the nation in the change. The plea of ill-health upon which Saionji retired was a subterfuge, and recognized generally as such, even though Ito from his post in Seoul issued a statement with the object of convincing the nation of its truth. Saionji's recommendation of Katsura as his successor was a result of the same compulsion which had brought about his resignation, but it served the purpose of

enabling the Seiyukai to save its face while it turned
to offer its support to the new Minister President.

The second Katsura Cabinet was composed in the
main of the members of the Yamagata faction, along
with three of Katsura's personal following, the only
Minister who had any Opposition party affiliations being
Komatsubara, in the Department of Education. Komura
was recalled from his post as Ambassador in London
to take up the duties of the Foreign Office. Katsura
filled the double rôle of Minister President and Finance
Minister, associating himself in the latter post with
Wakatsuki, a man of doubtful ability and little training,
but possessed of immense confidence in himself and
his wrong-headed financial ideas. Terauchi and Saito
were reappointed to the military offices, Okabe became
Minister of Justice, and Katsura's henchmen, Hirata,
Oura, and Goto Shimpei, were installed in the Departments of Home Affairs, Agriculture and Commerce,
and Communications.

As the problem of public finance, especially the *post-
bellum* programme, had been the chief source of the
outgoing Cabinet's unpopularity, Katsura turned his
attention to this field, and early in September announced
his policy. Expenditures and revenues were to be
balanced without resort to new taxes, new loans, or
the inclusion in the Budget of the anticipated increase
of the revenues of the year. Fifty million yen were
to be set aside annually for the reduction of the foreign
debt, and the period for the completion of the *post-
bellum* programme was extended from six to eleven
years. The Budget estimates were published two
months later, and showed an expenditure of 517,000,000
yen, a reduction of nearly 100,000,000 yen from the
figures of the preceding year, this immense curtailment
of expenditures being mainly accounted for by the
segregation of the railway accounts and their non-
inclusion in the estimates. As a matter of fact, in the
new Budget the *ordinary* revenues were increased by
28,000,000 yen, and the *ordinary* expenditures by

10,000,000 yen, as contrasted with the Budget of the previous year, but its intricacies served to emphasize the reduction in the total figures, and the people mistakenly concluded that a new financial régime had been initiated.

At the close of December the annual session of the Diet began, and after the recess the Seiyukai, at the request of Saionji, entered into an agreement with Katsura to support the Government. The session under these circumstances was unmarked by any incidents, except such as were created by the Shimpoto's futile opposition to the Cabinet's so-called *negative* financial policy. But outside the Houses a sensation lasting a little longer than the proverbial nine days was created by the " sugar scandal," [1] more than a score of members and ex-members of the Lower House being arrested, tried, and convicted, for having received bribes from the Japan Sugar Refining Company. This industrial corporation, with a capital of 12,000,000 yen, had come into existence in July 1906, during the boom which followed the war, and after a few years of apparent prosperity was declared bankrupt at the beginning of 1909. It had been so successfully looted by its directors that little or nothing remained of its immense assets. In examining its affairs the police discovered that more than a million yen had been spent in bribing members of the Diet during the years 1907 and 1908, with the object of securing legislation to create a Government monopoly of the sugar refining industry, in which event the directors anticipated being able to sell their plant to the State for twice its physical value, and with the proceeds cover up their own defalcations and malfeasance of the company's funds. The failure to secure the necessary legislation was mainly due to their lack of judgment in having approached mere members of the Lower House instead of Cabinet Ministers. The result was bankruptcy, followed by investigation, and the arrest and punish-

[1] See Uyehara, *op. cit.* pp. 255-61.

ment of both the bribers and the bribed, and for the time being the prestige of the House of Representatives was seriously affected. But scandals involving the members in dishonest practices were not rare, and the nation was not prepared to condemn its representatives. In fact, the whole middle class in Japan had always regarded politicians, with a few conspicuous exceptions, as venal, and members of the political parties as well as of the oligarchy were expected to be corrupt, nor have they ever failed to fulfil the expectations of the public in this respect.

During the next two sessions of the Diet the Seiyukai continued to support the Katsura Government. The questions which engaged the attention of the members were chiefly such as related to readjustment of the national finances. The Government during the session of 1909-10 continued to adhere to the "negative" policy initiated during the previous year. The Budget provided for an expenditure of 534,000,000 yen, an increase of 17,000,000 as compared with the disbursements of the previous year. Almost the whole of the increase came under the head of ordinary expenditures, for the Administration proposed to raise the salaries of officials by 30 per cent., the Civil List by 50 per cent., and the sessional allowance of members of the Lower House to 2,500 yen. When this programme was presented to the Budget Committee, the Seiyukai members decided to materially alter a number of the items. A reduction of 1 per cent.[1] of the land tax was voted by the Committee, and in order to balance the Budget it was determined to cut the proposed increase of official salaries in half, thus saving six millions, to reduce other expenditures by six millions, and to expunge entirely the grant for increased sessional allowances to the members of the House of Representatives. But the Government was unwilling to accept these amendments, and on Saionji's recommendation a conference was held between Messrs. Hara and Matsuda repre-

[1] This meant a decrease of between one-third and one-fifth of the tax.

330

senting the Seiyukai, and Katsura and Terauchi the Cabinet. A compromise was adopted, by the terms of which the Government submitted to a slight reduction of the land tax on the one hand and of its proposed increase of official salaries on the other.

In pursuance of this arrangement the Committee finally reported the amended Budget on February 12, 1910, and after an eight hours' debate the Lower House accepted the report. The only influential paper in Tokyo which had anything to say in praise of the compromise was the *Kokumin*. The *Jiji* called it a sacrifice of principles to prejudice, and the *Asahi* and *Shogyo Shimpo* declared that the interests of the mercantile community had been sacrificed to those of the agriculturists; the *Hochi*, which represented the Yellow Press, described the Seiyukai as " enemies of the people." To explain this almost unanimous hostility of the Press toward the Budget, it is necessary to keep in mind that the war taxes of every kind and description were still in force, and that the land tax during the war had been increased to a much smaller extent than had taxes on the mercantile class and the urban population in general. The Tokyo papers had advocated the abolition, in the first place, of the so-called " bad taxes," such as the salt monopoly and the textile consumption tax. But the members of the Diet, 80 per cent. of whom represented rural communities, insisted upon the reduction in the first place of the land tax, and the Government, whatever its preference may have been, was compelled to assent to the demands of the majority in the Lower House. Hence the *Jiji's* reference to the compromise as a " sacrifice of principles to prejudice."

Not only was any reduction of the burden of taxation borne by the mercantile class postponed in 1910, in order that the landowners might be relieved, but the Finance Minister in January called together the bankers of the country and disclosed to them a project,[1] which it was proposed to adopt immediately, for the conver-

[1] See *Japan Weekly Mail*, February 5, 1910, p. 163.

sion of the entire domestic debt upon a basis of a 4 per cent. rate of interest. This scheme, it is said, was one of Wakatsuki's devising. In his address to the bankers, Katsura, who knew little or nothing of the principles of public finance, justified the conversion to a lower rate on the grounds first, that the banks in Japan were contemplating the reduction of the rate of interest on deposits to 4 per cent., and second, that Japanese 4 per cent. bonds were selling in London at 92 and 5's in Tokyo at 93-5. He also adverted to the propriety of establishing a " national rate of interest," to be determined by the Government without reference to the conditions of the domestic money market. A more arbitrary measure, short of absolute repudiation of the debt, could hardly have been perpetrated against the investing public. The holders of Japanese domestic bonds were compelled to accept the new issue bearing 4 per cent. in lieu of their holdings which paid from 5 to 7 per cent. or else find other investments, and the banks were arbitrarily forced to subscribe for large amounts of the new 4's, which they were further pledged to hold in their vaults for two years lest the bond market should be demoralized by immediate liquidation on an unduly large scale. The result of this project was to reduce not only the incomes of investors but their principal as well, for the prices of the new bonds almost immediately dropped into the 80's, and the Government renewed its practice of redeeming its issues, not at par by lot, but by. purchase in the open market. The entire advantage accrued to the Government, as the interest charge for the service of the domestic debt was reduced, as was also the cost of redemption. As far as the bankers were concerned, a *quid pro quo* for the losses forced upon them was easily given in the form of increased privileges in Korea and Manchuria as well as in Japan. Few, if any, of the Japanese banks confine themselves to strictly banking business, as all of them are more or less engaged in the promotion of industrial enterprises, hence franchises and mining, timber and water rights are matters of great consideration to such institutions, and the acquisition of such rights was sufficient to offset completely any losses incurred by a reduction of the rate of interest upon their holdings of Government bonds.

Another of the features of the financial policy of the Katsura Government which was widely discussed both in the Diet and by the Press was the revision of the tariff. By the terms of the British Treaty of 1894, extra-territorial privileges were to be abrogated after five years and the conventional tariffs after seventeen, provided a year's notice was given to that effect by the Japanese Government. In 1910 the time had come for serving notice on the Treaty Powers of Japan's intention to revise her tariff of Customs duties, which was to come into force July 1, 1911. In connection with the matter the subject necessarily was brought to the attention of the Diet. In announcing the Ministry's policy of tariff revision, the Foreign Minister said on January 29: "It is the intention of the Government to conclude treaties based entirely upon the principle of reciprocity, eliminating from the future compacts all unequal engagements which appear in the present treaties, such as the unilateral conventional tariffs, the clause relating to permission of coasting trade to foreign ships, and the provision requiring that amendments to the statutory tariff shall be promulgated six months before they become operative." In the Budget Committee, in reply to a question, the Minister further stated that in determining the duties the necessities of the revenue as well as the question of protection for young industries would be taken into account, and also that in the matter of reciprocally advantageous treatment care would be taken to secure such benefits whenever possible. Questioned further as to what arrangements were to be made with Great Britain, Komura expressed the opinion that as Britain was a free-trade country it had nothing to offer in return for concessions, and therefore none would be made. On this indiscretion, which the Government attempted to explain away as a mere slip of the tongue, hinged the whole of the negotiations with Great Britain. Komura, who had an inveterate dislike for foreigners in general, and for the English in particular, had lapsed in public into an expression of his private sentiments, and this single slip wrecked his plan to achieve what he called " equilateral tariff arrangements." The Tokyo Press was not slow to print his address, and the correspondents of the London papers promptly telegraphed the Foreign Secretary's speech to their home papers. A storm of protest arose not only in England but in Japan also, and the outcome was a series of concessions [1] to the British cotton, woollen, and steel manufacturers, concessions which were enjoyed under the most-favoured-nation clause by all the other Powers. This incident not only helped to discredit Komura in Europe, but to increase also the growing distrust in England of the Japanese Government and its policies.

The interval between the sessions of 1910 and 1911 was occupied principally by the matter of the annexation of Korea, and the negotiation of the new commercial treaties incidental to the revision of the tariff. Both these subjects attracted much attention during the session of 1911 ; *ex post facto* consent was given to the Government's annexation proceedings, and the new tariff was introduced and passed, even though it included many concessions to the interests of the foreign merchants. The session was noteworthy, too, for the close alliance between the Government and the Seiyukai. The compromise between the two was based upon the postponement of the projects for standardizing the gauge of the railways and for further naval expansion. In return for these concessions the party, which numbered over two hundred parliamentary members, passed the Budget and consented to the enactment of a Factory Act and an Act granting rights of ownership of land

---

[1] See the text of Anglo-Japanese Commercial Treaty, *Japan Weekly Mail*, April 8, 1911, pp. 368–9.

under conditions which made it practically impossible for foreigners resident in Japan to acquire real estate.

One of the most interesting parliamentary debates [1] of the session occurred upon a private Bill, introduced into the Lower House by Matsumoto Kumpei, providing for universal manhood suffrage. The discussion of this subject brought out some of the finest speeches of the year, and what was still more gratifying, the Bill was passed by the Representatives, but in the Upper House the measure met with a very different reception. On March 15 a special committee reported against the measure as contrary to the spirit of the Constitution. Hozumi Yatsuka, Professor of Constitutional Law in the Imperial University, bitterly attacked the Bill, and Kamada Eikichi, President of Keiogijuku, supported it with equal spirit. In the course of his remarks Professor Hozumi gave expression to the views of the bureaucracy on the subject by saying, " Nowhere in our Constitution is it stated that the chief object in the creation of the Diet was to give expression to the will of the people." Another and even more zealous exponent of the official opinion went so far as to rhetorically demand that a notice be placed on the door of the Upper House refusing admission to all further Bills relating to the same subject. The unfavourable report of the committee was adopted by an overwhelming majority. The incident served to show very clearly how diametrically opposed were the views of the Representatives and the Peers on the question of constitutional reform, the former striving to advance toward democracy, the latter to preserve the predominance of the aristocracy.

In August 1911 the second Katsura Government resigned, having been in office for three years and a month. During that period many important national undertakings had been carried through successfully. The new commercial treaties had been negotiated, the

---

[1] See *Japan Weekly Mail*, March 25, 1911, pp. 315–16, and April 1, 1911, Supplement, p. 1, for a full report of the debate.

alliance with Great Britain had been renewed in a form consonant with the new alignment of the Powers in the Far East, Korea had been incorporated into the Empire, and Japanese interests in Manchuria consolidated. But in the field of domestic politics, especially in public finance and administrative reform, the Government had failed to effect any improvement. The downfall of the Government at this time was, at any rate, voluntary. None of the Japanese Cabinets had set a precedent for long terms in office, and Katsura was wise enough to withdraw after three years of sustained effort, in which time he and his colleagues had reaped a large monetary harvest and had bestowed upon themselves high titles and dignities. The retiring Prime Minister acknowledged that the people appeared to have tired of his Administration, and as he knew that it would be an easy matter to reoccupy his post at any time, he graciously withdrew, recommending Saionji as his successor in the highest office of state.

During the second Katsura régime the political parties had made no progress. The great party, the Seiyukai, had turned, obedient to its leader and with due recognition of the political situation, to support the Government. In each of the sessions of the Diet there had been a definite arrangement between the Cabinet and the party with regard to such projects of legislation as the Government should introduce ; by this process the Seiyukai sought to satisfy its supporters in the country, for it could point to various Bills which it had forced the Government to withdraw or postpone, the most important of all being the reduction in the land tax which it had wrung from the Administration in 1910. By such means did the party try to efface the stain of the sugar scandal and to dispel the public's suspicions that its support had been purchased for the Cabinet by a generous distribution of funds among its members. Nevertheless, it was widely believed in Tokyo, at any rate, that the parliamentary members of the Seiyukai had been busily occupied in

The End of the Meiji Era

enriching themselves with Government money and favours. That these suspicions were well-founded was demonstrated early in 1911, when a valuable franchise for the supply of electric light to the capital was granted to certain prominent party men. When the prospectus of the new corporation was issued, with Seiyukai men in all the important posts, the indignation of the Press was so loudly expressed that the original list of officers and directors was hastily withdrawn and the names of well-known business men substituted.

What the Seiyukai had done during the years between 1908 and 1911 was only what might have been expected under the political system in vogue, for it was inevitable that the rank and file should consult their own interests during the first year after the election of 1908, in order to recoup as rapidly as possible the immense sums spent to procure their seats. The venality of some of the members of the Lower House was disclosed specifically in the investigation of the sugar scandal, but while that *contretemps* had led to greater caution in accepting money bribes, it had hardly diminished the hunger for rewards which characterized Japanese politicians. As a new General Election approached the country had to be convinced of the party's usefulness, so increasingly harder bargains were driven with the Cabinet during the sessions of 1910 and 1911. In addition to personal bribes, the Seiyukai demanded as part of the annual payment for their support the passage of an occasional measure of public interest, or the withdrawal of certain Government projects which involved or threatened to involve an increase of taxation. The party gave the Cabinet least trouble in 1909, for in that year the members were under the immediate necessity of reimbursing their election expenses, most of them succeeding in obtaining an amount sufficient for the purpose. In 1910, the financial pressure on the members of the party having been largely removed, they had an opportunity to do something towards consulting the public's interest or to criticize outspokenly the programme of the Government. By 1911 the inevitable tendency of Japanese political parties towards obstruction had developed to such an extent that Katsura did not think it worth his while to continue any longer in office.

Such was the history of the Seiyukai's policy, an opportunist programme which had been carried out on former occasions with success. If such a policy was entirely lacking in high qualities of statesmanship or devoid of principle, it was at least successful in preserving the political peace ; it had staved off a dissolution of the Diet, which most certainly would have ensued if the party with its control of the Lower House had come to close grips with the oligarchic Cabinet. The first ten years of the parliamentary régime had been replete with dissolutions, which followed each other with a rapidity that is not only bewildering to the student but must have been ruinous financially to the members of the Lower House, but the second decade presents a scene completely devoid of such untoward events. The change was not due to any diminution of the oligarchy's determination to rule, but entirely to the policy of the Seiyukai and its leaders. Opposition for the sake of obstruction gave place to acquiescence in the Government's various budgets and programmes, with only that amount of hesitation which was necessary to bring out the money from the Ministry's bribery fund or to save the party's face before the country. The demand for money or its equivalent with members of the Diet in exchange for votes is always insistent, but it is strongest immediately after an election, and on the other hand, the necessity for obstruction is greatest just before a General Election. Even with Saionji in power, as in 1908 and again in 1912, the Seiyukai has shown itself capable of careful examination of the Budget in the sessions preceding an election. It is interesting to note that the country in 1914, after some fifteen years of Seiyukai predominance, has turned from the party, heartily tired of its opportunism and corruption, its lack of principle and its policy of allying itself readily with any Government which may be in power.

The new Saionji Cabinet came into office in August 1911, with only three of the members appointed from the Seiyukai. As in his previous Ministry, Saionji filled the Cabinet posts mainly from the ranks of the oligarchy, but far the most interesting appointment to office was that of Yamamoto Tatsuo, the President of the Hypothec Bank, who entered the Finance Department. Throughout the Ministry's short life Yamamoto remained the storm centre, for it is safe to say that Katsura's failure to effect any real improvement in the financial situation had been the ultimate cause of his Government's unpopularity. Except for the slight reduction in the land tax, nothing had been done to lighten the people's burdens, the objectionable war taxes having been allowed to stand. The general system of taxation in Japan, which traverses every canon of economic science, was left unreformed. The national debt had not been reduced, but rather increased in amount, for the 50,000,000 yen annually appropriated for the redemption of the bonds held abroad was more than offset by new domestic loans. The Japanese investors in domestic bonds found the value of their securities reduced into the bargain, as a result of the conversion to a 4 per cent. basis at a time when the rate of interest paid by the banks on funds left on fixed deposit was 6 per cent., and when money could not be borrowed for commercial ventures at less than 8 per cent. ; further, in effecting this arbitrary conversion, Katsura had more or less crippled the banks by compelling them to underwrite and hold large amounts of the new low interest bonds. The indirect taxes were likewise largely augmented by the new tariff which had come into force July 1, 1911.

The new Finance Minister began by alarming the nation, and the foreign bondholders also, for he uttered in the Diet a warning to the effect that the national finances were in a precarious condition, and that retrenchment and readjustment were the only means of avoiding bankruptcy. The pronouncement of such pessimistic views by the Finance Minister, whatever might be said of his honesty of purpose, was a tactical political blunder, for it shocked the nation and alarmed the foreign investors. The Japanese soon recovered their equanimity, but it took a pointed intimation that the Government did not intend to default to reassure the European bondholders. London, if the *Times* spoke for the City, preferred Katsura's finance with its specious policy of no new loans or taxes, 50,000,000 yen a year for amortization of the foreign debt, and the maintenance of a specie reserve in the Bank of England.

Yamamoto, however, was a banker, not a politician. The ultimate goal, as it appeared to him, was to place the national finances upon a sound basis; to bring about a real equilibrium of receipts and expenditures, by encouraging the productive industries of the people to an extent necessary to secure an excess of exports over imports, in order that the interest on the foreign portion of the debt might be paid in merchandise, and not, as hitherto, in specie borrowed in Europe and held in London, and by the same process to increase the taxable resources of the people so that the revenue of the State might be sufficient to defray all necessary expenses. He declared himself willing to adopt every legitimate means to accomplish this end. If capital for the development of the resources of Japan could not be obtained within the country, he saw no objection to borrowing abroad. The policy of allotting annually so large a sum as 50,000,000 yen for the redemption of Japanese bonds owned in Europe and America, when money was so urgently needed at home, seemed to him not only senseless but distinctly opposed to the nation's material development. His conception of the needs of the times was founded upon a firm conviction that the interests of the Japanese people should be consulted first, and that the best prospect for national solvency lay in the development of the productive industries and the export trade, whereas Katsura's policy had been to placate the foreign bond-holder and thus dull the edge of European suspicions as to the soundness of the financial condition of Japan.

If the ultimate object of the Finance Minister's policy was to develop the productive industries and thus augment the taxpaying abilities of the people, his immediate task was to readjust and reform the system of taxation which had been devised during the war and subsequently patched up by Sakatani and Katsura. In order to abolish the most objectionable of the levies, and yet maintain the equilibrium of income and expenses without resort to further loans, it seemed necessary to make sweeping reductions in the administrative expenditures. To this end the Cabinet organized a Bureau, with the Prime Minister as Chairman, to investigate all departmental accounts. From time to time the Bureau reported progress, and it seemed probable that the people would obtain some relief from their burdens. Every element of the nation outside of military and bureaucratic circles was disposed to sympathize with and support this undertaking of the Government. The Press reported the Bureau's progress and performed an immense service in educating the people in the art of public finance, nor could any better campaign literature have been issued than that which the Seiyukai gave out as it approached the regular General Election in 1912. But to those Japanese who understood their own system of Government it was obvious that the Ministry's project was almost certain to be rendered abortive, as, in fact, it was, owing to the peculiar powers of the militarist bureaucracy, opposed on principle to retrenchment.

The annual session of the Diet was opened on December 23 by the Emperor, and after the recess the Government introduced the Budget and the Minister

President made his annual address. Yamamoto, in bringing down the estimates, intimated that his guiding principle in framing the Budget had been to secure an income which would not only defray expenditures but provide a small surplus also, even though for the year 1912-13 a deficit of 18,000,000 yen was unavoidable. Speaking in the Upper House on January 23, Saionji referred with satisfaction to the new Anglo-Japanese Alliance, the revision of the commercial treaties, and the establishment of the Bureau for investigating the accounts of the various departments. Uchida, the Minister of Foreign Affairs, on the same occasion commented upon the friendly relations of Japan with the Powers, especially England and Russia, and declared that his Government desired only the restoration of order in China, at this time passing through the revolution which was to overthrow the Manchus.

The Budget, as usual, proved the most contentious part of the Government's annual programme. The failure on the part of the Finance Department to include in the estimates an appropriation for construction of battleships, amounting to 90,000,000 yen, spread over six years, and the rejection of the item to defray the expenses of an additional two Army divisions for Korea, completely alienated the sympathy of the military party and proved the undoing of the Cabinet. But during the session of 1911-12 the Seiyukai, by its adoption of the Budget as it was introduced into the Lower House, saved the Government for the time being and enhanced the party's reputation in the country. The Shimpoto, which had changed its name in 1911 to the Kokuminto, condemned the financial provisions as negative, and the Cabinet's foreign policy as weak and vacillating, especially with regard to China. Nevertheless, the session passed off quietly, the parties being more interested in the approaching elections than in the Government's legislative programme.

The End of the Meiji Era

The result of the election in May was the return of the Seiyukai with a slight increase of strength, and a considerable margin over all the other parties combined. The Kokuminto held its own. But it is impossible to attach much importance to the result of a General Election in Japan as a method of determining the sentiments of the country toward the Administration ; the elections are notoriously corrupt, the parties are only loosely connected with the Ministry, and the electorate is so limited that only about one in forty of the population has the right to vote.

After the election the Government took up the work of maturing plans for the retrenchment of administrative expenses, and practically no other political subjects were discussed in the Press during the month of June. But in July of this year came the Emperor Mutsuhito's death, most unexpectedly, for he died after an illness of only about a week, and for the time being the interest in politics was eclipsed by the nation's universal mourning. This untoward event and the arrangements for the elaborate funeral which ensued absorbed the Government's attention for nearly two months. By the end of September it was evident that the Government's days were numbered, and little headway was made with its cherished plans of financial reform.

The passing of the Meiji Tenno and the accession of his only son, Yoshihito, whatever else it may have involved, was the signal for a political upheaval such as had not been seen in Japan since 1873. Katsura, who had conferred upon himself the rank of Prince in 1911, had evidently incurred the jealous hatred of his quondam patron Yamagata. Both were Choshu men, but Katsura's power and wealth had increased to such an extent that Yamagata feared for his security as head of the Army, and he therefore determined to put his former henchman out of the way. Katsura had gone to Europe about the middle of the year on what was ostensibly a pleasure trip—afterwards seen to be a political mission to Petrograd—only to be hastily recalled by the Emperor's illness. He arrived in Japan some days after the Imperial demise to find himself the victim of an intrigue ; for on the very day of his return Yamagata secured his appointment as Court Chamberlain and Keeper of the Privy Seal. What this extraordinary appointment meant, who was responsible for it, and what Katsura thought of it, became the subject of so much speculation that to silence the Press he finally made public his determination to quit politics for ever and devote the remainder of his life to the personal service of the young Emperor. Having thus disposed of Katsura in a manner which admitted of no refusal, Yamagata turned on the Ministry. He was credited with the intention of ousting the Cabinet and substituting a clan Government, with Terauchi as Minister President ; but if he had any such idea, an essential part of his intrigue miscarried. On the other hand, Katsura's followers, though their leader was for the time being out of the way, were not disposed of, and they were privately making it known that they intended to be back in office before the end of the year. The general public knew nothing of these plans of the rival Choshu magnates until difficulties suddenly loomed up before the Administration. For the time being few recognized the possibilities of the cloud, in the shape of the renewed demand from the War Office for an appropriation to create two new Army divisions in Korea, which appeared on the horizon, but it grew larger, and by the end of November it had covered the whole political firmament. In the storm which broke in the first week of December the Government was swept out of office.

Saionji's resignation was caused by the military party directly and openly, and although he had the backing of the Seiyukai and the sympathy of the general public, his Administration was unceremoniously brushed aside because it stood in the way of the Yamagata faction. At no time in Japanese political history did the strength of the military clique stand out more

The End of the Meiji Era

conspicuously than in this crisis. According to the Constitution (Article LV), the various Cabinet Ministers are made individually responsible to the Emperor for the advice given to the sovereign. The rules for the appointment to high offices, formulated by the Privy Council in 1894 at Yamagata's instigation, limit the possible candidates for the War Office to Generals and Lieutenant-Generals in active service. When the Supreme Military Council, under Yamagata's control, compelled General Uyehara, the Minister of War, to resign his office because his colleagues in the Ministry declined to adopt the two divisions project, the Saionji Cabinet was crippled, and the Prime Minister's difficulty was to find a successor for Uyehara. The Army refused to furnish a qualified candidate except on its own terms, and as no civilian was eligible there remained no alternative but resignation. By means of a provision of the Constitution, supplemented by the above-mentioned rules of the Privy Council, it is possible for the military party to oust any Cabinet from office at their pleasure.

After Saionji's resignation the task of choosing a successor was taken in hand by the Genro, and for three weeks the process dragged on. As on previous occasions when the strife was acute within the inner circle, the office was offered in succession to Inouye, Matsukata, and Yamagata, all of whom refused it in turn, then to Terauchi, who likewise refused it. There was a faction in the Genro in favour of putting Saionji back again, but from the beginning Katsura was the most promising candidate. In the meantime the Press was busy denouncing the Genro and ridiculing their various shifts, incidentally discussing with an admirable grasp of the subject the constitutional questions involved in the overthrow of Saionji. The Seiyukai and Kokuminto united for the time being against the oligarchy, and their spokesmen displayed an activity and boldness unheard of hitherto in Japan, in discussing before large audiences in all the principal cities the defects of the national system of government. Ozaki, Inukai, and a host of lesser lights exposed the secrets of the clan system so cunningly devised to keep the military party in power, and they pointed out clearly the nature of the devices of the clans and the methods by which the Sat-Cho combination had been successful in retarding the growth of popular government. Yet nothing was more conspicuous than the complete absence of criticism of the Constitution. This sacred instrument, though the main bulwark of the oligarchy, passed through the ordeal unscathed, even unquestioned.

It was in the midst of this political ferment that Katsura and his Cabinet were sworn in on December 21, 1912, but from the first day it was evident that the Premier would have difficulties to face other than those created by the party politicians. In order to form his Cabinet it had been necessary to issue an Imperial order to Admiral Saito, commanding him to retain his office as Minister of the Navy, but at the time the significance of Satsuma's refusal to voluntarily supply an eligible candidate for the office had been cast into the shade by a companion rescript commanding Katsura to resign his offices at Court and enter politics once more. For more than a month the popular orators and the Press continued to denounce the clan system, until other events made it obvious that the emergence of Katsura was not a victory of the clans but a personal triumph which involved his repudiation of the clans and the clan system and his adoption of the principles of party government.

In due course the Diet met, on December 25, to organize for the session, and, after being formally opened by the Emperor, adjourned till January 20. As a sign of their hostility to the new Cabinet, the combined Seiyukai and Kokuminto refused to extend the recess till February 5, as the Government requested, but when the day for reassembling came the sitting was postponed for fifteen days by an Imperial order, and on the following morning, January 21, Katsura launched his new party,[1] the Rikken Doshikai (Constitutional Fellow-thinkers' Society), and invited the friends of the popular cause to join him. Katsura's sudden profession of faith in party government revealed, as by a lightning flash, the true situation within the clan councils. He had been ousted from the Choshu clique, yet by dint of his enormous power he had snatched the reins of office from both Yamagata and the Satsuma faction. The significance of the Imperial order to Saito became apparent, as well as that of the rescript extricating Katsura himself from

[1] The platform of the Doshikai was contained in thirteen articles as follows :—

1. That the dignity of the Imperial Court shall be maintained.

2. That the Anglo-Japanese bond of alliance shall be faithfully maintained and the Far Eastern peace preserved.

3. That the foreign policy shall be improved, efforts being made for the maintenance of Japanese rights in Manchuria, the solution of the Chinese question, and the abolition at a proper occasion of the Japanese declaration on the maintenance of the present Customs rates in Korea, in order to improve the economic relation between Japan proper and Korea.

4. That all schemes for supplementing either the naval or military forces shall be determined by a Defence Committee.

5. That industrial development shall be encouraged in order to promote the welfare of the nation.

6. That for the purpose of consolidating the basis of the State finances, 50,000,000 yen or more shall be saved in the expenditures of the general account, and 30,000,000 or more in those of the special accounts.

7. That the amount of Exchequer Bonds to be issued in any fiscal year shall be less than 50,000,000 yen, and that no railway bonds shall be issued for the time being.

8. The national bonds shall be redeemed each year to the amount of 50,000,000 yen or more.

9. That education shall be conducted upon the principle embodied in the Imperial Rescript on Education.

10. That the spirit of thrift and saving shall be encouraged among the people, and that money shall be available at low rates for investment for the development of industry.

11. That the Higher Civil Service Appointment Regulations shall be revised so that all able men may be eligible for appointment in Government service.

12. That efforts shall be made to harmonize relations between the rich and poor and to maintain good customs and habits in society.

13. That taxes shall be lowered to decrease the financial burden of the people.

the limbo of the Court. In defeating the intrigue of his enemies within the clans, Katsura was working along with the Opposition, but when he set up as a party leader the Seiyukai and Kokuminto turned against him, correctly interpreting his action as an attempt to break their power. The orators of the day and the Press were obliged to perform a remarkable *volte-face* on January 21, when they diverted their vituperation and violence from the Genro to the Prime Minister.

The Cabinet resorted to every device in its repertoire to build up a party. Money was freely distributed, two to five thousand yen being the price of an ordinary member and as much as fifteen thousand that of orators like Shimada Saburo. By February 5 the new party numbered between eighty and ninety adherents, drawn from the Chuo Club, the Independents, the Kokuminto and the Seiyukai. It was to the credit of the last-named that so few of its members yielded to the temptation put in their way, but with the Kokuminto the case was entirely different, for the party was split in two, and all of its leaders [1] except Inukai, and half of the rank and file deserted to the Government. Nevertheless, when Katsura faced the Diet again his position was hopeless. The House of Peers met on the morning of February 5

---

[1] Oishi, Kono, Shimada, Minoura, and Taketomi. In a manifesto issued at the time the former Kokuminto leaders explained their action. It began : "For many years past we have been constantly striving for the advancement of constitutional government, namely, for a responsible Cabinet which will conduct the affairs of state in a constitutional manner." After referring to other necessary reforms in connection with the conduct of the nation's foreign affairs, and colonial, educational, and industrial policies, the statement ended with the following paragraph :—

"These are what we have constantly advocated for many years past, as the general public knows. At this moment the authorities of the present Ministry are eager for political reforms. We met them twice and exchanged views, when we found that theirs perfectly agreed with ours. We are glad that our long cherished desires can thus be realized by these authorities. Here we are furnished with a good opportunity for the reform of our conduct of state affairs. For these reasons, we, who are always ready to make efforts for the improvement of constitutional politics, believe in the sincerity of these authorities, and have decided to co-operate with them in the organization of a new political party."

and heard the Minister President outline the Government's policy, but by the afternoon, when the Lower House assembled, an immense crowd had gathered in the streets surrounding the Diet buildings. These spectators, though quiet enough for the time being, were a source of strength to the Opposition and a terror to the Doshikai, for there was no misjudging the temper of the mob or its sympathies. Meanwhile, within the House the Prime Minister and the Minister of Finance repeated the statements which they had made in the morning to the Peers. Then followed an attack on the Premier, which was begun by Mr. Motoda, a member of the Seiyukai. Ozaki Yukio followed by introducing a motion of want of confidence, which ran as follows: —

" Prince Katsura Taro, the Minister President of State, importuning the Throne on several occasions for Imperial Ordinances, has confounded the Court with politics; also, using his official power for his private ends, he has canvassed in the interests of his new party. Moreover, he has arbitrarily suspended the sittings of the Diet at the very outset of the session. All this is opposed to the principles of the Constitution and exerts a prejudicial effect upon the political progress of the nation; nor is it the way to maintain the dignity of the throne and the felicity of the people. Therefore this House declares hereby that such a Minister President cannot enjoy its confidence." But before a division could be taken an Imperial order was received by the President of the House, adjourning the sitting for a further space of five days. From this time matters only grew worse for the Government. It was impossible for it to enlist any further recruits, for the fear of the infuriated populace had entered into every one. The *soshi* were already encamped upon the premises of every doubtful member of the Diet, threatening violence as the penalty for deserting the Opposition. When February 10 brought the next meeting of the House the mob once more assembled, and on the police attempting forcible measures a serious riot ensued. In the face of this demonstration of hostility the Government resigned. Thus Katsura, the self-proclaimed " last of the bureaucrats," the " convert to party government," went down amidst a storm of execration, broken not only politically but physically.[1] He had demonstrated that a strong man could form a Ministry in spite of the opposition of the Genro and the people, but his over-throw proved that no Government could remain long in office in the face of an unbribable majority of the Lower House, backed by an exasperated and lawless Tokyo mob. It was a victory for the Opposition and the populace over a dictator who had set himself up in spite of all the constituted forces of clans and parties, and who announced, as the vernacular Press reported, that he would " run the show with his own capital."

It is impossible as yet to be certain of the details of the secret intrigues which resulted in the setting up of the third Katsura Ministry, but it is obvious that in the process Yamagata and Katsura had parted company, and that for the time being the Choshu faction was in eclipse. Although the meeting of the Genro held on February 11, 1913, was attended by only three of its members, two of them Choshu men, no attempt was made to call a Choshu clansman to the helm of state. Admiral Yamamoto, the leader of the Satsuma faction, was immediately put forward as the next Prime Minister. It is clear that whatever Katsura might have accom-plished by way of temporarily shelving the Genro and abolishing clan influences, with his downfall these long-established forces asserted themselves once more, with this difference only, that Satsuma and not Choshu occupied the leading position.

The era of Meiji had ended in a period of absolute political calm, as befitted the end of the reign of the great monarch during whose lifetime Japan had been transformed from an unknown island State in the Pacific to a great Power which promised to dominate Asia.

[1] Long before the year was out Katsura died.

The End of the Meiji Era

But the calm presaged a storm of almost unprecedented violence. Within three months after the Emperor's funeral it had burst over the nation, threatening to uproot all the former institutions and place the control of the nation's destinies in the hands of the people's representatives. When the fury of this political typhoon had subsided, and the wreckage was cleared away, it was found that the fabric of the government remained intact. The clan system, built up on the Constitution, had evinced its immense strength, surviving both a quarrel within the oligarchy and a popular assault from the combined forces of the Opposition. The Genro had shown themselves almost as inviolable as the Emperor, for, having set up a Prime Minister who was howled down within a month and a half, they had immediately brought forward another, and their new nominee was straightway accepted. The Constitution had never even been called into question, but had been appealed to by the staunchest advocates of popular liberty. So far from being regarded as a stumbling-block in the path of progress, it had held its place as "an immutable law." The military bureaucrats had triumphed in the formation of the Yamamoto Cabinet, and all that had been accomplished under the most favourable circumstances by the advocates of popular government was merely a change from one faction of the military party to the other, from the domination of Choshu to that of Satsuma, from a policy of military to one of naval expansion.

CHAPTER XV

THE POLITICAL SYSTEM IN JAPAN

THE complete domination of Japan's political system by a military oligarchy is the most significant fact in the history of the later years of Meiji. Though an oligarchy it is true had ruled the nation throughout the whole of the modern era, until 1889 the development of the machinery of government, central and local, was the main interest of the ruling clique. With the promulgation of the Constitution and the other organic laws, prescribing the extent to which the popular element was to be admitted to a share in the control of the affairs of state, the constructive work of the civil oligarchy was completed. When in 1890 the Diet met for the first time, Japan stood at what seemed a parting of the ways. One road apparently led to popular government, the other to a perpetuation of the powers of the oligarchs. For four years both of the opposing sections in the Diet, the party politicians and the Government, strove to make progress, but in vain. Ito's institutions as embodied in the Constitution and the Law of the Houses proved impracticable. The Diet's powers of consent to legislation were too meagre to enable the parties to advance, and yet they were extensive enough to hamper the Government effectually. The oligarchy could no longer keep the nation interested in civil progress without making further concessions to the parties, thereby endangering its primacy in the State, nor was it possible to stand still for ever at the meeting of the ways. To amend the Constitution to the extent of abolishing the Diet was not possible, and to hand

The Political System in Japan

over to the politicians the control of the administration was unthinkable : there seemed no way out of the deadlock created by the Constitution. Attempts were made to discipline the Lower House by a series of dissolutions, and the elections were tampered with by the Government, but all to no effect. The parties came back from the country after each General Election stronger and more determined than ever to have their way. It was only after Yamagata, Matsukata, and Ito, the strongest of the oligarchs, had failed to enlist the co-operation of the parties that it was determined to introduce a programme of military aggression in China in order to distract the nation's attention from domestic politics. Since 1894 the power of the military clique has steadily increased and that of the political parties declined. Even when the military camp was divided against itself, at the end of 1912 and the beginning of 1913, the popular party was unable to take any advantage of this weakness, and it had to stand by and see first Katsura, a rebel from the Choshu faction in the oligarchy, and then Yamamoto, the leader of the Satsuma clique, installed as the Minister President of State. There had never been a more promising opportunity offered to the party politicians, and never was their failure to improve it more complete.

The strength of the military oligarchy is to be explained by the inherent chauvinism of the Japanese, to which almost every Government since 1894 has successfully appealed, while the weakness of the political parties is due to their lack of substantive powers and consequent absence of principles, to the venality of the politicians and the electorate.

Enough has already been said in explanation of the origin and progress of Japanese nationalism, whose beginnings are to be found in the pre-Meiji feudal soil. The Restoration was one of its earliest fruits ; the absorption of Formosa in 1894, of the Liaotung in 1905, of Korea in 1910, and the establishment of a virtual protectorate over South Manchuria in 1915 have likewise been the harvest of militarism, and in comparison the lack of domestic political progress has seemed to the people of little or no importance. To the world at large, and to the Chinese in particular, this sudden growth of the military power and spirit of the Japanese has been regarded with anxious concern, the most disquieting feature of the modern political situation in Japan being the absence of any constituted opposition to the military party. In the Diet the politicians vie with the Government in proposing schemes of further expansion, and among the people new societies continually spring up with the object of spreading the cult of Japan's destiny as the ruler of Asia, if not of the whole world. China, India, the Philippines and the islands of the South Seas, are all represented as fields for the spread of Japanese *kultur*. Of these societies the *Do-Kai* (Association of the Right Path) might be cited as an illustration, it being interesting to learn that the Right Path which the members of this organization have in view is one leading to the domination of the world by Japan. Speaking at a recent meeting of this Society in Tokyo, Mr. Oshikawa Hogi reached the climax of his argument in the following sentence : " With the most beautiful virtues which we have inherited from our forefathers, and splendid traditions which no other nation in the world has ever enjoyed, I conclude without any hesitation that we Japanese are the nation which has the responsibility of instructing and teaching the rest of the world, and are finally destined to become its dominant factor."

Militarism has for the present captured the various political organizations and silenced the demand for constitutional reform and popular government. Most of the men who since 1890 have fought the oligarchy are now ranged upon its side. Shimada Saburo, Ozaki Yukio, Oishi Masami, Kono Hironoka, are names which the world has connected with the cause of responsible government, yet all have been parties to the recent Okuma drive against China. Kato Takaaki, than whom

The Political System in Japan

no living Japanese was more highly regarded in London, was Okuma's Minister of Foreign Affairs until the middle of 1915, and he was then ousted by the Genro not because his policy *vis-à-vis* China was too strong, but because it was too weak. The question which inevitably presents itself to the minds of those interested in the affairs of the Far East, particularly of Japan, is, " What has happened to the political parties and their demands for responsible government? " To answer such a question it is necessary to examine the development of Japan's political system during the last two decades.

The brief annual sessions of the Diet afford the Opposition politicians their only opportunity of criticizing or modifying the Government's policy : during the rest of the year the Administration is free to take its own course. Thus in July 1910 Ito's policy in Korea was suddenly dropped and the military party effected the annexation of the peninsula as an integral part of the Japanese Empire, and the Diet's consent was neither asked nor given at the time. It was not until some time in the early months of the following year that the change in the status of Korea was sanctioned by the people's representatives.

The function of the Diet is to give its consent to legislation introduced either by the Government or by some private member of the Houses, and in exercising that negative power the Lower and Upper Houses are on a footing of perfect equality. But even this power of consent is not complete, for if the measures presented by the Government are of a financial character the Diet may obstruct their passage, but the Administration is empowered by the Constitution (Article LXXI) to re-apply the entire Budget of the previous year. Furthermore, if the Diet consents to laws of its own initiation, the Emperor upon the advice of the Cabinet is free to exercise his powers of veto. The legislative body is therefore limited in two directions : it cannot refuse supply, nor can it enact laws without the consent of the

Government. Under these disabilities the political parties are bound by the Constitution to carry on their work, and there is little cause for wonder in the fact that they become discouraged and cease to seriously oppose the Government.

The equality of the powers of the two Houses in legislation, with no provision for breaking the deadlocks that are likely to arise except a conference between delegates appointed by both or the personal interference of the sovereign, combined with the radically different ideas of members of the two Houses, has powerfully strengthened the hands of the Administration. During the greater part of their history the Peers and the Representatives have been working at cross purposes. The former has clung tenaciously to its aristocratic or bureaucratic traditions, while the latter has voiced to a certain extent at least the ambitions of the masses. Against all the efforts of the political parties to secure responsible government the Upper House has backed up the oligarchy, and has stood ready at the request of the Genro to block all legislation presented by a Government which was too closely allied with any party. Attempts at party government, therefore, have generally given place to government by the oligarchs with the support of the members of the parties, now in one combination, now in another, secured either by bribery or owing to their conviction that opposition was fruitless. In this way Ito in 1895 allied himself with the Jiyuto, and Matsukata in 1896 with the Kenseito. In 1900 Ito formed the Seiyukai, and that party, whether under his leadership or that of Saionji, until 1912 continued to support any Government which the military oligarchs chose to set up, receiving in return a few Cabinet offices and immense sums of money from the Government corruption fund.

In accordance with the terms of the Constitution, the Diet meets at least once a year for a session of three months' duration. That period may be extended by Imperial order, but, generally speaking, the business

The Political System in Japan

of the Diet is conducted with a view to concluding its discussions within the allotted time. The result is that in the Japanese Parliament little or no debate upon any measure is now heard. Even the Budget, the most important piece of legislation enacted during the session, is seldom debated for more than a few hours, though the division is often accompanied by disgraceful scenes of violence. In recent years practically all sessions of the Lower House have been marred by constant interruptions, so that a debate, even if the Government were willing to allow any extended discussion of a Bill, is no longer possible.

The Administration regards the session of the Diet as a constitutional nuisance which has to be endured, but to be made as short as possible. It has become a custom, therefore, to convene the Diet immediately before the New Year holiday. Late in December the Houses are organized and formally opened by the Emperor, and before any business is transacted an adjournment to about January 20 is moved and carried, almost a month being cut off the session at one stroke. It is further provided by the Law of the Houses (Article XXXIII) that the Government by Imperial order may suspend the sittings of either House for a period of not more than fifteen days, and upon numerous occasions this power has been exercised, especially when the Opposition has been particularly offensive in its obstruction. Again, the Lower House meets ordinarily on Tuesdays, Thursdays, and Saturdays, the sitting beginning at one o'clock and concluding before nightfall. It is an unusual session in which the Lower House sits on more than forty different days, and a day's sitting which lasts until six o'clock is almost certain to be commented upon by the Press as of extraordinary length. If the Budget is passed by the Lower House by the middle of February, as is usually the case, the interest in the session wanes unless there happens to be some other contentious measure included in the Government's pro-

357

gramme. As the middle of March approaches, the Houses give themselves up almost entirely to divisions, Bills being rushed through their various stages at the rate of a score a day, provided the Government has bought up a solid majority of the members ; if it has not so fortified itself, obstruction develops, and the session ends in stalemate or dissolution. The formal closing of the session is effected by an Imperial message of thanks, which is read by the Prime Minister to the members of the two Houses assembled to hear it in the Peers' Chamber. A few days are spent in post-sessional banqueting, the junketing which marks the close of the session having come to be recognized as an essential part of the reward of a member for his support of the Government, and thereafter the members disperse. Not only are the wines paid for out of the National Treasury at these functions, but the fulsome flattery of the humble member which constitutes the main part of the post-prandial oratory of the Minister President and the members of the Cabinet is welcomed by the rank and file of the party.

Two or three days before the formal opening of the sessions the Houses meet for the purpose of organizing. In the Upper House the process includes the creation of the *sections*, the appointment of a Chairman of the Committee of the Whole House, the selection of the members of the Standing Committees, and within each Committee the election of a Chairman. The President and Vice-President of the House are appointed by the Emperor for terms of seven years. In the Lower House the same organizing process occurs. The members are grouped by lot into eight or nine *sections*, the Chairman of the Committee of the Whole House is elected and the Standing Committees are set up and officered. Of the Standing Committees, that on the Budget is the most important. Since 1902 it has numbered sixty-three members, who are divided into six or seven *sections*. The other Standing Committees are those on Petitions, with forty-five members, on

The Political System in Japan

Settled Accounts with the same number of members, and on Discipline with twenty-seven members.

If a new Lower House has been elected since the last session, a further detail of its organization is the election of a President and Vice-President. Three candidates for each of these offices are chosen by the members of the House from among their own numbers, and the Emperor, upon the advice of the Cabinet, makes the appointments from the list provided. The duration of office of these two functionaries is coterminous with the life of the Diet, which is four years unless prematurely dissolved by the Emperor. As a matter of fact, no Diet before 1900 lived out its full legal term of years, though since that date, as the result of the Seiyukai's complaisance, General Elections have occurred at regular intervals until 1915. The choice of the House for the office of President and Vice-President usually falls upon some member of the dominant party, though on occasions men have been chosen for their conspicuous abilities rather than for their party affiliations.

The duties of the President are not merely to preside over the sittings of the House and preserve order ; his discretion extends to the compilation of the " Order of the Day " and to the application of the closure, and hence he is in a position to prevent a debate either from being begun or continued. Impartiality is therefore not likely to be one of the cardinal virtues of the President of the Lower House. Repeatedly his desk has been the centre around which storms have raged in the House, and on more than one occasion the President himself has suffered personal violence at the hands of some enraged member.

The two Houses having organized, the formal opening ceremony is performed a few days later, this exercise consisting of the reading of the Speech from the Throne and the presentation of humble replies thereto. The Representatives assemble in the Upper House about ten o'clock in the morning, the Emperor arrives in

state half an hour later, and, taking his seat upon the
throne, receives from the Prime Minister a written
address which he proceeds to read. At the present
time the Address adheres strictly to a form which
has become traditional : the country is congratulated
upon the ever-increasing friendliness of Japan's relations
with the foreign Powers, and if the occasion requires
some specific references are made to a new treaty ; then
follows a paragraph foreshadowing the main features
of the Government's programme. For example, in
1906 the Emperor said : " We have ordered Our
Ministers to determine plans such as are essential to
the development of the national strength and the completion of the country's defences, and to submit for
consideration the Budget for the fortieth fiscal year,
based upon those plans, together with various projects of law." In the earlier years of the Diet's history
it was customary for the Speech to say that the Diet's
function in legislation was to give its *consent* to the
measures proposed by the Cabinet, but that practice
has been discontinued, doubtless in deference to the
feelings of the members, though in its reply the Lower
House seldom has failed to draw attention to its inadequate powers by speaking of its " duties of consent."
The Speech concludes by exhorting the representatives
to perform their work with diligence and in a spirit of
harmony.

When the Speech has been read the Emperor immediately withdraws. No word is spoken except by the
monarch or his staff, and no eye is supposed to be
lifted to his face, Peers and Representatives alike standing with bowed heads. When the Emperor has
departed from the House, the Representatives return
to their Chamber, and both Houses, acting separately,
proceed to sanction a loyal Reply. This item of business
is soon dispatched, for the draft has been prepared
beforehand by the Chief Secretary of either House
and is voted *pro forma*, the President being com-
missioned to bear the document to the Palace. The

reply of the Lower House in 1906 was, in part, as follows :—

" Your servants will bring to the discharge of their duties of consent a spirit of circumspection and sincerity so as to comply with your Imperial Majesty's behests and discharge the trust imposed upon them by the nation."

The procedure connected with the annual Speech and the loyal replies is, like so much else in Japan, an adaptation of a foreign custom. Previous to the establishment of the Diet the Emperor had spoken to the nation at large in various Imperial messages, such as the rescript addressed to the Chihanji in 1871 abolishing the *Han*, the Parliamentary Rescript of 1881, and on numerous other occasions when a crisis impended. Other rescripts were issued subsequent to 1890 ; for example, the often-quoted one on education, the one on thrift, and the addresses to the people upon the occasions of the wars with China and Russia. To all of these no replies were necessary, but when the Diet was set up the custom of making an annual Speech from the Throne was adopted as part of its procedure. In imitation of the English practice the Speech was dictated by the Cabinet, and generally regarded by the Houses as an outline of the Ministry's policy, but since it was the Emperor who read the Address, no attempt could be made to discuss its contents, and instead of occupying a couple of weeks in debating the Reply, as is the custom in the House of Commons, the Japanese Diet disposes of the subject in as many minutes—in fact, it has become a mere matter of routine. This formalizing of the Speech and the Reply in adapting them to Japanese needs created the necessity for a statement by the Government of its programme, at a meeting in which objections could be made and questions asked, even though no general debate could be raised on the subject. Hence the first regular sitting of the Houses after the New Year recess has been taken up, since about 1900, by the Minister President and the Ministers of Foreign

Affairs and Finance in expounding the general policy of the Administration. Usually the estimates are brought down, and at least some of the Bills relating to taxation are introduced. It is customary for questions to be asked and answered, but nothing resembling a debate ever occurs at this stage.

When the Budget Committee has started its work, it may be said that the most important operations of the annual session are under way. This Committee meets almost every day, and its sittings are attended by the Ministers of State or the Government delegates. A few days are spent discussing the general outline of the Budget, then the Committee breaks up into sections, to each of which is assigned the task of examining in detail the items included in the estimates of one or more of the Departments of State. Thus, Section I may begin work upon the estimates of the Finance Department, or Section VII upon those of the Department of Agriculture and Commerce. At the meetings of the sections the Government Delegates are present to explain each item and endeavour to secure its favourable reception. After the whole of the estimates have been dealt with in the various sections, the Committee meets as a whole and determines its course with regard to the Budget. A report is prepared and submitted to the House upon a day appointed. The debate upon the report is likely to be either listless or much too animated, but whatever the state of feeling in the House, a division is brought on after a few hours, and it is a rare occasion when the Committee's report is not accepted.

Three weeks of the session are thus spent by the Budget Committee of the Lower House, and during that time the regular sittings are occupied in the discussion of the taxation Bills or some non-contentious measures. During this period the work of the Diet is very light, especially in the House of Peers, where there is hardly anything to do. The Budget reaches the Upper House during the last ten days of February, and is referred

The Political System in Japan

to the Committee, which is instructed to report on a specific day in March. The Budget Committee in the Peers proceeds in exactly the same way as its counterpart in the Lower House, and the House ordinarily concurs in the report after a formal debate. If the Upper House amends the Budget in the slightest degree, the Representatives receive it back and either accept the changes or reject them. In the latter case a conference is held and some compromise acceptable to the Government arranged. If the Houses change the estimates in a radical manner the Government may refuse to concur, and if one or other of the Houses remains obdurate the Cabinet either resorts to a dissolution as a punitive measure, or allows its Budget to lapse and reapplies the estimates of the previous year.

The serious business of the Diet is, therefore, transacted in the committee-room. Except when the Cabinet is being impeached the sittings of the Houses are uninteresting, and even upon such occasions it is not the debate so much as the outcome that holds the attention. In the early nineties the Lower House was a genuine debating chamber, speeches two hours long being not infrequent and the closure sparingly enforced. Takahashi, Inouye, Ozaki and Shimada made their reputation as orators in those days. But a change came in 1895, when speech-making ceased, and the floor of the House was deserted for the committee-room. In that year the oligarchy entered into an alliance with Itagaki Taisuke and his party, and from that time on the Government has contrived to arrange for the support of a majority of the Opposition politicians. For that matter, after Yamagata and Katsura had debauched the members with bribes, oratorical displays were useless. No amount of eloquence could win votes for the Opposition against the money or franchises so lavishly distributed by the Ministry.

The procedure in connection with the passage of a Bill through the House is ordinarily two readings, a committee stage followed by a report and a third reading. But in the process of "railroading," which takes place during the closing days of every session, the procedure is abbreviated, and consists of merely a committee stage and the report. Literally scores of divisions are taken every day, and while the work of the committee protects the Houses to a certain extent, a vast amount of ill-digested legislation is issued annually, this defect of the system, however, being largely offset by the Government's veto powers. Bills which have been carried against the Cabinet's wishes may be vetoed by the Emperor, or if that method seem too drastic, the Government can delay indefinitely publication of the distasteful Acts in the *Official Gazette*, or fail to provide in the Budget the funds necessary for their enforcement. By any one of these methods Acts which are passed in due form by the Houses may fail to become law. There is no occasion for alarm, therefore, over the enactment of laws that are injurious to the interests of the people, except in the case of Government Bills, and similarly little cause for rejoicing in the passage of highly beneficial legislation, for an affirmative vote of the Diet is no guarantee to ultimate inscription in the statute books. Since the establishment of the Diet, only about 5 per cent. of the privately initiated Acts have been incorporated into the law of the land. Even Government Bills to which the Diet has given its consent are often slow in being enforced. The Factory Act of 1910, though it received the Imperial sanction and was published in the *Gazette*, remained a dead letter for a period of five years.

From this description of the powers and procedure of the Diet, it is obvious that the creation of representative institutions in 1890 has afforded the advocates of popular government but few opportunities to influence the course of Japan's subsequent political development. The brief annual sessions, the perfunctory debates, the arbitrary powers of the Government, the independence of the Cabinet, and the general constitutional limitations upon the Diet's powers over legislation, have all combined to render nugatory the sporadic efforts of the Opposition to set up responsible government. Not only have the party politicians failed to make progress toward popular government—a failure that was inevitable under the existing Constitution—but in yielding to the temptations placed in their way by successive Cabinets since 1898 they have forfeited the esteem, if not the confidence, of the people. By deserting their party principles, as outlined in 1890, and by selling their support to the oligarchy, the parties have immensely strengthened the latter's position, and at the same time postponed the realization of responsible government for a generation or even longer.

The decline and fall of the political parties was the result of the system of government created by the Constitution. From the outset of the parliamentary régime the failure of the parties to control the Administration was a foregone conclusion. The framers of that instrument were members of the oligarchy, whose minds were imbued with the theories of the native policy and fortified by a study of the mediæval institutions of Tudor England and Hohenzollern Prussia, and they conceived it wisdom to perpetuate an absolute monarchy, operating through a bureaucracy dominated by the members of their own group. The Constitution was drawn up and ratified in the profoundest secrecy, and promulgated ostensibly as the gift of a benevolent autocrat to a grateful nation. The system was established by a process which made all criticism of it treasonable and modification wellnigh impossible ; nevertheless the members of the political parties in the early sessions of the Diet promptly began to attack its provisions. One dissolution followed another with a rapidity which proved the determination of the oligarchs to maintain their position at the head of the Administration. Four General Elections were held before the Chino-Japanese War, and the expenses of these frequent campaigns threatened to ruin the party candidates. In 1896 and 1897 the experiment was tried, first by one and then by the other of the two leading Opposition parties, of working with the oligarchy, but without success. In 1898 the two parties united and formed an Administration, which shortly fell to pieces because of the lack of harmony among its members.

The events of these eight years proved conclusively that the political parties were no match for the Cabinet as long as it was armed with arbitrary powers of dissolving a recalcitrant Diet, that the union of a party and the oligarchy meant merely the subservience of the former to the latter, and that no party, no matter how numerous its supporters in the Lower House, could successfully conduct the Administration. Despair of success in achieving responsible government, which meant to the politicians succeeding to office and the spoils thereof, was followed by an almost universal willingness to sell their support to the Government.

The epidemic of bribery and corruption in the Diet in 1898 and 1899 was the result of the peculiarities of the Japanese political system and the Japanese character. If the representatives of the people in the Lower House were unable to control the policy of the Government, they could at least, by refusing their consent, prevent the Government from carrying out its measures, therefore the Government was forced to purchase a sufficient number of votes. A punitive dissolution, while it meant financial embarrassment for the politicians, did not directly accomplish the Administration's purpose, for it delayed the passage of its measures for a year, while to the parties it was evident that a General Election could not possibly result in placing them in office. Under these circumstances it was considered only wise on the part of the Cabinet, and prudent on that of the Opposition, to compose their differences on the basis of monetary considerations given and received. Hence in 1898 and 1899 Yamagata for the oligarchs and Hoshi Toru for the Kenseito arranged terms satisfactory to every one concerned. In return for the votes of the party and the enactment of its own programme of legislation the Government handed over valuable considerations in franchises and money. These transactions need not be regarded as an indication of moral degeneration in the Japanese politicians, whether members of the parties or of the oligarchy. The former had endeavoured to wrest the administrative power from the latter from the very inception of the Diet in order to profit by the spoils of office ; the latter had resisted in order to retain those spoils for themselves, and the arrangement of 1898, by which the Yamagata Cabinet secured the support of the Kenseito, was merely a division of the spoils. On that basis the Government of Japan has been carried on ever since. During its remarkably successful career the Seiyukai, except in January and February of 1913, has consistently supported every Administration upon the understanding that its members should receive a share of the favours.

That the party men have been no more venal than the oligarchs is not difficult to prove. The moral guilt is as great in offering as in receiving bribes, and the Japanese law, recognizing this, makes the offence equally heinous. But other proofs are not lacking Few party politicians have made as immense fortunes out of bribes as have the Cabinet Ministers, and it is only necessary to point to the list of Japanese millionaires to prove the point. A few of them are business men—the Mitsuis, the Iwasakis, Okura, Shibusawa, Furukawa, Yasuda—others are the descendants of the great Daimyo families, who at the beginning of the Meiji Era were already in possession of great wealth, and the remainder are the so-called Elder Statesmen and Cabinet Ministers. These latter were originally in almost every case either poor samurai or the sons of men of very modest fortune, and have been all their lives in the service of the State, drawing small salaries. Their present immense properties are not the result of savings wisely invested but of peculations and bribes.

The devices by which the members of the Administrations, past and present, have made their money are not unknown in other countries, but some of them are so interesting as to be worth recording. The foundations of the Inouye and Okuma fortunes were laid in very early days. Inouye during his incumbency of the Department of Public Works had charge of the building of all railroads and telegraphs, and according to officially compiled reports of the Railway Bureau the construction expense per mile was cut in half after his resignation. Okuma, who while in the Finance Office was called upon to provide the means for carrying on the campaign against Satsuma in 1877, adopted the expedient of an issue of paper money, and it is commonly reported in Japan that he carried off several cartloads of the script which remained in the Treasury after the rebellion had been suppressed. The official careers of both these men had ended about 1881, though they have occupied Cabinet offices for short periods since then, and from that time they devoted their energies mainly to serving the interests of the great business houses of Mitsui and Iwasaki respectively. The first issue of the *Japan Year Book*, published in 1905, in a section made up of short biographical sketches of the influential men of the country, refers to Inouye as the Mitsui's representative in the Council of the Elder Statesmen.

But even more astonishing were the methods of the late Prince Katsura. When he died in 1913 his estate was reported to be worth 15,000,000 yen. His only official post in the Cabinet previous to 1901 had been that of Minister of War, and his term of service in that office only about three years; his accumulation, therefore, must have proceeded at a very rapid rate, and as an example of his methods the following story is illuminating. In 1911 two rival gas companies, the Tokyo and the Chiyoda, sought permission from the Home Office to effect a combination in order to restore the monopoly which had long been enjoyed by the former company. Permission was refused on the ground that the Chiyoda had been chartered mainly for the purpose of creating competition. Katsura is reported to have been approached by the interested parties, and to have demanded 1,500,000 yen as his price. But the sequel to the story is even more astounding. As soon as the money had been finally paid, and safely deposited to his account, Katsura is said to have driven immediately to the Palace and resigned his office, without obtaining the signature of the Home Minister to the charter of amalgamation.

The venality of the members of the Lower House, when contrasted with the peculations of the official class, appears extremely sordid. The bribes are smaller, and the transactions almost invariably take place in disreputable resorts in an atmosphere of vulgar dissipation. The official reports of the preliminary trial of the members of the Diet implicated in the sugar scandal of 1909 present the revolting details of a debauch lasting through the whole session. But it is impossible to blame the party politicians more severely than the Cabinet officers. All alike have their price, and are willing to sell their services in the interests of the highest bidder. There are and were some notable exceptions, but these merely serve to emphasize the almost universal corruptibility of the Cabinet and the Diet.

From the highest political circles corruption has filtered down to the electorate. The ordinary voter, though he must be a man of some property in order to qualify for the exercise of the franchise, has never been interested in the politics of the various parties, and there is nothing in their platforms that serves to differentiate them from one another, nor has there ever been a genuine Government party of any importance. The electorate has been appealed to often enough, but never by a party which has had even the smallest hope of actually being carried into power by popular support. In the four years which followed immediately upon the creation of the Diet the people supported the opponents of the Administration, in the mistaken expectation that the Opposition could and would establish a popular form of government, but after the disruption of the Okuma-Itagaki coalition in 1898 the electors followed the candidates into the morass of corruption. Knowing that the Government divided a rich harvest of spoils with the members of the Diet, the average voter saw no reason why he should not secure some of the rewards for himself : he set a price upon his vote and sold it to any purchaser, not once but as often as possible, in every campaign thereafter. So flagrant did the abuse of the franchise become that election-brokers periodically established themselves in regular offices, and engaged in the business of buying votes and selling them in blocks to the candidates. When this practice was suppressed by the police the evil persisted in other forms. After 1902, when the electoral districts were made coterminous with the Fu and Ken, it was possible for a candidate, knowing exactly the number of votes which he required for election, to dispatch agents throughout the constituency to arrange for the purchase of his seat, either by bribing individuals or buying up whole villages and towns. The author himself has on more than one occasion listened to a member of the Diet describing the incidents of his particular campaign, how in a certain village ten votes were bought for 40 yen and yet not one polled for him, and to his complaints about the exorbitant demands of the voters in recent years, making the cost of a seat four or five times what it was in 1900. From 5,000 to 10,000 yen was sufficient then, but now 30,000 yen is about the minimum figure. On inquiring how the candidate was to reimburse himself for such large outlays, the answer has been the one word " bribes."

How this habit of corruption is to be overcome it is impossible to say. All that the member of the Diet knows is that when the business ceases to pay him he will enter some other profession in which a living can be made : his philosophy runs no further. The

The Political System in Japan

electors, likewise, know that they will sell their votes as long as there are buyers in the market. The Administration will continue, in fact, must continue, to disburse five or ten millions a year in order to retain office, and as the money does not come from their private purses, but out of the public funds, it is nothing to them. Bribery is a national institution. The Cabinet provides the funds out of the taxes to buy the support of the Houses. A Cabinet cannot expect to retain office unless it can carry its programme through the Diet almost every year ; the members of the Houses must be supported, for politics is their profession, and seats in the Lower House are expensive. The ordinary voter takes his toll at each General Election, not because his vote costs him anything, but because it has a value in the estimation of the candidates. There apparently is no ethical question involved, no moral degradation. Loyalty to the sovereign and filial piety are the great virtues of the race—inculcated by the Educational Rescript, the Japanese moral code, and to consider the giving or receiving of a mere bribe as immoral is to think in terms worthy of a pettifogging attorney. The Japanese point of view is as simple and natural to them as it appears cynical and degraded to the Anglo-Saxon.

It is impossible, therefore, to regard the universal prevalence of bribery as a sign of the moral obliquity of the Japanese nation : in its modern form, political corruption is the inevitable concomitant of their system. The members of the Administration under the Constitution are appointed and removed by the Emperor, and while in office are responsible to him for all his and their acts. Such responsibility would be tolerable if it were not for the Genro, whose influence with the Court is supreme. The Genro not only interfere to direct the policy of the Government in great crises, as in 1905, when they brought the hostilities with Russia to an end upon terms that were most unsatisfactory to the people, but they continually meddle in domestic politics, and in formulating its programme the Cabinet must always satisfy the Genro or submit to removal from office. It must adopt certain policies —for example, the continuous expansion of armaments, both military and naval, since the Elder Statesmen have distinctly militarist leanings—and it must carry out its programme in such a way as to win the support and goodwill of the country. But even the Japanese people, patient as they are, look upon increases of taxation or additions to the national debt with displeasure. The Cabinet's course is consequently extremely difficult. In 1906 it adopted the Genro's *post-bellum* programme, but failed to carry it through because the necessary funds could not be raised without recourse to fresh taxes or borrowing, the result being dismissal from office. In 1912 exactly the opposite course was pursued, the Ministry refusing to accept the Genro's plan for two new Army divisions, and dismissal again ensued. Moreover, the Cabinet finds it difficult to bribe the Genro, not because its leading members are incorruptible, but because of their already enormous accumulations in wealth and honours. Money has little attraction for them, since they are already surfeited with it, and there are no higher honours to be bestowed than those they already enjoy.

There is another characteristic of the Genro that demands attention. They all are members of the Sat-Cho clan oligarchy, with the exception of Marquis Saionji, whose membership is only nominal, consequently they favour those Cabinets which are dominated by their henchmen. Katsura's Administrations were much less likely to be interfered with than Saionji's, for the reason that Katsura, at any rate until 1912, was a staunch adherent of the clan system, whereas Saionji was closely affiliated with the leading political party, the Seiyukai. When Katsura turned demagogue in 1913, he found himself opposed by the Genro in addition to the Diet and the people; hence the short duration of his third as compared with his first and second Administrations. In the Genro's estimation, political orthodoxy consists in adherence to the principles of clan domination ; Prime Ministers who subscribe to this confession of faith are protected, and those who do not must contend against constant intrigue in the Court, for the Genro never rest until they have ousted the heretics.

But the Cabinet has not only to live at peace with the Genro ; it must also manage the Diet. The complexity of that problem arises from the conflicting traditions of the two Houses, the Upper House being aristocratic or bureaucratic in its sympathies, the Lower democratic, and during the greater part of their history the two Houses have been at daggers drawn. On more than one occasion their disputes have had to be composed by Imperial messages addressed to the one or the other. The Peers have throughout the whole parliamentary régime supported the clan oligarchy ; the Representatives have opposed it. Clan Cabinets since 1901 have had to buy the support of the Seiyukai in the Lower House, while the Saionji Cabinets have been compelled to bribe the Peers.

The attitude of the Peers toward the Administration is to be accounted for merely by the composition of that House. Its dominating principle is the preservation of the autocracy of the existing régime under the Constitution. Hence any Government which is even slightly tainted by party affiliations is anathema—though that curse may be removed by cash. In the Lower House the case is somewhat different. The parties still look forward to the establishment of responsible government, which means to them office and patronage far more than a radical change in the foreign or domestic policy of the country. There is no political party at present, nor has there been one during the last decade, opposed to militarism and to an indefinite expansion of the Japanese power in Asia. The views of all the parties are in harmony on the subject of foreign policy, and in domestic affairs there are no serious differences, both Seiyukai and Doshikai agree-ing in demanding financial and administrative reform, the development of industry and commerce, and the destruction of independent Cabinets. Nevertheless, the dominant parties for a consideration have consented to support the Cabinet, at times because the Ministry has a certain party complexion—as, for instance, during the various Saionji Administrations—at other times, as during the first two Katsura régimes, because oppo-sition was futile and unprofitable. The Diet's place in the political system is an impossible one. It is divided against itself ; the two Houses are mutually antagonistic and fail to accomplish any positive result ; their powers of consent only serve the purposes of obstruction and provide an excuse for corruption and manipulation by the Cabinet, which in its turn suffers from its subservience to the will of the Elder Statesmen.

It is to this pass that Ito's arrangements, as embodied in the Constitution, and the clan oligarchy's tenacity in clinging to power have brought the govern-ment of Japan. Two remedies alone seem to be adequate to cure the " disease of government pro-ceeding from multiform centres," [1] either to abolish once and for all the Constitution and the Diet and revert to a system of absolute and autocratic monarchy, or to amend the Constitution in the sense of placing the control of the affairs of state in the hands of a Cabinet responsible to the dominant party or com-bination of parties in the Lower House. Either of these changes would produce a form of government that could be easily understood and operated. If the time has gone by when the first of the suggested remedies could be safely applied, the present or the immediate future seems a favourable opportunity for the application of the second. Only two or three of the Meiji statesmen remain, and they have all reached an advanced age. The House of Peers could be so

[1] *J. G. D.*, p. 33

The Political System in Japan

reconstructed, or its powers so reduced as part of the project of constitutional revision, as to make it subservient to the Cabinet and the Lower House.

Even if responsible government were established in Japan, there would still remain to interest Europeans and Americans the question of the nation's foreign politics. Japan's predominance in Eastern Asia has become the foundation of the national policy. "Nibbling at China" is no longer the propaganda of the military party alone : that policy has come to be universally accepted as leading directly to the realization of the nation's destiny. Korea, Manchuria, Mongolia, and, finally, the Middle Kingdom itself— this is the order of conquest in the minds of the Japanese, not only among the dreamers or the professional militarists, but among the rank and file of the people also.

The passing of the Genro, the amendment of the Constitution, the establishment of party government— these would probably only accentuate the rampant Imperialism of the Japanese nation. As Okuma has taken advantage of the present European situation to initiate the most recent as well as the most flagrant attempt to violate China's sovereign rights, vastly more dangerous than Ito's attempt in 1894, so other Cabinets in future may be expected to follow his lead. The policy is popular in the country, and opposition from without alone will stop the process. In the event of China's inability to defend herself, what Western Power will intervene to save her?

INDEX

377

Index

Index

Index